Freudian Thought for the Contemporary Clinician

This book uses clear language, modern contexts and key psychoanalytic concepts to exemplify how Sigmund Freud's thinking and legacy is directly relevant to contemporary therapists.

Interweaving theory with history, *Freudian Thought for the Contemporary Clinician* allows readers to take a walk in Freud's shoes, offering a new framework for understanding his arcane language and the cultural mores of the early 20th century. Robert Mendelsohn explores topics including sexuality and gender, racial injustice and cultural differences with direct reference to Freud's cases, demonstrating how traditional psychoanalytic ideas may inform solutions to issues we face today.

Featuring clinical examples and philosophical explorations delivered in an accessible style, *Freudian Thought for the Contemporary Clinician* will be a key text for psychoanalytic clinicians in practice and in training. It will also be of great interest to academics and scholars of psychoanalytic studies, the history of psychology and the history of ideas.

Robert Mendelsohn is Professor of Psychology and former Dean at the Gordon F. Derner School of Psychology of Adelphi University, USA.

Freudian Thought for the Contemporary Clinician

A Primer on Psychoanalytic Theory

Robert Mendelsohn

Routledge
Taylor & Francis Group

LONDON AND NEW YORK

First published 2022
by Routledge
2 Park Square, Milton Park, Abingdon, Oxon OX14 4RN

and by Routledge
605 Third Avenue, New York, NY 10158

Routledge is an imprint of the Taylor & Francis Group, an informa business

© 2022 Robert Mendelsohn

British Library Cataloguing-in-Publication Data
A catalogue record for this book is available from the British Library

Library of Congress Cataloging-in-Publication Data
Names: Mendelsohn, Robert, 1943– author.
Title: Freudian thought for the contemporary clinician : a primer on psychoanalytic theory / Robert Mendelsohn.
Description: Milton Park, Abingdon, Oxon ; New York, NY : Routledge, 2022. | Includes bibliographical references and index.
Identifiers: LCCN 2021020041 (print) | LCCN 2021020042 (ebook) | ISBN 9780367774431 (hardback) | ISBN 9780367774417 (paperback) | ISBN 9781003171393 (ebook)
Subjects: LCSH: Psychoanalytic counseling. | Psychoanalysis. | Freud, Sigmund, 1856-1939—Influence.
Classification: LCC BF175.4.C68 M46 2022 (print) | LCC BF175.4.C68 (ebook) | DDC 150.19/52—dc23
LC record available at https://lccn.loc.gov/2021020041
LC ebook record available at https://lccn.loc.gov/2021020042

ISBN: 978-0-367-77443-1 (hbk)
ISBN: 978-0-367-77441-7 (pbk)
ISBN: 978-1-003-17139-3 (ebk)

DOI: 10.4324/9781003171393

Typeset in Times New Roman
by Apex CoVantage, LLC

This book is dedicated to Gordon Fredrick Derner (1915–1983), my teacher, mentor, colleague and friend

Contents

Figures

Foreword

These are challenging times for psychoanalysis. In the era of evidence-based practice and managed care, psychoanalytic ideas appear to have fallen out of favor among contemporary clinicians, and among academics as well. But appearances can be deceiving. Psychoanalysis has not disappeared, it has simply gone underground – still influential, and still widely used, but not discussed as openly as it once was. A number of scholars have documented the pervasive (albeit unacknowledged) influence of psychoanalysis in contemporary clinical practice and research. Moreover, the powerful pull of psychoanalytic thought is not limited to clinicians and researchers, but includes students as well. For many years, trainees at a behaviorally oriented doctoral program not too far from Adelphi have, *sub rosa*, sought out opportunities for supervision from psychodynamically oriented clinicians to supplement the behaviorally focused supervision they receive on campus. The behavior of these incipient behaviorists reveals a simple but powerful truth: It is hard to imagine being a clinical psychologist and not recognizing that patients are complex, conflicted, self-deceptive creatures – as are we all. The utility of psychoanalytic ideas is beyond question, but a significant challenge remains: How can one present the teachings of Sigmund Freud and others in a way that makes these ideas relevant and compelling to the next generation of clinicians? How can one make psychoanalysis relevant for psychologists today – especially psychologists early in their careers who will be the caretakers of Freud's legacy during the coming decades? That is the challenge taken up by Dr. Robert Mendelsohn in this remarkable book.

Freudian Thought for the Contemporary Clinician: A Primer on Psychoanalytic Theory presents a series of 11 lectures delivered by Dr. Mendelsohn in The Freudian Legacy, which has for many years been a required first-year course for doctoral students in the Derner School of Psychology at Adelphi University. The course has attained what can only be called legendary status at Derner, and rightly so. It is the experience that initiates the transformation of our incoming cohort of students into psychodynamically informed clinicians, and eventually, clinical colleagues. It's an ambitious undertaking. In this course, and in these lectures, Dr. Mendelsohn casts a wide net: In addition to discussing psychoanalytic theory and therapeutic technique, he weaves into his presentation issues related to gender, culture and diversity, empirical research (from outside psychoanalysis as well as within) and contemporary challenges in diagnosis, assessment and treatment.[1]

It will not take long for the reader to notice one of this book's most compelling features. Because Dr. Mendelsohn's lectures (including the students' questions and comments, and the dialogue that ensues) are presented almost verbatim – that is, transcribed during four consecutive years (the fall semesters of 2017, 2018, 2019 and 2020) and then integrated so that they maintain sequence and rhythm –the book has a spontaneous, in-the-moment immediacy that one rarely finds in discussions of Freud's work. In his Preface Dr. Mendelsohn notes that one goal of his course is to help students experience what it was like to walk in Freud's shoes. The reader will experience something similar, and they will also experience what it is like to be one of Dr. Mendelsohn's students, and to walk in his shoes as well.

After reading an earlier draft of this manuscript, my first reaction was that *Freudian Thought for the Contemporary Clinician* has many of the best features of a live album. And no wonder: Prior to becoming a psychologist Dr. Mendelsohn was an accomplished musician, collaborating with Al Kooper and with the Ronettes, among others. Dr. Mendelsohn still plays the drums in his spare time; music is still a key part of his life. It also informs what he does in the classroom, and as Dr. Mendelsohn notes in the book's Preface, "My musician days helped me to become a performer, a skill that I hope has added to my teaching abilities." This unique blending of musical sensibility and psychological insight illuminates every chapter of this book.

It is rare to find a master clinician who is also a master teacher, but Dr. Mendelsohn is such a person. In reading these chapters one not only benefits from Dr. Mendelsohn's clinical wisdom but also appreciates his thought processes, and those of his students, as ideas and issues get worked out in the moment, during the course of each lecture. The process is not always straightforward. Like clinical work, teaching may occasionally lead down an unpredicted path, or circle back to take up an issue that had seemed, at first glance, to be fully resolved. But that's part of the challenge, and that's part of the fun, and as any musician can tell you, if someone should happen to break a guitar string, or a drumstick takes flight midsong, the band plays on.

Robert Bornstein
Distinguished University Professor
Adelphi University

Note

1 Dr. Mendelsohn is not the first to see value in committing the spoken word to written form as a way of capturing the essential truths of psychoanalysis. In fact, there is a long history of presenting seminal psychoanalytic ideas and concepts in the form of a series of lectures, the first being Freud's *Five Lectures on Psychoanalysis*, based on his talks at Clark University in 1909. This was followed by Freud's *Introductory Lectures on Psychoanalysis*, originally delivered at the University of Vienna in 1915, and later, toward the end of his career by 1932 *New Introductory Lectures on Psychoanalysis* (which were actually not lectures at all, but by this time Freud had recognized the power of presenting his ideas in lecture form). Anna Freud, Rudolf Steiner, Joseph Sandler, Ernest Hilgard, Ralph Greenson, and others also published psychoanalytic works based on talks presented to various professional and lay audiences.

Preface

My goal for this book is to make Freud's theories accessible to the uninformed reader. The book is a series of transcribed and edited lectures presented to first-year doctoral students in clinical psychology during the fall semesters of 2017, 2018, 2019 and 2020 in a course known as The Freudian Legacy. This course is required of all beginning doctoral students in clinical psychology at the Derner School of Psychology of Adelphi University. I had long wondered why so many of Freud's ideas been either co-opted or discarded.

Here are two reasons: (1.) Freud's language is arcane, and (2.) Freud lived and worked within the cultural mores of more than a century ago. With regard to this second reason, Freud was a Jew who spent most of his life in an anti-Semitic country (Austria). It was not until the year 1867 (when Freud was 11 years old) that the Austro-Hungarian Emperor Franz Joseph I gave the Jews the right to vote (Beller, 1990). Freud credited his Jewish background and outsider status with helping to develop and maintain a different perspective, and hold onto it despite opposition. Freud attempted to apply psychoanalysis to cultures outside western Europe but was unsuccessful.

A bit of my history

My academic interest in Freud began in the 1970s when I joined the faculty at The Derner School of Psychology of Adelphi University, working with Drs. Donald Milman and Gordon Derner. However, my *exposure* to Freud goes much further back, to the early 1950s (I was born in 1943), when my mother's younger sister, Aunt Mildred, would tell me stories about Herr Professor Dr. Sigmund Freud. Mildred heard these stories from Dr. Theodore Reik, her teacher and mentor (he referred to Mildred as his protégée). Reik received a Ph.D. degree in psychology from the University of Vienna in 1912. His dissertation was only the second psychoanalytic dissertation written, coming one year after one penned by Dr. Otto Rank. After receiving his doctorate, Reik devoted several years to studying with Freud. Freud financially supported Reik and his family during this time. Reik was himself psychoanalyzed by another of Freud's early students, Dr. Karl Abraham (Falzeder, 2002).[1] Reik's most important book, *Listening with the Third Ear*

(Reik, 1948), describes how psychoanalysts intuitively use their own unconscious minds to decipher the unconscious of their patients.

With Mildred for my academic inspiration, I finished my undergraduate studies in New York (and also left my other career as a rock and roll musician playing drums in music clubs in New York City).[2] In 1964 I began doctoral studies in clinical psychology, and in 1969 I received a Ph.D. in clinical psychology from the University of Massachusetts at Amherst,[3] (Harmatz et al., 1975; Mendelsohn & Harmatz, 1977) and then spent a year teaching psychology at Hobart and William Smith Colleges, in Geneva, New York. In 1970 I returned to Long Island; for several years I was Supervising Psychologist at the Nassau University Medical Center while pursuing postgraduate study in psychoanalysis at another Long Island institution, Adelphi University. At Adelphi I completed two postdoctoral training programs: a four-year postgraduate program in psychoanalysis and a three-year postgraduate program in group psychotherapy. In 1976, while a post-doctoral student, I also began teaching an introductory course (now called The Freudian Legacy, it was previously known simply as The Freud Course) to all first-year students in Adelphi's clinical psychology doctoral program.

I have been teaching Freud's ideas to bright, talented and demanding doctoral cohorts continuously for 46 years. I have been fortunate to work in an intellectually supportive environment at The Derner School of Psychology, to have had coursework and clinical presentations with visiting professors such as Drs. Lewis Aron, Habib Davanloo, Reuben Fine, James Grotstein, Earl Hopper, Masud Kahn, Otto Kernberg, Robert Langs, Donald Meltzer, Stephen Mitchell, Adam Phillips, Harold Searles, Peter Sifneos, Hyman Spotnitz, Vamik Volkan, John Warkentin, Alexander Wolf, and Benjamin Wolstein. I also enjoyed clinical supervision with Dr. W.R. Bion (Mendelsohn, 1978).[4]

The Derner School of Psychology at Adelphi University has been my professional and intellectual home for much of my lifetime. I cherish all of the mentors, colleagues, students and friends that I have made along the way.

Note

1 Karl Abraham May 3, 1877–December 25, 1925) was an influential German psychoanalyst and a collaborator of Freud who called Abraham his "best pupil" (Falzeder, E. 2002).
2 My college student days also included time as drummer for the rock and roll singing group The Ronettes. The Ronettes were a girl group from New York City and they became one of the most popular rock and roll groups of the 1960s; one of the Ronettes' most famous songs (recorded after I left for my graduate studies) is "Be My Baby." When I played in their band, the musicians included Al Kooper-leader (rhythm guitar), Paul Harris (piano), Harvey Brooks (electric bass) and Elliot Randall (lead guitar). Our band backed The Ronettes at the Café Bizarre in NYC around the years 1962/1963. My final professional gig (meaning that I was paid in *money*) was in a band playing at the 1964 World's Fair in Queens, New York. For many years I had convinced myself that the name of that band was The Greenmen, but about 15 years ago, when I emailed Al Kooper and wrote about these memories, he confirmed all of them, but corrected me

about this last fact; the name of my final group was The Clubmen . . . but I was paid in *green*. My musician days helped me to become a performer, a skill that, I hope, has added to these lectures, but may not have done a lot for my memory.

3 My doctoral training in clinical psychology combined behavioral and psychodynamic approaches (Harmatz & Mendelsohn, 1975, Mendelsohn & Harmatz, 1977).

4 Dr. Bion supervised several of my cases, one of these appears in the article, Mendelsohn, R. (1978) "Critical factors in short-term psychotherapy: A summary"

References

Beller, Steven. (1990). *Vienna and the Jews*, 1867–1938: *A cultural history*. Cambridge: UK: Cambridge University Press.

Falzeder, E. (Ed.) (2002). *The complete correspondence between Sigmund Freud and Karl Abraham* (1907–1925). London: Karmac Books.

Harmatz, M. G., Mendelsohn, R., & Glassman, M. L. (1975). Gathering naturalistic, objective data on the behavior of schizophrenic patients. *Psychiatric Services*, *26*(2), 83–86.

Mendelsohn, R. (1978). Critical factors in short-term psychotherapy: A summary. *Bulletin of the Menninger Clinic*, *42*(2), 133–143.

Mendelsohn, R., & Harmatz, M. C. (1977). Length of stay and behavior patterns of hospitalized schizophrenics. *Psychiatric Services*, *28*(4), 273–277.

Reik, T. (1948). *Listening with the third ear*. New York: Grove.

Acknowledgments

I am fortunate to work in an intellectually supportive environment at The Derner School of Psychology at Adelphi University, to have been mentored by the late Drs. Gordon Derner and Donald Milman, to work with psychoanalytic/psychodynamic scholars such as Drs. Jacques Barber, Robert Bornstein, Laura Brumariu, Wilma Bucci, Morris Eagle, Jerold Gold, Mark Hilsenroth, Karen Lombardi, Christopher Muran, Joseph Newirth, Michael O'Loughlin, George Stricker, Kirkland Vaughns and Joel Weinberger. I am also appreciative of the work done by a number of psychoanalytic authors who have looked deeply into both Freud's ideas and his personal life, and have made him accessible to me so that I can make him accessible to my students. In this regard I am particularly grateful to Dr. Reuben Fine (1963)[1] for his books and his seminar at Adelphi University, where he showed a depth of understanding of Freud's theories. I am also appreciative of the work of Dr. Ernest Jones (1957),[2] whose biography of Freud is both comprehensive and emotionally gripping. This is no surprise; Jones worked closely with Professor Freud during much of the master's life and work.

Please note that Figure 2.1 is included with permission from Blue Q, designers and manufacturers of products that are profound, interesting and funny!

For their work in recording, transcribing and editing these lectures, I would like to thank the following doctoral students: Firouz Ardalan, Nicole Belletti, Jessica Kovler, Margaret Peebles-Dorin and Elizabeth Uribe. This book would not have been possible without your efforts.

I especially wish to thank Dr. Jacques Barber, Dean, and Dr. Chris Muran, Director of Clinical Training, who urged and encouraged me to undertake this project.

I want to thank my editors at Routledge: Alexis O'Brien has championed this project and been a cheerleader for me from its beginning; and Alec Selwyn, Adam Woods, Ellie Duncan and Susannah Frearson all helped to smooth the manuscript's transition to Routledge.

John Knecht's editorial assistance has been invaluable; I don't know what I would have done without him!

Drs. Richard Billow and Joel Weinberger have been generous in every way in offering both editorial and much-needed theoretical/scientific advice, and many

of their suggestions that have been incorporated into this book. Dr. Robert Bornstein has also offered editorial, theoretical and scientific advice; his generosity has
touched me beyond words.

I want to thank the students who have enriched my professional life and allowed
me to a part of theirs as they learned to become psychology scholars and clinical
practitioners. Each of you has touched me and I have learned so much from you
over the many years that I have been teaching Freud's ideas to you. I will briefly
mention only a few of you, although all of you have made me proud:

Anthony Bossis, Ph.D., is a clinical assistant professor of psychiatry at NYU
   School of Medicine investigating the effects of psilocybin, a naturally occurring compound found in specific species of mushrooms.

Peter Caproni, Ph.D., is an associate professor in the Department of Clinical and
   School Psychology and Director of Training in the Postdoctoral Residency
   Program at Nova Southeastern University.

Francine Conway, Ph.D., is Chancellor/Provost and Distinguished Professor of
   Psychology at Rutgers University-New Brunswick.

Mary Gail Frawley-O'Dea, Ph.D., specializes in clinical work with survivors of
   sexual abuse. In 2002, Frawley-O'Dea was the only psychologist to address
   the United States Conference of Catholic Bishops as they crafted a response to
   the sexual-abuse crisis in the Church.

G. Rita Dudley-Grant, Ph.D., MPH, ABPP, is a clinical psychologist in private
   practice with Island Therapy Solutions and a member of the Behavioral Health
   Advisory Council in the Virgin Islands.

Jerold Gold, Ph.D., is a professor at the Derner School of Psychology of Adelphi
   University and one of the founders of the field of psychotherapy integration.

Beverly Greene, Ph.D., is a professor in the Department of Psychology at St.
   John's University.

Bruce Hillowe, Esq., Ph.D., is an attorney emphasizing mental health care law
   and health care law.

Lavita Nadkarni, Ph.D., is the director of forensic studies at the University of
   Denver's Graduate School of Professional Psychology. She has participated in
   and provided specialized training in the assessment of psychological sequelae
   of torture and other forms of human-rights abuse.

Lourdes Rigual-Lynch, Ph.D., is director of mental health services at New York
   Children's Health Project of Montefiore Hospital. She joined a federal team of
   mental-health professionals to meet the family of Cuban refugee Elian Gonzalez-
   during an international custody and immigration controversy involving the
   governments of Cuba and the United States. She also consulted on the transfer
   of Gonzales to his home in Cuba.

Mary Trump, Ph.D., is an American psychologist, businessperson and author. She is a niece of former U.S. president Donald J. Trump.

Kirkland Vaughns, Ph.D., is senior adjunct faculty and director of the Derner Hempstead Child Clinic at the Derner School of Psychology of Adelphi University. He is also the founding editor of the *Journal of Infant, Child and Adolescent Psychotherapy*.

To all of you, and to the hundreds of other students who have taken my Freud course over the decades – including the class that completed the course with me on December 16, 2020 – I thank you all for giving me this most wonderful opportunity.

I also want to thank Marc Harris Miller, MFA, for his wonderful graphics in Figures 2.2, 3.1, 6.1 and 7.1 and for the photo on the book cover.

Finally, I want to share with you my answer to the following question: What is a family?

A family is a group of people who support one another through the cycle of life. My family has been a support to me over many years – and especially during this time of stress over the COVID-19 pandemic – while I have taken precious time to write this book. Our family contains people from the ages of three (my granddaughter Juliet) to 78 (me), and they include Elise Mendelsohn; Dr. Chelsey Miller and my son-in-law, Marc Harris Miller; Tyler Mendelsohn and her partner, Trish Causey; my precious grandchildren Stella Rose Miller and the aforementioned Juliet Lennon Miller; and finally, the love of my life, Dr. Robin Mendelsohn: my sidekick, my companion, my wife.

Robert Mendelsohn, January 10, 2021

Notes

1 Fine, R. (1963). *Freud A Critical Evaluation of His Theories*. New York: Routledge Taylor & Francis.
2 Jones, E. (1961). *Sigmund Freud: Life and work* (L. Trilling & S. Marcus, Eds.). New York: Basic Books (an abridgment of the preceding three-volume works).

Introduction

Why a Freud book?

This is a reasonable question; there are, after all, some very good Freud primers. Yet we still have trouble understanding Freud's work, which slightly preceded the beginning of the 20th century (1896) to the beginning of the Second World War (1939). So why keep trying? There are many reasons. Here's one: Freud developed talk therapy. Here's another: Freud devoted study to complex issues of humanity, the connection between our desires (the unconscious) and our conscious minds (rational will).

In the current understanding of Freud's work, there are two criticisms leveled at him:

(1.) Freud's work is an example of scientism (too much emphasis on science as an explanation for complex human phenomena);
(2.) Freud's work is not scientific enough.

There is some substance to each of these. The reality is, Freud's ideas are not accessible to the current practicing clinician and modern student. Here's another reason: Freud did his best theoretical work when connected to basic clinical data, the data that includes the unconscious/preconscious process. As a corollary, the further Freud strayed from this data, the less accessible his ideas and the less defensible his observations.

My plan is to make Freud more accessible

In this book I review the major theoretical ideas Freud developed, the ideas that directed his understanding of psychopathology, the human mind and personality. In the lectures I apply Freud's wisdom to our 21st-century cohorts. After they complete these lectures, the new generation is actually better disposed toward Freud.

DOI: 10.4324/9781003171393-1

Some words about format

This book is a recorded, transcribed and edited version of my one-semester course The Freudian Legacy. The lectures were recorded and transcribed during four consecutive years (the fall of 2017, 2018, 2019 and 2020) and then integrated so that they maintain sequence and rhythm. As with all clinical psychology doctoral programs, our enrollment has become diverse with regard to race, ethnicity and gender; I've added content that reflects these changes (the student questions you will hear reflect these changes as well).

I urge these students to walk in Freud's shoes. If they can, they soon understand the reasons Freud has not been accessible: Freud was a product of his time (1856–1939). Freud was patriarchal, misogynistic and sexist. He was Victorian, and therefore a prude. All of this makes his sexual theories even more remarkable. While walking in Freud's shoes won't make his wrongheaded ideas go away, it does allow us to create a space between ways of thinking that are now considered socially wrong and attitudes that were considered acceptable then. By the end of our final lecture, I hope to have presented enough material to whet the appetite of those clinicians and students who have read this book, to leave them with a more-than-cursory understanding of Freud's work, and to make them wonder: What are the connections between what Freud said then, and what we do today?

Chapter 1

The exploration of the neurosis and the early origins of psychoanalysis

Source: Studies on Hysteria, 1895

Welcome to The Freud Lectures.

In order to learn about Freud's theories in the context of his time and to apply them to our time, I ask that you put yourself in Freud's shoes:

Putting yourself in someone else's shoes

For those of you who plan to do clinical work, it's helpful to learn how to put yourself in the shoes of another. This is called the theory of mind.[1] As we will see with many of the principles of dynamic psychology, the theory of mind is understood by studying those who have trouble taking the viewpoint of others. We learn the most by looking closely at those who *cannot* put themselves in another's place. Studying people diagnosed as narcissistic, and on the autism spectrum, we learn the theory of mind.

Freud and his history

Let's practice the theory of mind by viewing Freud in historical context. A major idea of Freud's time was Darwin's theory of evolution (Darwin, 1859) as the driving force in adaptation to life.[2] This idea is the underpinning behind all of Freud's thought. In parallel, Darwin's theory was the *driving force in Freud's entire intellectual project*.

This course is divided into three sections. The first is called Id Psychology, the study of the biopsychological drives. Following this is Ego Psychology, the study of that which modulates the drives. In the final section we talk about Freud's case histories. We discuss his important cases and the role of clinical material in deepening his understanding of the mind. Then we briefly summarize the major theoretical/technical extensions and elaborations of Freud's theory that led to

DOI: 10.4324/9781003171393-2

post-Freudian ego psychology and object-relations theory (as well as offshoots of these: self-psychology and relational psychoanalysis).

Exploring the neuroses

Today we both begin and complete our study of the first period of Freud's work before he developed psychoanalysis: exploring the neuroses (1886–1895).

A brief history

Freud was born to Jewish parents in Freiberg, then part of the Austro-Hungarian Empire (now the Czech Republic), on May 6, 1856. He qualified as doctor of medicine in 1881 at the University of Vienna. In 1885 he was appointed a docent (lecturer) in neuropathology at the University of Vienna, and in 1886 he went to France to study with the famous neurologists Charcot[3] and Janet.[4] Freud became an affiliated (adjunct) professor at the University of Vienna in 1902. He lived and worked in Vienna until the final year of his life, having set up his clinical practice there in 1886 after returning from France. In 1938 Freud left Austria to escape the Nazis, and he died in exile in England on September 23, 1939.

After Freud finished studying in Paris, he began to collaborate with Dr. Josef Breuer, the most senior neurologist in Vienna, who was working with hysterical patients. When they began their work, the study of hysteria (neurosis) was in chaos. Only a few people were doing work of value (Liebeault and Bernheim at Nancy, France; Charcot and Janet in Paris; and Breuer in Vienna). Liebeault, Bernheim, Charcot and Janet's contributions were using hypnosis to both demonstrate and treat hysteria (Gay, 1988). Each of these clinicians put patients under hypnosis, paralyzed a limb, and through hypnosis showed, using words, that one can alter a somatic experience. Following their work, Josef Breuer from 1880 to 1882 treated a young woman, Anna O. (her real name was Bertha Pappenheim.[5] She later quipped that it was *she* who invented psychoanalysis, not Freud. She believed that the most important part of her treatment with Breuer had not been the hypnosis, but instead the talking that occurred before and after each trance state). We will soon see, by the way, that Anna O. was actually not entirely wrong: As Freud later understood, and psychoanalysts who followed Freud reinforced, every psychoanalytic treatment hour is cocreated by the interchanges between the doctor and the patient (see the work on relational psychoanalysis; Aron, 1996).

Freud learned that Anna O's improvement was the result of two factors: The first is the release of repressed/blocked emotion, which Breuer and Freud called *abreaction*. The second is the making conscious of what had previously been unconscious, which they labeled *insight*.

Psychotherapy researchers still study these factors:

(1.) Releasing pent-up emotion;
(2.) Understanding the deeper (nonconscious) meaning of events in one's life.

With some kinds of patients it's the first (emotional release) that's the primary curative factor. For those struggling with obsessive-compulsive disorder, abreaction – that is, getting emotions released, helping the patient to express emotions when they can't do so (often, helping the patient to realize that they *have* emotions) – is the major goal.

With other people, such as those overwhelmed by their feelings (that is, they can't control feelings, which is the case with people suffering from hysteria or borderline personality disorder), helping them to have insight, presenting them with meaning and sublimations (expanding their understanding of their confusing life) helps them.

That said, there's still controversy in psychotherapy about which is more important, abreaction or insight. Later, clinicians added another factor to this, an equally important third factor: the experience of the therapeutic relationship.

However, Freud did something more than the presentation and exploration of abreaction and insight. This is the major reason that we study his work. Freud carried Breuer's observations further. He reasoned that the road to understanding neurosis is in the mind as well as in the brain. Neurosis – and ultimately all of psychopathology – can be best understood by studying psychology, not just biology and neurology. This is all the more remarkable when we consider that Freud had been trained in medicine, particularly in neurology.

In fact, Freud struggled throughout his life with ambivalence as to which of these variables (the mind versus the brain) was the more important. As we see throughout the lectures, he never fully embraced either view; he never fully dealt with his ambivalence about this – and it affected his ideas. We'll have more to say about this throughout these lectures.

To continue, Freud suggested that clinicians treating neurotics suffering from hysteria could describe hysteria, and work with hysterical neurosis, in a psychological way. Most of us now realize that mental-health issues/psychopathology are at least partly psychological. In Freud's time, the most common "theory" was that any kind of mental illness was the result of a combination of several factors, among them evil spirits/the devil, moral degeneracy, or a hereditary or acquired physical disease. One scientific finding at the time bolstered the hereditary, or acquired physical disease, view: The physician Gray wrote a book called *Gray's Anatomy* (the current popular TV show *Grey's Anatomy* is a play on words using this famous textbook as a foil). The real Dr. Gray performed autopsies on the brains of people who had died while suffering from end-stage syphilis. Prior to their death, these patients exhibited psychotic symptoms. Gray found massive lesions in the brains of these patients and drew a strong correlation between brain lesions (biology) and severe emotional problems (psychology). I'm not suggesting that there's no connection between the brain and the mind. However, while Freud was ultimately unable to find the ultimate connection between the two, he did show us the relationship between neurosis and the psychological mind.

Currently, psychoanalysts recognize that there is at the least a relationship between emotional problems and temperament. The psychoanalyst Otto Kernberg suggests that early attachment problems and parent/child misattunements occur when there are temperamental (biological) differences between mother and infant. In the 19th century, psychopathology was believed to be the result of an unknown brain lesion or bacterial infection. Therefore, one couldn't effectively treat neurotics. You could merely make them comfortable while waiting for a biological cure. If the sufferer was wealthy you might refer them to a retreat house, where they could "rest their nerves" (this was called the "rest cure" because the belief was that if the person could rest the nerves, that might help them). Some people taking these rest cures did improve, at least temporarily, because they were removed from their family. Keep in mind as future psychologists that this viewpoint (mental problems are entirely biological) has not been abandoned. We understand that all of the complications of one's background affect the person's psychic life. The variables are complex. What we also now know is that with certain patients the combination of talk therapy and medication works best; with others, medication works better than talk therapy; and with a third category of patients, talk therapy works better than medication (Strauss et al., 2015).

Studies on Hysteria

In 1895 Freud and Breuer published *Studies on Hysteria*, Freud's first major work (Breuer was collaborator). The book shows the origin of Freud's thinking about neurosis and revolves around this clinical observation: Neurosis is a defense against the intolerable. From this observation, Freud later developed the idea of "primary thoughts," the thoughts also found in dreams (they're the unseen forbidden thoughts pushing to become conscious; they cause an "intolerable experience"). A second group of thoughts are "secondary thoughts" (thoughts that are defensive because the organism finds the primary thoughts to be intolerable). Freud went on to rework this idea into "the pleasure principle" and "the reality principle." Later still he reformulated them into "the ego" and "the id."

Freud never actually changed his basic understanding of how the mind processes, functions, defends and gratifies human needs. He reworked it, elaborating and expanding upon it. In hysterical neurosis, Freud found that an intolerable experience is connected in some way to the patient's past. Freud believed that the neurotic adult suffered a trauma in childhood and hasn't dealt with the trauma effectively. While a "normal" person might have a trauma, release toxic emotion connected to it, and store the intolerable experience away in the mind as a memory, neurotics can't let go of the trauma – and the trauma's associated emotions. The neurotic remembers the trauma unconsciously. The trauma returns to haunt the neurotic through symptoms or inhibitions.

STUDENT: Can you clarify release of emotion?
DR. M: Yes. When my daughter told her two-year-and-six-month-old (my granddaughter) that this child was going to have a sibling, my granddaughter said "Oh." She calmly walked into her bedroom, and then threw her toys all

around the room while yelling. When she returned to her parents' room, she was calm, even happy. It was going to be better for her to have released some emotion, than if she had never expressed any emotion at all.

Freud expanded on the work of Charcot and Breuer, which was the work of hypnosis: abreaction (releasing emotion) and insight (making the unconscious conscious). However, Freud soon abandoned hypnosis for two reasons: first, he wondered if the memories that the patient produced might be suggested to the patient – and therefore hypnosis might not be reliable or valid. Second, Freud's patients could not always be easily hypnotized and he wondered why. Freud began to believe that there is a psychological force that blocks the hypnotic process in the patient, and that this force has something to do with the relationship between the hypnotist (doctor) and patient. These were the first observations of what Freud would later call "resistance" and "transference" (Fine, 1987). Resistance is the blocking force, and transference is the relationship. Freud discovered something that he called "free association." Free association is a technique where the patient is asked to say everything that comes to mind, no matter how trivial the thought(s) might appear to be. Freud was following an assumption of science: that every association has a cause.

Freud and Breuer said that the intolerable experience comes from the past. "The neurotic suffers from reminiscences." They meant that the neurotic suffers from unconscious, undischarged memories. First, Freud saw the hysteric's intolerable experience as any kind of emotional experience. Later he narrowed it to sexual feelings/thoughts. Freud noted that many neurotics presented with sexual dysfunctions such as frigidity and/or coitus interruptus. Freud's first theory of neurosis was a sexual theory, the "toxic" theory of neurosis. Freud's understanding was that in each human there is an amount of sexual chemical, and if it is blocked, what occurs in the blockage is similar to what can happen to wine when it is left uncorked, the wine converts to vinegar. Later, Freud broadened his understanding of what sexual pleasure is, likening it to bodily pleasure of all kinds such as eating, eliminatory functions and genital stimulation. We'll see that anxiety is at the root of all these neuroses. Sometimes it shows itself directly, as in hysteria, where the person is overtly anxious. However, in another kind of hysteria – hysterical conversion – the anxiety converts to a physical symptom or a phobia or panic attack and, sometimes it's blocked and the person doesn't have any anxiety or emotion at all (this is what we see in the obsessive-compulsive person: no manifest anxiety or emotion).

Before we go further, one characteristic of Freud seen in his writings has led to a bit of trouble in understanding his work. Freud was somewhat ambivalent about psychology. Words like "ambivalent" have been co-opted by the public. "Ambivalent" is mistakenly employed with the intent to use the word as a substitute for "negative affect." "Ambivalent" is a combination of "ambi" and "valent"; it means having two opposite feelings of equal strength, positive and negative. In this context, Freud was very positive about psychology. He was also negative about it at the same time. Freud didn't yet have sufficient medical explanations for the mental processes he had trained for. Thus he was ambivalent about relying entirely upon the psychological. We'll see the struggles in Freud's theories: First he makes a brilliant psychological observation, then he pushes this observation into some presumed biological base, twisting and turning logic to do so.

Summary of lecture I

An idea of profound influence to Freud was the belief in scientific positivism as determined in Darwin's theory of evolution as *the* driving force in adaptation to life. In 1895 Breuer and Freud published *Studies on Hysteria* (Breuer & Freud, 1895), Freud's first major work. This work marks the beginning of what became psychoanalysis. This and all that followed revolves around the observation that neurosis is a psychological defense against the intolerable. Freud suggests that the neurotic's intolerable experiences (thoughts/feelings) come from the past. The neurotic suffered a trauma and represses (forcefully forgets) the traumatic thoughts and feelings. But these thoughts/feelings can break through the repression and become converted into anxiety, psychological symptoms and inhibitions. Freud originally used the hypnotic method he'd learned from Charcot, but soon abandoned it. He did so for two reasons. Freud found results obtained from hypnosis to be unreliable. Relatedly, he began to suspect that the heightened state of suggestibility associated with hypnosis raises the risk that the repressed memories recovered during the hypnosis might be false memories. Freud moved away from inducing trance states in his patients via hypnotic suggestion. Instead, he used free association. The patient is told to say everything that comes to mind without censoring, selective editing or suppression. Freud followed an assumption based on his belief in psychic determinism (there are cause-effect relations in the mind connecting all of the associations). Freud also noticed that certain people couldn't be hypnotized. These people appeared to have strong feelings about the doctor that seemed to block hypnotic process. Freud later turned these observations into processes called resistance (blocking) and transference (feelings about the doctor).

Notes

1 *Theory of mind* is the ability to attribute mental states – beliefs, intents, desires, emotions, knowledge – to oneself and others, and to understand that others have beliefs, desires, intentions and perspectives different from one's own.
2 Charles Darwin (1809–1882) was an English biologist best known for his contributions to the science of evolution (1859). He proposed that all species of life result from a process called natural selection in which the struggle for existence has a similar effect to the artificial selection involved in selective breeding.
3 Jean Charcot (1825–1893) was a French neurologist best known for his work on hypnosis and hysteria. His work greatly influenced the developing fields of neurology and psychology.
4 Pierre Janet studied under Charcot at the Psychological Laboratory – Salpêtrière Hospital in Paris. Janet was one of the first to suggest a connection between events in one's past life and a present-day trauma; he coined the words "dissociation" and "subconscious."

5 Gay (1988) suggests that the neurologists Liebault, Bernheim, Charcot and Janet helped Freud recognize the importance of the unconscious.

References

Aron, L. (1996). *A meeting of minds: Mutuality in psychoanalysis.* New York: Routledge.

Black, M. J., & Mitchell, S. A. (1996). *Freud and beyond: A history of modern psychoanalytic thought* (2nd ed.). New York: Basic Books.

Breuer, J., & Freud, S. (1895). On the psychical mechanism of hysterical phenomena: Preliminary communication from studies on hysteria. In J. Strachey et al. (Trans.), *The standard edition of the complete psychological works of Sigmund Freud, Volume II (1893–1895): Studies on hysteria.* London: Hogarth, 1–17.

Darwin, C. (1859). *On the origin of species by means of natural selection, or the preservation of favoured races in the struggle for life.* London: John Murray.

Fine, R. (1987). *The development of Freud's thought: From the beginnings (1886–1900) through id psychology (1900–1914) to ego psychology (1914–1939).* Lanham, MD: Rowman & Littlefield.

Gay, P. (1988). *Freud: A life for our time.* London: J. M. Dent & Sons Ltd.

Gray, H. (1918). *Anatomy of the human body.* Philadelphia: Lea & Febiger.

Strauss, B., Barber, J. P., & Castonguay, L. G. (Eds.). (2015). *Visions in psychotherapy research and practice: Reflections from the presidents of the society for psychotherapy research.* New York, NY: Routledge Press.

Chapter 2

Dreams
Psychoanalysis begins

Source: The Interpretation of Dreams, 1900

Today we discuss the roots of Freud's masterpiece *The Interpretation of Dreams*. When Freud published *Studies on Hysteria*, he was a neurologist practicing in Vienna, specializing in neurosis. While Breuer and Freud developed some interesting concepts (i.e., the notion of the defensive conflict in symptom formation), they were two of several neurologists struggling to understand what was then considered a physical/neurological disease, neurotic hysteria. From the publication of *Studies on Hysteria* in 1895 to 1900, when Freud wrote *The Interpretation of Dreams*, he evolved from neurologist to psychoanalytic psychologist, developing the technique of psychoanalysis. As a prelude, Freud undertook a personal psychoanalysis, or self-analysis.

Most psychoanalysts now focus not only on understanding the patient's unconscious processes but also their own. They do so by having the experience of a personal or training psychoanalysis with a senior colleague. Freud was the only psychoanalyst who ever attempted to psychoanalyze himself. It is unclear how successful Freud was, yet considering the time and place, this was creative and courageous. Why did Freud pursue his self-analysis? This is not clear, but Freud later said it was related to the death of his father (it was also probably related to Freud's substitute father/son relationship to Wilhelm Fliess).[1] Speculations aside, the reason for Freud's undertaking a self-analysis is what psychoanalysts now call "overdetermined." Whatever the reasons, during this self-analysis, perhaps under the pressure of neurotic anxieties, on July 24, 1895, Freud had his Irma dream.

In a preamble to the discussion of the dream (this preamble is now called the day residue), Freud mentions that he'd been treating a young woman (Irma) psychoanalytically; she'd been struggling with doubts about their treatment. On the day before the dream, Freud was visiting with a junior colleague/friend who'd recently seen Irma. When Freud inquired about her, he detected a reproach in his friend's words and tone. Freud felt annoyed by this. That night, Freud had the Irma dream (he noted that he was fortunate to write down the entire dream immediately after waking).

DOI: 10.4324/9781003171393-3

In interpreting this dream, Freud showed that he could apply the method of free association to himself.[2] Freud realized there are unconscious wishes in the dream. Further, in this dream, which is about guilt and anger, Freud realized that he was tortured by feelings of guilt, anger and competition toward his patients, colleagues, family and friends. In his understanding of this and other dreams, memories from Freud's childhood appeared. Freud became convinced that the unconscious thoughts that appear in dreams come from memories of childhood, as well as from events of the previous day.

With the realization that dreams are an expression of the unconscious, Freud acquired a deep understanding of the unconscious. Others before Freud had posited the idea of a relationship between dreams and the unconscious, even those of very early civilizations such as the Sumerians of Mesopotamia (Kramer, 1961).[3] However, Freud's psychoanalysis brought a new understanding and new way of working directly with the mind. While others saw dreams as meaningless occurrences, over 120 years of clinical work, as well as work in neuroscience, has demonstrated that dreams are the product of both the mind *and* the brain.

In this regard, after *The Interpretation of Dreams*, Freud referred to psychoanalysis as the "psychology of the depths," the deepest levels of the mind, the unconscious. Freud first observed the unconscious when performing hypnosis with patients. He practiced hypnosis into the late 1890s but, as mentioned earlier, he gave up treating patients with hypnosis. Freud realized that he didn't need to alter the patient's state of consciousness: If he simply asked the patient to say whatever came to mind, without attempting to censor it, the person would associate, leading to memories. Memories from childhood emerged and were understood as the opening to the person's entire unconscious psychology. Freud gave up hypnosis because hypnosis encourages a person to be suggestible. (Later, in the 1980s, the issue of suggestibility led to controversy when some therapists presented examples of what they called recovered memories of childhood sexual abuse (Loftus & Ketcham, 1996; Whitfield, 2001).[4] Freud decided he needed a nonbiased field and abandoned hypnosis. In hypnosis, the subject is given a suggestion to carry out after they come out of the trance and told that they won't remember this suggestion. As we see in stage hypnosis, the suggestion is often inappropriate to the situation, and the person is told they're not going to remember the suggestion. This is called post-hypnotic suggestion/posthypnotic amnesia. Clinical hypnosis, by the way, remains a useful adjunct in the treatment of certain kinds of trauma/PTSD (Cf, McWilliams, 1992). The next area where Freud recognized the unconscious is the treatment of the neuroses. In psychotherapy, the patient's associations are seen as an avenue to the unconscious. These phenomena are confined to psychopathology and treatment. However, when Freud focused on dreams, he was dealing with normal psychology: Everybody dreams. *The Interpretation of Dreams* represents for Freud a transition from the study of the abnormal to normal psychology. Manifestations of the unconscious can be found in hypnosis, neurotic symptoms, free associations, daydreams, dreams and slips of the tongue (as in: "my Freudian slip is showing"), errors of omission and commission; all are examples of the unconscious.

Another example of the unconscious is an obsessive-compulsive episode:

> A young/overwhelmed mother is about to leave home for an errand. A baby-sitter is there with her children. However, this mother begins to ruminate (that is, to obsess):
>
> "I hope that I put all of the sharp knives away, from the dishwasher into the drawer. I don't want a sharp knife around that'll cut one of my kids."
>
> She goes to the drawer and counts out 14 knives, because she knows there are 14. However, she doubts herself:
>
> "Oh, I think there are 15 knives."
>
> She counts again, but her count is 13. She counts again – *just to be sure* – now her count is 14. This goes on for 10 minutes.

What do you make of it? She's in conflict. This is what can happen when one is unaware of an (unconscious) conflict; it's called doing and undoing, an obsessive-compulsive ritual or a symptomatic act. A symptomatic act is not a full-fledged neurosis, but a temporary interference with one's functioning resulting from an unconscious conflict that's attempting to become conscious. What is the conflict in this case? We'll guess this woman's exaggerated concern: *harm might come to her children* suggests that it's her aggression or its expression that concerns her. Perhaps responsibility for the children is overwhelming her; they are a burden. She is struggling with the idea that they keep her tied to a husband she is *ambivalent* about (there's that *ambivalent* word again). This is what I meant when I said things are determined by a number of different roots; they are overdetermined.

If our hypothetical mother could laugh sarcastically at herself (Figure 2.1) and at her dilemma, she would be using sublimation – she wouldn't be suffering – but she can't laugh.

What could happen if this woman went to a uninformed cognitive behavioral therapist (CBT), that is, someone who simply prescribed assertiveness for the release of angry feelings without recognizing the internal struggle, the struggle to protect herself against upsetting thoughts and feelings?

One danger with such an approach might be that it places her in an even more precarious emotional position. If she's attempting to protect/defend herself against negative thoughts about her children, and is unaware of these powerful pushes and pulls in her, what might happen if such thoughts were artificially increased? She might need to defend her *self* with more drastic measures to keep these ideas/ feelings out of awareness. On the other hand, a person informed about these processes might first work with this woman's perfectionism – her need to be "good." Later, a guided assertiveness training and encouragement to express negative feelings (particularly toward her spouse) might be helpful. This approach is informed CBT and it would be an example of psychotherapy integration.[5]

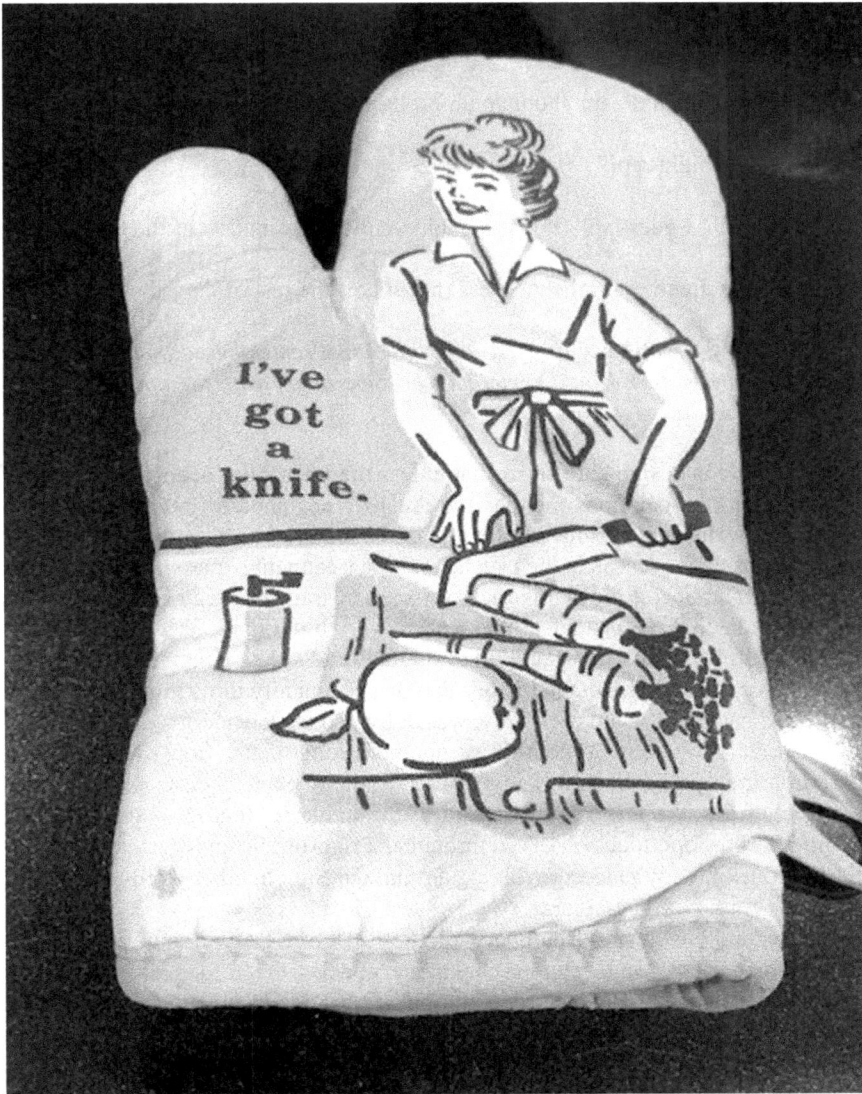

Figure 2.1 Hypothetical mother

To continue, Freud believed the unconscious is understood only when the associations of the dreamer are provided, so a chain can be formed from a particular idea (such as a dream or slip of the tongue) to its unconscious origin. Only when you listen to the dreamer's associations can you actually understand the unconscious contents.

For example, a dreamer might say: "I had a dream last night. I was holding an umbrella . . . that's all I remember."
Their friend says:

"Oh, you had a dream about an umbrella, you think it's going to rain today."

The dreamer might reply:

"Oh, yeah, I guess so" (this is a cookie-cutter explanation of the dream).

However, the dreamer might suppress (not share) the rest of their thoughts:

> *You know, I won't say this out loud, but I just remembered that when I was young my mother would sometimes become angry with me and hit me with her umbrella.*

This example is designed to show that unless the interpreter hears the entirety of the dreamer's associations, neither the dreamer nor another interpreter will be able to know the unconscious meaning(s) of the dream. The best place to see these processes as they occur is in the psychoanalytic treatment situation. That said, the very idea of an unconscious mind was rejected by most of Freud's colleagues. As he later realized, Freud had dealt the world a very bitter blow.

Black and Mitchell (1996) remind us about Freud's statement – that there were three major thinkers in human history that dealt humanity three great blows to its collective narcissism, and each blow was delivered by science.

The first blow came from the astronomer Copernicus. Copernicus' theory, based on the science of astronomy's observation of planets, destroyed the common belief that the Earth is the center of the universe; that all planets revolve around Earth. Copernicus observed through the rigorous means of a telescope that Earth is one of many planets revolving around our Sun. In other words, our planet is not the center of the universe.

The second blow came from Darwin (1859). Before Darwin, our same narcissistic human species said "Humans are a finer species, better than any other – certainly better than an amoeba, or a common slug." Darwin ruined that for us also. Darwin's observations suggested the origin of our species is not drastically different from the origin of every other species. While we're advanced in that we have consciousness and the ability to learn and communicate knowledge via language, we are not in other ways different (in biological process) from the slug.

Then those same narcissistic humans said: "OK, what you are saying is: we're not the center of the universe, we're not biologically different from a slug, but at least our consciousness makes us different/superior, because we're in control of our own minds.

"Not so fast!" said Freud. There's a vast unknown world inside each of us, and that world often determines how we think/feel; we're *not* in full control of our minds. This was the third and final blow to human narcissism.

Freud's negative correlation in the mind

In describing the power of the unconscious mind to influence our functioning, Freud introduced what I call "the mind's negative correlation." By this I mean that when powerful emotion presents itself on the surface (such as extreme politeness, being too agreeable, or being overconfident), this has a psychoanalyst reasoning that the opposite emotion is probably struggling beneath the surface. Thus, the overly polite person is often a bore, the too agreeable a controlling bully, and the overly confident filled with insecurities. While Freud was the first to study this process psychoanalytically, writers (e.g., Shakespeare) always understood this.

Freud's metapsychology[6]

In order to understand the processes occurring in the mind, Freud suggests we use a metapsychological point of view. "Meta" means "beyond/transcending/overview." Freud's metapsychological point of view is concerned with three processes:

(1.) Topographic;
(2.) Dynamic;
(3.) Economic.

The topographic process looks at the three mental processes of consciousness:

(1.) The conscious;
(2.) The preconscious (we talked a bit about this during the last lecture);
(3.) The unconscious.

The word "topographic" is from *topography* (map reading). Looking at a map of the mind, the first layer (the part facing the outside world) is the conscious, the second layer is the preconscious and the third layer the unconscious. Freud suggests that the conscious is the perceptual system and that it looks something like this (see Figure 2.2). In this model the conscious is the smallest piece of the mental apparatus, as it is simply a perceptual crust over the rest of the mind. The preconscious is a bit larger because it holds those memory experiences yet to be conscious (to be perceived) as well as defenses the person employs to keep upsetting thoughts and feelings from consciousness. Beneath the preconscious in this model is the unconscious. As can be seen, it's very large: it contains every memory, every perception the person has ever had. That is, every memory, every experience and every perception the person has had since they began to perceive as a newborn. For example, if you're 25 years old, there are millions of experiences and momentary excitations that you've experienced.

The second process of the mind is the dynamic. I assume that you've heard this term before. Freud borrowed it from the science of physics. "Dynamic" means

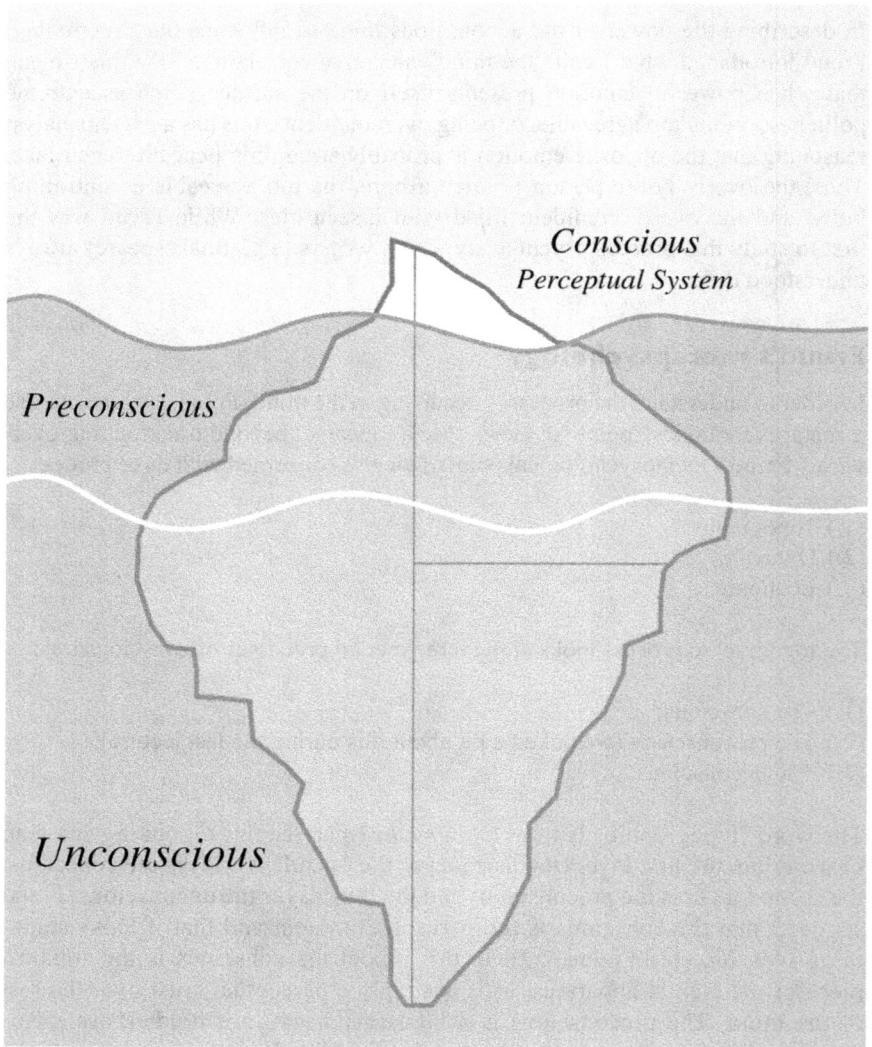

Figure 2.2 Early model of the mind

there are forces pushing toward and forces pulling away. For example, here's an idea in a dynamic relationship:

"I hate my mother."

This idea might be pushing toward becoming conscious, while also being held back for reasons of discretion. Thus, there are forces pushing and pulling this idea.

The dynamic aspect suggests that mental phenomena concern the interaction of forces.

In this case, a part of the person wants to make this idea conscious, perhaps during a fight with the mother, and the idea *I hate my mother* begins to enter consciousness, but somewhere they know this isn't a good thing to think or say (it's also only one part of the relationship to one's mother). One part is pushing this idea into consciousness. Another part – a powerful force – is pushing back to keep the idea from consciousness.

You might remember that I alluded to this process in the anecdote about a mother, her children and the kitchen knives. I implied that the mother had ambivalent feelings about her children. On the one hand, it would be horrifying for her to think she wishes her children harm, because her basic narrative is that she loves them. Yet sometimes the children are frustrating and difficult (all children can be). Worse, perhaps, the children keep her tied to a husband she doesn't want to be married to. This woman is leaving home for an errand – some part of her wishes to not return! Yet that would unacceptable to her basic psychological narrative. Then she has another thought: the knife. There is one knife, lying around, that's going to cut those little bastards. It won't be her fault, it will be the babysitter's: There is another perpetrator. On the other hand, this woman (a person of decency) is trying hard to make sure this "accident" *doesn't* happen. Yet, *if* this terrible thought became conscious, that would be even more horrible. Thus she is a tortured soul. This is the kind of person who may very likely consult a clinician for help.

What is the clinician going to think when they meet with her? The clinician needs to understand the deeper meaning of this symptom, understand the difference between thinking/feeling versus acting/doing. While it would be a moral transgression for her to cut her children, she hasn't done that; she is a tortured soul needing understanding and help. Further, there are three agencies: the conscious, the preconscious and the unconscious. These disturbing thoughts are from the unconscious (these thoughts – a wish for relief, a wish for freedom from the burden of motherhood – push to become conscious via the preconscious) that we can think of as a great switchboard holding wishes back. (Later, Freud describes the preconscious as "cilia," that is, tiny hairs that reach into the unconscious and "feel" upsetting thoughts, sending a signal to the preconscious to actively shut the thoughts down.) This gets clearer when we look at the next agency. The third and final process of Freud's metapsychology is the economic. The economic process describes what happens to amounts of excitation in the mind. Excitation is either pushing toward the discharge of a particular idea ("cut children") or pushing away from it ("don't cut children").

For the mother in our story, all three aspects tell us she's feeling frustration, anger and the powerful pull of inhibition of feeling at the same time; it's driving her crazy. She has conflicting (dynamic) feelings/impulses (economic) she's unaware of (topographic). The result is that she requires lots of mental energy. Think about starting a car, putting one foot down on the brake pedal, placing the other foot way down on the gas pedal. The car won't move but burns lots of energy (gasoline). If you're unaware of these processes, you'll be feeling anxious, tortured and tired.

Back to metapsychology: Freud wonders what happens to excitation (the economic aspect) in the mind. The unconscious is filled with ideas; these ideas are filled with energy and are attempting to be released into consciousness. Some of these ideas are filled with positive energy, some with negative energy, meaning that some are desired while others are feared. Freud says the positive ones are filled with positive cathexis, while the negative ideas are filled with negative cathexis. The term *cathexis* is confusing, like a number of terms that come from Freud's medical background. It would have been better if he had labeled them positive and negative emotional charges. That said, the unconscious consists of many ideas, positively and negatively cathected. Freud will later call cathected ideas "wishes." These positive and negative wishes are attempting to become conscious so they can be discharged. How are they discharged? When awake, they're discharged by motor behavior: I have a craving for chocolate (wish). I remember it's in the kitchen cupboard. I walk to the kitchen (motoric system), open the cupboard, unwrap the chocolate. I put it into my mouth and eat it. There are also other ways to discharge: through neurotic symptoms, dreams, daydreams, in symptomatic acts: e.g., the worried mother.

The mental functioning that occurs in the unconscious is called the primary process. The primary process is different from rational thinking. Its chief characteristic is striving for immediate discharge of cathected thoughts and associated feelings. When we observe somebody who is very disturbed, we see the primary process much more clearly. For example, on a hospital ward an inmate has been diagnosed as bipolar I (manic); the person is talking rapidly. What's coming out of their head/into their mouth is a kind of free association: one thought after another, primitive thoughts. In the primary process, the person is unable to hold back the cathected wishes. They're discharging cathected energy.

There are two major tools available to this primary process: condensation and displacement. In condensation, one idea comes to stand for many; that is, the person condenses several ideas into one. Why would a dreamer use condensation?

Here is an example: What if you dream about love?
How do you dream about a concept?

Dreams are visual images and sound (sometimes smell). How does one convey concepts via a picture? One way is to dream that you're hugging a loved partner. In this example, you have condensed a whole series of complex ideas into a single image. Condensation is a shorthand way of being able to communicate the concept of love (or some other concept) much as a work of visual art communicates several ideas to the viewer.

The second device used by the primary process is displacement. Displacement occurs when a person, thing, behavior or idea is replaced unconsciously by something more acceptable (for example, one's mother is replaced in a dream by a strange and younger woman in order to avoid the dangerous idea of seeing Mother in a sexual way).

Displacement is also a process in neurotic symptoms. When one says that they are afraid of heights, it may be trauma-based (they had a bad fall from a height). However, for others it's more complex. Being afraid of heights may represent a whole series of other kinds of fears condensed and displaced. For some a fear of heights may actually signify that they are fearful about the wish to "fly off" in a new direction, perhaps become more separate (get a promotion in a job, or get engaged/married). In other words, they are fearful because they fear a certain freedom (with accompanying loss) that is unconsciously connected with the experience of success. The message, from one part of the mind to another, is *I'm scared that I may be flying off untethered into space.* The fear of success has been displaced onto a fear of heights. In effect this person is saying: *It is easier for me to think about being afraid of high places than to think about other complex collections of wishes and fears, wishes I'm not emotionally equipped to think about.* That is, one might say that the connections are associative rather than rational.

Also, one can have a fear, or a phobia, about something that stands for a number of conflicts; this is called overdetermination. As an example, the most common fear – in fact, higher on the list of fears even than the fear of death – is fear of public speaking. Why, might you ask, don't I have a fear of public speaking? Because in this instance I am what one would consider counterphobic. By counterphobic I mean that I push myself into the kinds of situations (like speaking to a large group) in order to master my fear. This is one reason why I became a professional musician, and later a teacher.

When we start looking more closely at dreams (and associate to them), we see condensations and displacements work. As we saw in the Irma dream, the process of displacement makes ideas become attached to other ideas that seem in no way alike. It is because of these processes of condensation and displacement that the unconscious can seem unintelligible.

In contrast to the primary process, there's the secondary process. The secondary process is the mind's attempt to hold back the discharges of the cathexis. From this point of view, consciousness (and by consciousness I mean the perceptual system and the preconscious) is like a kind of sense organ that protects each of us from certain material from the unconscious, material that would be too disturbing for us if it were to become conscious.

The secondary process is the operation of consciousness, the ability to use logic. In particular, as seen with dreams, it is tied to time, place and person logic. The person moves from associative reasoning to rational reasoning. When one has a dream, the dreamer might dream that they are another person, and/or that they are in another place, in another time. Interestingly for our clinical purposes, when working with a psychotic patient – perhaps a recently hospitalized psychotic person who hasn't yet been stabilized by the safety of the hospital, the talk therapy and medication – the clinician wants to access whether the patient is oriented to the three spheres: The shorthand way of seeing this is: "oriented 3X." The clinician asks: "Do you know *who* you are? *Where* you are? *When* it is?" If the person does not, and the person also shows other signs of a psychotic process, then we reason that they're in a kind of altered, dreamlike state. The secondary process keeps us from being flooded by upsetting ideas from the unconscious and allows our conscious waking thoughts to be orderly and coherent. However, unconscious material that *is* too disturbing occasionally breaks through. Freud, with some drama, calls this material "the return of the repressed." In other words, Freud sees repression as a protective process used by "consciousness" to ward off unpleasant experiences from the past, located as memories in the unconscious. This model originates from Freud's first observations in *Studies on Hysteria*, where he observed that neurosis is a defense against the intolerable. Neurosis is a defense against experiences that are intolerable to the conscious mind. In *The Interpretation of Dreams*, Freud expands this phenomenon by suggesting that repression isn't confined to the neurotic; it's found in all human beings. Repression, by keeping painful ideas from becoming conscious, helps to avoid pain while we achieve some modicum of pleasure.

STUDENT: When we don't remember dreams, is that a form of repression? Is that an active process?

DR. M: To restate your question, I think that it would be: "Why don't we remember *all* of a dream?" The answer is that we don't remember a specific dream or series of dreams when repression is working well, not enough of the dream material is retrievable. Our dreams are full of upsetting ideas that we have to screen out; we need to work these ideas over. Therefore, here is one thing that I encourage people to do: when one has a tragic loss, I suggest that the person focus on remembering their dreams. They say, "But I'm not dreaming." If it's been a tragedy, a trauma – no loss is good, but with a very tragic loss, the person doesn't *want to* dream, because the dream will be about their upsetting loss. I say, "Well, whatever you remember, write it down." This exercise does several things: it gives the person a task to do when they are about to go to bed. I don't know if anybody here has suffered a traumatic loss, I hope not, most of you are relatively young. The death of each of my parents was sad, but not unexpected because of their ages and their state of health, but my most tragic loss was the sudden loss of my sister; she was in her fifties. This was a devastating blow. I felt like I couldn't dream. It was hard for me to take my own advice. I kept working on it, kept trying to capture my fleeting dreams. Later you will understand why it is that one can't remember their dreams after a tragic loss and why it is that I encourage one to do so.

Given what we have discussed thus far, a natural question would be: Why do we remember dreams at all? We do so because the state of sleep reduces the power of repression. Why not then remember the entire dream? Because there is enough repression at work to make the dream tolerable enough, but not so much as to present it in its complete form. If one remembers a dream in its most vivid and primitive state, this might suggest that the person is probably suffering from a traumatic disorder, or that they are disturbed and have weak repressions. Soon

I'll tell you a dream that a patient presented in our first meeting, a dream that was troubling. It confirmed my worry that he was very troubled.

STUDENT: Are there dreams that we don't remember?
DR. M: We remember parts of them.
STUDENT: Can dreams lead you to explore the type of trauma? Because I feel like some dreams are just too random/not significant.
DR. M: Freud is suggesting to us that through the processes of *condensation* and *displacement* the preconscious is attempting to *trick* our consciousness, so the dream seems random/not significant. In the unraveling of the dream content (as seen with Freud's Irma dream) major themes emerge. In this regard, people have had, at certain times in their history, the same (or similar) dreams over their lifetime.

For example, I would suggest that everyone in this room has had a dream that concerns being in a classroom for a final exam in a course they didn't take and/or didn't study for. I am suggesting this because Freud proposed this kind of dream is predictive of success in school. You got to be doctoral students in clinical psychology, so you were successful in school. All of us have had this kind of dream, and we have awoken with: "Oh my God, I didn't register for this course and it's the final." *(Students nod in agreement.)* Freud says that this is an anxiety dream about being successful. Most of us – can I say *all* of us? – have some ambivalence about being what we might consider *too* successful; being ambitious and successful has perhaps been paired in our history with our feeling better than others. Being better than others might be associated with being arrogant, with not being liked by others.

STUDENT: So what's the wishing in that dream, that "anxiety dream"?
DR. M: I would suggest that in this classroom test dream, the wish is to be the best in the class. It's a dream of ambition and the desire to be intellectually powerful. This is an important theme. I would bet that you are probably going to have some dream that has in it the theme of starting doctoral studies. What a great guesser I am! I say this because you're starting doctoral studies! It's a change, a transition, and an important one. Although the dream's content at first might appear to be neutral, the *trick* of the dream is that it seems random so it doesn't let your conscious know what it's about. Perhaps this is a good time for us to return to "the Irma dream continued." To return now to Freud's analysis of the Irma dream, he says that in order to understand a dream one needs the dreamer's associations. These associations always lead back to the hidden material: that material is always the expression of a wish. (I understand that this is an extremely difficult concept for you to learn, and for me to teach, as it is counterintuitive).

Every dream is the expression of a wish by the partial gratification of that wish through the expression of hidden content in the dream. The dream is a hidden and disguised way of expressing the following: "I wish" in a dream is replaced by "It is true." Here's an example: "I wish I were Emperor of the Universe." In the person's dream, this might become: "It is true that I am Emperor of the Universe."

STUDENT: What about dreams that are scary?

DR. M: Freud calls these *anxiety dreams*. We'll talk about them when we get a better understanding about why Freud believes dreams are created. For now, anxiety dreams are attempting to do what a typical dream is able to do: that is, a typical dream is able to gratify part of a hidden wish. However, in anxiety dreams, the dream is having difficulty doing this.

STUDENT: How would something scary be a wish?

DR. M: This is why this is such a difficult concept. For whatever reason, in the dreamer's history expression of this particular wish is associated with danger of some kind.

STUDENT: Little kids sometimes experience night terrors.

DR. M: Yes, and for them, most of their dreams are very simple expressions of wishes. It's only later in preadolescence that children begin to understand more about their world and, as a result, their dreams become more upsetting. At the age when a child begins to be a bit more physically and emotionally independent, they also become more scared about it. That's when the night terrors start. With regard to Freud's entire model of the mind, your question is prescient, but I can only tease by saying this because too much material needs to be learned before my comments make more sense. That's why we need to study Freud developmentally.

STUDENT: What do you say to people who think that dreams are just a processing of residue from the previous day?

DR. M: As you will soon see, in a way these people are correct, but that's only one part of the story. That said, I believe that what you are suggesting is what a number of psychoanalytic thinkers, such as Fine (1987) call "the Ebenezer Scrooge theory of dreams." Ebenezer Scrooge is a fictional character from *The Christmas Carol*,[7] a book by Charles Dickens, later made into the movie the *Christmas carol* (Desmond-Hurst, Director 1951). Scrooge is a miser transformed into a kinder man. The story is interesting for our purposes because it is about both the power of dreams and also how dreams serve as wonderful psychotherapy metaphors. Scrooge has a scary dream and then suggests that it was "just a bit of "undigested beef" or "potato." In other words, the Ebenezer Scrooge theory of dreams says dreams are only a biological anomaly related to the residue of the previous day, in this case, Scrooge's dinner.

Of course, in the functioning of the brain, everything is biological, but this also depends on what level of observation you want to have. Psychological observation of the mind suggests dreams also have purpose and meaning. Their biological purpose is that they eliminate the day's residues and the desires that these residues have stimulated, so that the dreamer can sleep.

STUDENT: Is the feeling you have when you're experiencing a dream as important as the content itself? Because you could be flying and terrified or flying and happy.

DR. M: Yes, it could be that you started by being happy, but that the happiness made you terrified. Or you could have started by being terrified but underneath you were happy. In other words, it's hard to know in each case, unless we go back to, retrace, the dream and residue to unravel the unconscious wish. This is a very difficult concept. Why would you wish for something that causes you to wake up with anxiety? I'm going to be able to offer Freud's answer to that question. We begin to achieve some self-consciousness about the dream as we're waking. Self-consciousness is the result of two newer processes that I'm going to talk about today: we've heard about condensation and displacement, when waking the dreamer also employs:

(1.) Secondary revision;
(2.) Secondary elaboration.

What these mechanisms do is that they add time, place and person aspects to the dream processes. When we observe psychotic patients on a hospital ward, they often don't know *who* they are, *when* it is, or *where* they are. They've lost what is called the three spheres, and this is exactly like dream life. Freud will later say that in dreams the normal person becomes psychotic every night. In other words, dreaming is our way of granting/gratifying the dream wishes; it's made up of a manifest content and a latent content. The manifest content of the dream is the dream as it appears to the dreamer upon waking, while the latent content is the dream as it's ultimately unraveled. It's actually a wish attempting to become conscious but being restrained (or more accurately, partially restrained) by the censorship (the preconscious). The censorship's job is to restrain this wish. At this stage Freud is talking about the censorship/preconscious, and he uses these terms interchangeably.

There is always a point of contact in between the dream and the previous day. This point of contact is called the day residue. During the course of the day, experiences that have been upsetting leave a kind of residue on the preconscious mind. This residue has triggered wishes in the unconscious. For example, let's remember that Freud felt a colleague slighted him the day before he had the Irma dream. When one traces the latent content, the dream – as it's ultimately unraveled – is the wishful thoughts attempting to break into consciousness while the censor is trying to block them from consciousness. The dream is triggered by something that happened within the past 24 hours (an incident from the previous day created a residue that stimulated latent wishes).

As I've suggested, if the analysis of the dream goes deep enough, we soon find that the dream is a mixture of both the day residue and some early childhood experience/memory. I'm going to explain why. Right now this may not be making sense to you. Suffice it to say that the dream is some combination of the current life (the day residue) and a childhood scene or memory. In its manifest content the dream is linked to the day residue and in its latent content the dream is linked to childhood.

STUDENT: Is it possible that if you had some type of traumatic experience later, after childhood, that your dream would reflect that? Or is it just specifically early childhood?

DR. M: In earliest childhood wishes are granted in fantasy, that is, you wish for something and it happens. We see this in the presentation of children's stories. This way of thinking is the way young children process the world. The concept of cause and effect comes later in the child's cognitive development. Our earliest model of thinking is the following: I wish for something and it comes true. When we dream, we revert (regress) to this earlier model of thinking, when all of our wishes were granted by magic. We can say that dreaming is a regression to an earlier way of solving problems by wishing them solved. An adult who has addictions or other impulse problems might be employing the same regressive defenses, and one might say to a gambling-addicted person: "If wishing could make happen what you want to happen, you could gamble your way out of the jam you've put yourself into." In other words, addicted people "solve problems" through wishes in the same way that the young child believes that Mommy grants all wishes.

When an infant is hungry, it is "starving" (it is also crying). The infant doesn't know that it's crying and it certainly doesn't associate its crying with getting fed. At some point it smells the scent of mother, sees her smile, and sees/feels/experiences a breast or a bottle. It feels, smells and tastes the milk and soon it feels full and no longer in distress. Then it falls asleep. After some period of growth and development, each time the infant gets hungry it imagines a picture image of a breast or bottle and the smell and feel of its mother. For us as adults, we understand that the mother's ministrations have been paired with diminished feelings of anxiety and hunger and increased feelings of satiation and pleasure. This is a kind of instrumental conditioning since the baby is reinforced for crying and imagining. For the young child, the earliest learning is that wishes are granted by wishing them. That's the earliest way we learn how to "think" – that wishes lead to gratification. Thus, when you have an upsetting dream it is because the dream has not fulfilled its function, the function to satisfy your need state by granting your wish via fantasy.

STUDENT: Manifest is what we remember and latent is what actually happens?

DR. M: Latent is how the dream is seen after it is unraveled and we discover what the hidden (latent) wishes are.

STUDENT: How is this different, then, from what actually happens in the dream?

DR. M: The latent content is changed, all prettied up by condensation and displacement. Then, as we are waking up, in order to begin to make sense of the dream, we subject the dream to secondary revision and secondary elaboration.

For example, in a dream where the adult person dreams of themselves as a young child flying through the air unaided, and then awakens, they think, *Oh, I couldn't have been flying unaided; I must have been in an airplane, looking out the window at the clouds.* Further: *It couldn't have been when I was a young child. It must have been when I first flew by myself as a passenger in an airplane and I felt anxious and childlike.* In other words, these processes add time, place and person dimensions to the dream's narrative. As I said previously, in a mental status interview with a person that the clinician suspects is psychotic, we will assess whether or not the person is oriented to the three spheres of time, place and person. We do so to assess whether the person is thinking rationally.

Another way to understand this is that the manifest content is connected to the day residue. The latent content is connected to our hidden childhood mind's way of gratifying wishes through primitive modes of "thinking."

The process by which the latent content is transformed into the manifest content is called the dream work. This is the use of condensation and displacement. These mind tricks are used by the preconscious to make the dream's latent content more acceptable to consciousness, since the dream has to evade the preconscious censorship. In order to do so, displacements are used, but these have to be produced in a visual way. Images and visual symbols are used. No one dreams of love in the abstract. How would one dream that? But in your dream you can produce a dream image that you are embracing someone you wish for. In other words, with condensation of the dream, a symbol may have many meanings. As I have said, we call this overdetermination. Overdetermination is an important concept in psychoanalysis because when we see overdetermination "in action" we understand that neurotic symptoms are also overdetermined. This means that the person has a neurotic symptom and we see that it serves a number of purposes, so as to prevent the person from having different kinds of suffering than they are currently having, though the person is suffering nonetheless.

Thus, while a person may suffer a lot of anxiety about speaking in front of a large group, they might suffer even more if they didn't have this phobia but instead had a full-fledged anxiety attack. The symptom may also have some secondary value in that the person gets sympathy from others. So there are a number of different roots (the roots are overdetermined). In psychoanalysis we look at the different roots that this dream or symptom presents and we do so by the process that I just called reconstruction. Finally, the dream is made acceptable to consciousness by the two processes I mentioned: secondary revision and secondary elaboration. In any production such as a dream, a daydream, a slip of the tongue, a symptomatic act or a neurotic symptom – when you have to deal with an unconscious process and you're attempting to make the contents conscious, you're reworking it in your mind so that it meets the criteria of time, place and person dimensions. Early memories, slips of the tongue, dreams and symptoms are complex phenomena, but once one breaks the code, Freud's ideas become clearer. What I have just been talking about (slips, memories and minor mistakes), by the way, is what Freud later calls the psychopathology of everyday life. We'll also discuss this unconscious process.

STUDENT: Are secondary revision and elaboration different words for the same thing?

DR. M: No. Secondary revision suggests that you are revising history, that is, the image that you remembered upon waking is being changed on the spot because you can't reconcile it with the time, place and person aspects of reality. With secondary elaboration, as you elaborate you are constantly and continually changing the image of the dream by adding features that weren't there before. So, you weren't flying, you were viewing a friend who was flying, and he was a close friend. And he wasn't actually flying – he was talking about going to flying school and you were jealous of this, etcetera. In secondary revision you change (revise) the story, and you are aligning it with the 3X, but in secondary elaboration you are adding to the story, adding features that are designed to further confuse you, keep you from the original latent material. The goal of revising and elaborating is to make the latent content all the more disguised so it is acceptable to consciousness. If a person were to remember a very upsetting dream that was unfiltered, or a barely filtered dream – the manifest content of the dream was available but the latent content was also available – this would be a dream that most people don't typically remember. Here is an example of a dream with upsetting content.

The context of the telling of the dream

At the time that this occurred, I had just begun to add couples therapy to my clinical practice. I got a call from a young woman. She wanted to see me with her boyfriend for a consultation. We worked out the time and I gave her directions to my office. At the appointed hour, I expected to see both of them, but when I opened the waiting room door, her boyfriend was there, she was not. Where was she? She had driven them both to the session, he'd gotten out of the car, and she said to him: "You need help. I don't want to be with you anymore. You see the psychologist." Then she drove away. This is what he told me. He seemed like an emotionally damaged person; he could barely talk. Of course, he was now traumatized, but he also seemed quite odd. Then, during the course of the session he said, "I had a dream last night." He had known that he was going to have a session with a psychologist, so I call the dream a transference dream (his upcoming meeting with me influenced the dream).

Here is the dream:

PT.: "I was walking in the woods and my foot knocked into a canvas bag. I opened the bag and there was a dead body. I realized I had to hide the evidence. So I ate it (the body)."

That was the dream. There was no elaboration. Hearing this dream was upsetting to me. I thought to myself: *Holy XXX, he's not supposed to remember dreams like this.* In other words, the latent content was barely filtered/barely hidden from consciousness. Thinking quickly, I said:

ME: "What an interesting dream. I'll bet you're the kind of person who eats yourself up alive when you're upset."

PT.: "That's right."

He showed some signs of relief, and we spent the rest of the session discussing
how he was too hard on himself; that he felt he could never get things right. At the
end of the session, I asked if he wanted to return. He said he couldn't afford to see
me – he and his girlfriend had been planning to share the cost. I gave him a list of
clinics to apply to for treatment, and asked him to make contact with me after he'd
arranged to do this. Fortunately (one has little control over this), he did call after
he made an appointment at a recommended facility.

I want you understand that this dream was unusual because the dream work
did not adequately disguise the manifest content from the latent content. I also
want to tell you what *I think* the dream was about. I think the dream represented
that he believed he killed every meaningful relationship through his inadequacy,
hate, envy and greed (eat), and that he had to hide the evidence of another failed
relationship. I think he saw the breakup coming. I have no proof of the accu-
racy of my understanding of the dream and only could have had this (at least
partially) confirmed had he and I worked on the dream together. However, I
believe that this is an example of why Freud called dreams "the royal road to the
unconscious."

Summary of lecture 2

In 1899, Freud published *The Interpretation of Dreams*. This is often considered Freud's greatest work. It was stimulated by Freud's analysis of the dreams
of his patients as well as by his self-analysis. In interpreting both his patients'
and his own dreams, Freud recognized that he could apply the free-association
method to dreams. A dream is made up of a manifest content and a latent content. The manifest content is the dream as it appears to the dreamer upon waking and the latent content is the dream as it is unraveled after the method of
psychoanalysis is applied (free association and detailed inquiry). The manifest
content involves the dreamer's most recent needs, worries and concerns (called
the day residue: events of the past 24 hours have left a kind of residue of
experience inside the dreamer), while the latent content concerns unconscious
childhood memories of wish fulfillment that have been used to discharge these
wishes. In presenting this model, Freud suggests that dreams are not the result
of random brain activity. In this way, Freud was agreeing with the writers of
antiquity who believed that dreams contain meaning. However, Freud was also
suggesting that, although to the ancients the meaning of the dream comes from
outside the self, to Freud the dream's meaning is psychological and comes
from within. Freud also proposed that dreams have a second purpose: They
preserve sleep by discharging powerful emotional experiences that have accumulated during the day.

Notes

1 Wilhelm Fliess (1858–1928) was a German otolaryngologist who practiced in Berlin. He developed highly eccentric theories of human biorhythms and a possible "nasogenital" connection that have not been accepted by modern scientists. He had a close friendship and theoretical collaboration (primarily via letters) with Sigmund Freud, a controversial chapter in the history of psychoanalysis.
2 "Free association to himself." As can be seen in the lecture, the use of logical reasoning to explore unconscious/irrational processes had been used in psychiatry to understand the patient, but now Freud was employing it in the service of also understanding the clinician. J. D. Sutherland (1957) has pointed out how great Freud's achievement was in analyzing himself, even to the point of seeing the meaning of his own Oedipus complex. Sutherland suggested that among the factors that enabled Freud to accomplish this were: the particular structure of Freud's family; the fact that Freud was such a good dreamer; Freud's ability to use his relationship with Wilhelm Fliess in much the same manner as patients may use the transference; the death of Freud's father, which acted as a stimulus in the mobilization of childhood feelings; his mother's ability to confirm many of Freud's own recollections; and finally, Freud's ability to use his observation of the behavior of his own children.
3 Dream interpretation was prominent in early civilizations (Kramer, 1961). Thus, the ancient Sumerians in Mesopotamia left evidence of dream interpretation dating back to at least 3100 B.C.E.
4 In the 1980s, the issue of suggestibility led to controversy when some therapists presented examples of what they called recovered memories of childhood sexual abuse, (cf Loftus, E., & Ketcham, K. 1996).
5 Psychotherapy Integration-Informed behavior therapy is a psychotherapy practiced by a person who employs psychotherapy integration (see Stricker, 2010, *Psychotherapy Integration*). Integrative psychotherapy is the integration of elements from different schools of psychotherapy in the treatment of a patient. Integrative psychotherapy may also refer to the psychotherapeutic process of integrating the personality uniting the affective, cognitive, behavioral and physiological systems within a person. Psychotherapy integration had its beginning in several places, one of which is here at Adelphi University, under the guidance of Drs. George Stricker and Jerrold Gold.
6 Psychoanalytic metapsychology is concerned with the fundamental structure and concepts of Freudian theory. In the 1910s, Freud wrote a series of 12 essays, later collected as *Preliminaries to a Metapsychology*. Five of these were published independently under the titles "Instincts and Their Vicissitudes," "Repression," "The Unconscious," "A Metapsychological Supplement to the Theory of Dreams," and "Mourning and Melancholia."
7 *The Christmas Carol* (Renown Pictures, 1951) *Scrooge* (released as *A Christmas Carol* in the United States) is a 1951 British Christmas fantasy drama film and an adaptation of Charles Dickens' *A Christmas Carol* (1843)

References

Black, M. J., & Mitchell, S. A. (1996). *Freud and beyond: A history of modern psychoanalytic thought* (2nd ed.). New York: Basic Books.

Darwin, C. (1859). *On the origin of species by means of natural selection, or the preservation of favoured races in the struggle for life.* London: John Murray.

Desmond-Hurst, B. (Director). (1951). *A Christmas carol* [Film]. George Minter Productions.

Dickens, C. (1843). *A Christmas carol. In prose. Being a ghost story of Christmas.* London: Chapman & Hall.

Fine, R. (1987). *The development of Freud's thought: From the beginnings (1886–1900) through id psychology (1900–1914) to ego psychology (1914–1939).* Lanham, MD: Rowman & Littlefield.

Freud, S. (1900). The interpretation of dreams. In J. Strachey et al. (Trans.), *The standard edition of the complete psychological works of Sigmund Freud, Volume IV.* London: Hogarth, ix–627.

Freud, S., & Breuer, J. (1895). *Studies on hysteria. Standard edition 2.* London: Hogarth, 255–305.

Kramer, S. (1961). *Sumerian mythology: A study of spiritual and literary achievement in the third millennium B.C.: Revised edition.* Philadelphia, PA: University of Pennsylvania Press.

Loftus, E., & Ketcham, K. (1996). *The myth of repressed memory: False memories and allegations of sexual abuse.* New York: St. Martin's Griffin.

McWilliams, N. (1992). *Psychoanalytic diagnosis.* New York: Guilford.

Stricker, G. (2010). *Psychotherapy integration.* Washington, DC: American Psychological Association.

Sutherland, J. (1957). Freud's life and work: An appreciation of Ernest Jones' biography. *British Journal of Medical Psychology, 29*(2), 77–81.

Whitfield, C. L. (2001). The "false memory" defense: Using disinformation and junk science in and out of court. In C. L. Whitfield, J. L. Silberg, & P. J. Fink (Eds.), *Misinformation concerning child sexual abuse and adult survivors.* New York: Haworth Press, 53–78.

Chapter 3

Dreams

Where psychoanalysis begins; an early structural model of the mind

Source: The Interpretation of Dreams, 1900

Today we discuss Chapter 7 of Freud's *The Interpretation of Dreams*, but before we do I want to talk a bit about what is called psychoanalytic epistemology.[1]

Several of you had questions about my interpretation of the cannibal dream from last week, questions such as "How do you know?" "What does it mean to say that you know something in psychoanalysis?" "What makes you *believe* that your interpretation is justified?" and "How do you know what you know"? First, I want to remind you that what I suggested was a provisional hypothesis about the dream. That said, your questions are important for psychoanalysis. Freud avoided addressing such questions of interpretation because they stirred up a conflict for him due to his positivist scientific ideals.

Beginning with David Rapaport (1960), there was a shift in the science of psychoanalysis, from positivist to post-positivist points of view. Rappaport played a prominent role in developing psychoanalytic ego psychology (we will study ego psychology this semester). In his book Rapaport (1960) *The Structure of Psychoanalytic Theory*, he organized ego psychology into an integrated, systematic and hierarchical theory capable of generating empirically testable hypotheses. Rapaport (1960) suggests that psychoanalytic theory is a biologically based general psychology, and it explains the entire range of human psychological functioning (e.g., memory, perception, motivation, behavior). He believes this is consistent with Freud's attempts to do the same (e.g., what we see later, not only in Freud's studies of dreams, but in jokes, and the "psychopathology of everyday life").

However, Schulman (1982) suggests that writers in psychoanalysis haven't successfully incorporated this shift in the epistemology of psychoanalytic science into their approaches to psychological understanding. Scientific knowledge in many fields where interpretation plays an important role is not dependent on controlled studies, but rather upon the care with which multiple and redundant checks are applied as work proceeds. The psychoanalyst recognizes how this error-checking process is so much a part of their daily work.

Do experienced psychoanalysts have a special kind of expertise? Schulman suggests that studies of expertise in many fields show that the most important difference

DOI: 10.4324/9781003171393-4

between experts versus those less successful is the extensive, detailed knowledge of the experts. This permits them to focus on problem solution rather than follow set methods. Problem-solving strategies employed by experts tend to be carried out with flexibility. They don't use cognitive methods identifiably different from those used by others, but they demonstrate what Schulman calls a well-stocked mind. It's rare that the exact nature of the expertise can be stated in many fields, as in psychoanalysis. The clinical situation, where the psychoanalyst has an extensive and wide exposure to the mind and life of each long-term patient, constitutes a very special form of expertise about patients, one that is often underestimated and not often studied.

Now to Chapter 7: In this chapter, Freud describes in detail the mental structures of the unconscious that account for dreams. Keep in mind that these are not literal structures. There is no actual structure in the brain stem that is the preconscious; the preconscious is a series of functions and processes. Freud proposes a kind of structural metaphor. Using this metaphor, Freud describes a structural model of the mind in the unconscious to account for dreams. To do so, he asks a question that a number of you have asked during these first lectures: "How do we know whether or not we're really remembering a dream correctly?" His answer is that we don't know for sure. But he argues the following:

(1.) The extent of forgetting of dreams is overestimated;
(2.) It doesn't matter whether or not we remember a dream correctly, since from a positivist point of view, mental events, like physical events, are also determined.

What we forget and what we remember – and what we later remember – are each important in different ways. Freud labels this determination process *psychic determinism*. He reasons that there are cause-and-effect relationships in the mind just as there are cause-and-effect relationships in other scientific inquiry, such as in biology, chemistry and physics. What we might remember of the dream has meaning, but what we don't remember – or what we later remember – is just as meaningful as what we do remember now. Freud continues that forgetting of the dream has to do with the censorship. What he's calling the censorship he also begins to call the preconscious; and later still, Freud will say that this preconscious censorship is part of something called the ego. For now it is the censorship.

Next, Freud asks: Why do we dream at all, if we have a censorship? He suggests that this is because the state of sleep reduces the censorship. The next concept Freud introduces – first in a biochemical way and later in a more psychological way – is called the regression. Regression is an important concept in psychoanalysis because a lot of what occurs in normal and in pathological processes is hypothesized to be the result of someone regressing from a current state to an earlier state. In a dream, thought is objictified; that is, a situation is presented where a wish is granted: *I wish it was true* becomes *It is true*. In this way the wish is "gratified." Thought is objictified in that it becomes a visual image and sometimes it is the experience of speech. In this regard, some people have dreams that involve talking and other sounds. Also, certain lucid dreams have this as a feature. As I promised in the last lecture, this background will soon help us to understand so-called anxiety dreams. By the end of this lecture we'll be able to understand why it is that I have said that anxiety dreams are nothing more than failed/failing dreams. They have failed in the major function of dreaming: to keep you sleeping by partially gratifying hidden wishes that have been stimulated during the previous day via the day residue. This is now understood as the result of the process called embodied cognition (Vacharkulksemsuk & Fredrickson, 2012).[2]

In the dream, thought is *objectified* into visual images and sometimes into speech. This differs from how thoughts are experienced in waking life. In waking life, psychological processes move from the perceptual end of the diagram to the motor end. For example, let's say Student X is eating a piece of cake. I see (perceive) this cake and want it. I walk over to Student X, who has the cake, and grab it away and I eat it.

STUDENT X: "You could have just asked."

DR. M: "Can I please have that imaginary piece of cake?"

STUDENT: "Yes."

DR. M: "Thanks (gobble, and gobble!). By the way, I didn't *ask* for the cake because speech is a secondary process behavior, and in this example I am presenting the most primitive actions. As you can see in this example, the process is from perception to motor, or to put it in psychological language, from stimulus to response. This is called the reflex arc (you've all learned about this process from psychology courses that you took)."

In this model **(Figure 3.1)** Freud shows a system where in the front, the person receives perceptual stimuli, just like what occurs when you are awake. Stimuli are coming in. You retain no trace of these stimuli, because if you remembered every single percept that has been perceived by the perceptual system for every waking minute of your life, your brain couldn't process all of this information.

The dream is Created in the Unconscious

AWAKE

See Cake	*Perceptual System --- PCS Memories*	*Motor System (S-R) Get Cake*

ASLEEP

Perceptual System --- Preconscious //// Unconscious Memory Images (Dream Is Created) //// Motor System Is Blocked

Figure 3.1 Model of waking versus dreaming mind

STUDENT: The perceptual system is conscious?

DR. M: Yes, but the preconscious part is not conscious. This part protects the person from overload. As with many kinds of normal processes, one often learns more about them by studying abnormal versions of the process. Neurologists have seen patients who have no memory because of certain kinds of brain pathology. If one does not have the ability to retain in memory the millions of perceptions we experience during our waking life, then the person will be flooded and overloaded with perceptions. Thus, we see the first system, the perceptual system, as well as a second system, where all of these momentary perceptions are stored: a memory system. Behind that there is something like a large warehouse where all memories are kept. Thus, the person perceives perceptual stimuli but retains no trace of them, no memory. Then, behind this is a second system where the energy is transformed from momentary excitations to what will become permanent traces (they're transformed into permanent memory traces). This system is the preconscious. Freud also suggests in this model that the mind is divided into three topographic systems: the conscious, preconscious and the unconscious.

Let's return to Figure 3.1. In Figure 3.1 we can see that the left side is the perceptual system and the right side is the motor system. Percepts lead to memories or permanent traces, which are unconscious and stored in memory.

STUDENT: Does Freud believe that everything you experience is stored?

DR.M: Yes, stored in memory. Stored but not necessarily available to consciousness.

STUDENT: Literally everything?

DR. M: Keep in mind that in this hypothetical model, not everything you have experienced occurred when you had the words and therefore the cognitive ability to "remember" it. This is why Freud and later psychoanalysts talk about experiences that are called "preverbal," that is, experiences that survive in each of us just as they were first stored when we didn't have cognitive understanding of the experience or the words to describe it. Think, for example, about what the newborn and then the infant experiences in the feeding situation, what they experience and what they recall. In this regard, cognitive psychology now talks about implicit and explicit memory.[3] These are seen as qualitatively different, in different parts of the brain. Research now suggests that explicit memory does not mature until about ages three to four. Implicit memory is present from birth.

STUDENT: Is all of it retrievable?

DR. M: We're going to find out that it is, but it's not retrievable in the same cognitive ways that we learn in later childhood, latency, adolescence and adulthood: it is retrievable as an image in a dream, or when one is psychotic and regresses (but then these images are called hallucinations and appear to the person but seem to make no sense). As we have previously discussed, the preconscious "pretties up" the dream images, and thus makes the images acceptable to the dreamer, without presenting an image (that is, an idea or series of ideas) that would be too upsetting. If the image is too upsetting, the dreamer will be forced to wake up with a spell of anxiety.

To remind you, in the previous lecture I presented the upsetting dream of a young man. The dream contained primitive imagery of cannibalism and was upsetting to me because his preconscious was not making the dream more tolerable and disguising it for him. Keep in mind, we are laying the groundwork for later work on Freud's structural model of the mind. In future lectures, Freud will tell us that the perceptual system and the preconscious work together, and he'll call these processes a structure: the ego. The ego will be defined as a kind of alarm system that protects one from both internal and external danger (that is, the preconscious will be seen as protecting us from the danger of our internal impulses while the perceptual system will be seen as protecting us from dangers in the external world). For now, this structure that is alternately called the censorship or the preconscious is the system that protects us from dream images that might be too upsetting for us and force us to become awake.

To restate: The unconscious is accessible to consciousness only through the preconscious; it can't become conscious directly.

Freud now asks, "Where are dreams constructed?" He answers that they are constructed in the unconscious. Here is the model (let's return to Figure 3.1): In waking life, excitation moves in a forward direction (progressive), perceptual to motor, while in dreams, excitation moves in a backwards direction (regressive), motor to precept. That's why Freud calls this mode of cognition "regression." In my exercise before, when I'm awake my mental process moves from percept (I see the cake) to motor (I take the cake). The person has a need, or their perception stimulates a need, and they perform a motoric act to gratify the need. What happens if I get a need when I am asleep? During sleep one's motor system is blocked. So I have a need and attempt to gratify it via my motor system, but my motor system is blocked. I regress to the perceptual system and I create a dream image. Where do I find an image that will gratify my need? In the unconscious.

As I have suggested, the unconscious is a warehouse of old need-gratifying images. Keep in mind that this is merely a hypothetical model developed by a neurologist in 1900 who was studying the proposed neurological processes in neurotic illness. That said, perhaps you have noticed that when you wake from a short nap, your muscles might feel very tight? If you are waking from a dream, you might remember to try to do the following: hold your muscles perfectly still: the resulting dream images will be richer and clearer. Why is this? It is a bit of data that suggests that Freud may have been correct. Because the motoric system is blocked and the need (wish) is attempting to be gratified, the sleeping person cognitively regresses to the unconscious where the wish creates a dream image that gratifies (serves as substitute gratification for) the person's desire.

To repeat, why is the person doing this in order to stay asleep? Why do we need to sleep? Humans who are deprived of sleep for a long period present as if they are psychotic: their cognitive processes are regressive; they hallucinate. For whatever reason(s), we need to sleep. Dreams help us sleep. Maybe we need to sleep because we need to dream. So sleeping helps us dream. While this is circular, what we do know is that if a person doesn't sleep, they will start dreaming while awake.

To continue: (*said with sarcasm*) "I'm sure nobody here ever felt that they had to 'pull an all-nighter' for school." If you found yourself in that awful circumstance, perhaps you began to experience hallucinations, hearing noises that you interpreted. When previously awake after a restful sleep, you would have dismissed these sounds as momentary random occurrences. Now they began to become part of a disturbing narrative, even perhaps a narrative with ominous meaning. This is what can happen when we don't sleep: We deprive the brain/mind of sleep and therefore of the opportunity to dream, so we begin to "dream" while awake.

I'll repeat Freud's hypothesized formula for the process of making a dream: In the dream state (1.) The person moves from percept (desire) to motor. (2.) The motor system is blocked because the state of sleep has blocked it. (3.) Therefore the desire (need) moves to the unconscious in order to find an image, to gratify this need state. (4.) The person creates a need-gratifying dream image that serves as a substitute for the desire, a dream image with gratifying content. (5.) The dreamer continues to sleep.

DR. M: You have tried sleeping and blocking your motor system?

STUDENT: I've noticed what you describe. When I lay in the same position I was in the night before . . . I don't know if that's related?

DR. M: Yes, it's probably related, because your position emphasizes that you are blocking your motoric system . . . and you have a more vivid dream. Freud is saying that in dreams the excitation is backwards: motor to sensory. Not progressive sensory to motor. Instead of stimulus-response (sensory to motor), it is response (motor response blocked) to sensory, and this is why Freud calls this process regressive.

Why doesn't this backward direction happen when we're awake? Because the excitation/desire that motivates behavior can be discharged in motor behavior. Also, when we're awake there are lots of stimuli meeting the perceptual system. Relatedly, there is a research paradigm that was quite popular in the 1960s and 70s called sensory deprivation (Solomon et al., 1961),[4] where people are put in a situation with minimal outside stimuli and they begin to hallucinate. I participated in this research in the 1960s and found it very interesting, as both a former musician with experience with substances similar to what I was experiencing in the study and a research subject in clinical psychology research; this was interesting and ironic to me. Similar to the work with sensory deprivation, by the way, one of our Derner doctoral alumni, Dr. Anthony Bossis (2015) has been working in a research program with terminally ill patients (see this article in *New Yorker* magazine at http://nyr.kr/1vH5CSY) using psychedelic drugs in a "guided trip" to ease their emotional suffering and offer them a sense of inner peace.

To summarize, the excitation in the dream moves in a backward direction, that is, from motor to percept. Because the motor system is blocked, the dreamer produces a perception (dream image) instead of an action in the environment (the kind of action that one would perform in waking life). There are times, however, when one is awake but might also experience this regression; in this instance the person is experiencing a hallucination. When these are not substance-induced hallucinations and we analyze them, we see that the images that are experienced are repressed memories. That is, repressed memories have broken through the censorship. In dreams it may be that the dream's thoughts that are transformed into visual image and speech come from memories.

STUDENT: What about sleepwalking? It's kind of the reverse where the motor is activated while you are asleep.

DR. M: What is sleepwalking? Sleepwalking is the same as if the person is having an anxiety dream, or a command/lucid dream. In other words it is a failing dream, failing in that it hasn't kept the dreamer totally asleep. What the person is experiencing is a semiconscious state. It's what Schacter (1976) and others call a hypnogogic state a state in between dreaming and wakefulness. In the sleepwalker, the motoric system is not blocked enough, so there is movement, but it *is* blocked enough so that the person is not achieving full consciousness. This is the same process as with certain people who we call dissociated. That is, it is a kind of dissociated state, where you're neither awake nor asleep and seem conscious. For example, a self-cutter is a person who self-mutilates. The person seems to go into a kind of hallucinatory state. This is some intermediary state between waking and sleep. The censorship isn't working hard enough to block the motor system, and therefore some of the drive is being discharged in this way.

STUDENT: Is it that the censor is weak or the impulses are strong?

DR. M: Freud never answered this question directly. One could make the case that it's one, the other, or both. What he did say is that it is optimal for a successful night's sleep that the dream not fail in its primary task: to be able to discharge enough of the impulse (the cathected energy) to keep you sleeping. In this model, sleepwalking, anxiety dreams, command dreams (dreams that present the dreamer with the belief that they're actually controlling the dream, which is a rationalization), all of these are the result of a failure of the dream work. In this regard, a dream where you have a narrative such as, "Now I'm going to do this . . . now I'm going to do that," is the kind of dream that contains ways to reassure the dreamer that the dream isn't so upsetting, and with dream thoughts such as, "If this dream gets too upsetting, I'm going to wake up." These are lucid or command dreams, and they can be considered a semisuccessful example of the dream work attempting to keep the dreamer sleeping.

STUDENT: So the information that comes about in a dream . . . are we not supposed to know it, or are we supposed to know it? Is the goal to work with that information in some way or is it that we are supposed to keep it from ourselves?

DR. M: For Freud, the dream is fulfilling a psychobiological function: to keep you sleeping. It does so by allowing just enough disturbing material past the censor. But exploring dreams also offered Freud a way into the patient's unconscious. So, for example, if one is having a recurrent dream that is upsetting, they're probably better off knowing a little bit about what the dream means. In the example that I gave last week, each of you might currently be having recurring dreams about starting graduate school and this doctoral program. If you're having dreams that are a little disruptive – that are making you anxious – that is most likely because the day residue is related to your being in this program. You come here for classes, and when you don't come here, you are more than likely consumed by this program in several ways. When each of you goes home and goes to sleep, you have been exposed to material that has presented very powerful day residue. The kind of dream(s) that you have are then determined by your characteristic ways of dealing with this kind of stimulation (residue) and this kind of stress. As we learn over the course of these lectures, Freud at first looked at these processes with less concern about the mind and more concern about these experiences as energy-driven psychobiological processes, but in this example I am describing how one's character (personality) can intervene and affect one's dreams. This then becomes about one's defenses, which are the characteristic way(s) one deals with intolerable experiences. Later, Freud will focus on these defenses. In this regard, current psychoanalysis as a treatment is designed to help the patient develop more successful defenses. In our last lecture, I presented a young man who had primitive content in his dream (the cannibal dream). Primitive content means primitive defenses. In psychotherapy he might be helped to use less primitive defenses, such as rationalization, intellectualization and sublimation. In other words, a lot of what therapy does in terms of our cognitive and affective functions is that it provides us with new kinds of mechanisms to reassure ourselves, comfort ourselves, soothe ourselves and also to understand things differently and act differently because of this changed understanding.

To continue with Chapter 7, the dream that's been transformed into visual images and speech comes from memory. What does this mean? Freud is suggesting that the dream is a substitute for an infantile scene/memory that's been modified to recent experience. The infantile memory can't be revived directly. It has to be satisfied to return as an image in a dream. Dreaming is a regression to early childhood. It is a return to the time when all of our instinctual impulses dominated, and most importantly, it is a return to a time when the method of expression of our needs was not to perform using our motor functions on the environment (we were too immature to have, much less to use, such abilities), nor was it to call for our caretakers to help us (we were also too immature for this). The expression of our needs was available to us only through wish fulfillment. In other words, we wanted something so we wished it. Talk to a young child about how they understand causality and you'll see that they believe that wishing will make their needs satisfied. Many stories of childhood – in order to appeal to the child reader – encourage this view of magical wishing (remnants of this are also seen in people who gamble and who are impulse-ridden borderlines, psychopathic personalities and abusers of substances). Ask a character-disordered person why they do something and you'll see that their belief is that wishing will make it happen. This is one reason that many disturbed characters, without regard for the reality consequences of their actions, gamble or abuse themselves into ruin. They are confusing their wishes with reality. In a certain way, they've never grown up.

STUDENT: So what I don't understand is perceptual to motor for when you're awake. For dreaming is it motor to perceptual or unconscious?

DR. M: As I said, this is confusing! In waking life it is percept to motor: see cake, want cake, take cake, eat cake. In dreams the motor system is blocked. The person went to bed desiring cake. In the night while asleep the person craves cake but also craves sleep. The desire for cake, because your motor system is blocked during sleep, travels to the next available place: to the unconscious. Why there? It goes there because the wish seeks out an old storehouse of memories, a storehouse where needs are granted by simply wishing them. It goes backwards to an earlier time, an earlier way we were able to get our needs gratified: We got them gratified by wishing them.

In my many years of teaching this course, the concept of wish fulfillment is the hardest concept for you to grasp. For students who have spent your lives, for the most part, deeply grounded in reality, and then to have me suggest that dreams are about getting what you want by wishing it, is a tough sell. Further, how could it be that something that I say you want is often experienced in the dream as anxiety? How is that getting you what you want? The wish that's represented in the dream is an infantile one from the unconscious. Why is the unconscious filled with wishes? The answer to this is speculation, as we have not interviewed newborns. But decades of observation of newborns and young children (Beebe, 2018; Spitz, 1945, 1951) leads us to this: In the earliest of infancy, when the infant is hungry it cries. What happens when it cries? Hopefully it will soon see the mothering one's face, smell her scent and become enveloped by the warmth of her body. It will also feel and taste the nipple of her breast or the nipple of the bottle. Soon, the infant will feel satisfied. If none of this happens, there will be other kinds of trouble. Typically it does happen. By the way, it isn't just the milk that these babies begin to need; it's the whole experience, as we know from the research of attachment theorists, such as René Spitz (1945, 1951). This was research on the observation of abandoned babies who were in foundling homes during World War II. It was noted that when these infants were fed, but not held and cuddled, they became depressed and hopeless. If we follow these notions to their conclusion, for those infants who have been nurtured in infancy, when they are hungry they want to be satiated. However, soon, when these infants are hungry, they quickly imagine the "mothering one" experience. They picture the mother being there and the images of the mothering one become a source of gratification, even when she has not yet appeared. (When older children and adults are upset, by the way, it is helpful and soothing to imagine a calming scene of a person in one's head to feel better). Fortunately, the mothering one also hears the infant's cries and this is what actually brings the mother and gratification to the crying infant, but the infant doesn't know this (and regressed and disturbed people don't know it either). When the mother comes, the infant doesn't know the difference between thinking (reality) and hallucinating (fantasy). What we believe the infant experiences is satisfaction. Another way to say this is: for an infant and for a young child, thinking is the same as hallucinating; that is, the earliest form of thinking is the gratification of need states via hallucinating. To expand these ideas, when we call someone psychotic because they are exhibiting hallucinations, we are also saying that the person is regressed. The person has regressed to an earlier time in their cognitive and emotional development, when all their needs were "gratified" by hallucination. A dreaming, nonpsychotic adult is, by way of wish fulfillment, harking back to an earlier way of "thinking" where wishes are granted by simply picturing them. This is an important concept for you as beginning clinicians, because when you conduct a clinical interview, particularly when you interview people who are disturbed, you'll begin to understand how much the disturbed patient's thinking is dominated by earlier ways of thinking, thinking based upon the gratification of wishes from childhood, without regard for the constraints of reality.

Here is an example:

> I once interviewed a young man, slight in stature but expansive in gait, who had been an attorney but had been disbarred because he had embezzled money from his clients. He hadn't come to me about this issue, as his disbarment had occurred several years before and he was (surprisingly) dismissive about it. What he came for was he had been told by his internist that he should talk to me because of his level of stress! "Stress" can often be a code word used by physicians about someone that the medical doctor doesn't know what to do with (nor should they unless they've been psychologically trained). This patient was not stressed, although he should have been! Instead, he told me with great enthusiasm about what sounded like a Ponzi scheme[5] involving selling certain stock when these were at an artificially high value and then dumping them so they lost value (while I didn't quite get the technical language he was using, I knew that what he was doing was probably a crime, and he did too).

I listened politely. (I tend to be active in sessions, even in first interviews, but I felt that there was very little that I could say to this man that would have any effect on him.) At the end of the session I said the following:

"I'm not going to charge you any money for this meeting because I don't really have anything of value to say to you. What I mean is that I might have something to say that you might not see as valuable. I also think that you would not want to hear what I might want to say." (I actually thought that these comments were of great value for this man, but as I assessed that he had very strong narcissistic and psychopathic features, I chose to devalue my comments in advance, by myself, rather than allowing him to do it. Also, I was sure that he wasn't going to like what I had to say.)

Next, I said the following:

"If wishing for things could make them happen, then all that you have suggested to me would work out well for you with these plans, plans you have presented with such great enthusiasm. However, I don't think that it will."

From what you just heard, I don't think that you would confuse this with your grandfather or grandmother's psychoanalysis. However, in this example I applied a psychoanalytic understanding to this man's problems and I attempted to have him understand that his wishing would not make his schemes happen the way he wanted them to, any more than wishing in a dream will make the dreamer's reality any different when they awaken. I *was* hoping against hope that my comments would intrigue this man enough for him to want to come back, but this was not to be. I will return to this case example in another lecture to show how I also tried some other psychoanalytic comments during the hour, in my attempt to engage him in constructive clinical work.

STUDENT: So this is wish fulfillment as well? That he could do whatever he wants?
DR. M: Yes, and that wishing would get him whatever he wants! That's the wish fulfillment; this man believed himself to be omnipotent – all-powerful – wanting it and, therefore, getting it. He could do whatever he wanted and he could control the outcome because he wanted to. All humans have a bit of omnipotence; the defense is called omnipotent control. We also have a bit of narcissism. Otherwise we wouldn't have any pride in ourselves. But his omnipotence was wild, and his family dynamics pulled for this, as he was a very damaged person who had been enabled and encouraged to have no limits. The point that I am making here is that in this case I was applying concepts developed by Freud in the 1890s, but doing so in 21st-century terms.

To return to Freud's Chapter 7, Freud says that releases of pleasure and unpleasure are discharged or they are held in check by the preconscious. The blockage, direction and flow of energy here is what Freud called the economic factor of his "meta-psychological model of the mind."

Later, we will learn more about this economic factor. For now, Freud's economic factor suggests that an unconscious wish is either held in check or discharged in movement. However, if you're asleep, then the preconscious binds up the unconscious wish and prevents its discharge in movement (this is why we remember a dream better if we keep our muscles perfectly still). Also, if one isn't able to discharge some of the energy by way of the dream, then the person will be forced to wake up and discharge the wish motorically. For example, while I'm sure that what I now say will *not* have anything to do with any of you: Although each of you went to college, I'm confident that none of you ever drank too much beer (*said with sarcasm*). However, if you had, the experience you would have had is that you would have needed to awaken to urinate frequently during the night. Then, at some point, you would have gotten dehydrated and therefore become very thirsty. You would have either had to repeatedly wake up and drink lots of water, or you might have had a dream with some content such as this: You are in the desert and thirsty, and perhaps crawling along, when suddenly you see (you dream) a water fountain, a giant fountain. It is filled and ready to dispense your favorite beverage. If you didn't have this or some similar dream, you'd need to repeatedly awaken to quench your thirst.

STUDENT: Yeah, I have been in that situation, and it's not usually something as clear as being thirsty and seeing a water fountain in the desert.

DR. M: Yes, that is why the psychoanalyst helps the person to unravel it (just as Freud did with the Irma dream). As the psychoanalyst and the patient unravel it, the patient will say: "Wait a minute . . . this particular image makes me think of X, Y or Z." The psychoanalyst might then say: "Well, that reminds me of what you said happened yesterday . . . that seems important." Or, "Remember when you mentioned your childhood memory of you and your older brother?" Then the patient may start to think about a key moment the day before that now resonates with the dream content. Often this will lead the patient to memories from childhood. In effect, what the patient is learning is that dreaming is a way that we return to our childhood to use the methods that were available to us at that time to solve problems. The current problem that the dreamer is trying to solve is the problem of trying to stay asleep while being buffeted by powerful or upsetting needs and feelings.

I want to add that the man who believed that he was above the law had also returned to childish ways of thinking to solve problems: by wishing. Unfortunately he did so while awake! I gave you the example of frustrated physical needs because, as you said, those are easy to solve in the dream and the day residue is relatively easy to unravel: "I drank too much beer." It is typically the emotional ones that are more hidden. With Freud, it was the rebuff by a colleague in the Irma dream; or for one of us it might be a fight with a friend, or a very disturbing conversation with somebody that you love, or that you hate. The dreamer needs to find a way to deal with this day residue and the upsetting or intolerable feelings that have been triggered, so they can continue to sleep.

STUDENT: This psychic energy . . . is that what's going to be known as the libido?

DR. M: Yes.

STUDENT: I have a second question: Do neurotics tend to have a lot of nightmares?

DR. M: Everyone dreams. The current research on rapid eye movement[6] – we'll talk about it at the end of this section about dreams – suggests that the average person dreams four times per night. Not everyone remembers their dreams. Some people have nightmares. Some neurotics remember all of their dreams, some don't. For instance, an obsessive-compulsive neurotic might dream a lot and not feel anxious about their dreams. But a hysterical neurotic probably would feel anxious. I know that these distinctions don't make a difference yet, but they will. When we talk about the different psychopathologies we'll delve into this more. For now, the major issue for a neurotic who's obsessive-compulsive is that they do not experience feeling, are not feeling *touched* by the experience.

STUDENT: Is it possible to have masochistic wishes, wishes that aren't as happy as all these we've been talking about, like: "There's a part of me that wants to be sad, that doesn't want to have great relationships," and then that could be in the dream?

DR. M: Yes. This is an important question. I was not going to talk about that yet, because it is a much more difficult area for beginning doctoral students to hear about, but one kind of anxiety dream might be about the wish for mastery. Another kind of anxiety dream might be about the wish for punishment and suffering.

STUDENT: What about nightmares where everything is just terrible and you can't really identify a wish or anything that feels like a wish?

DR. M: If you start to ask about the day residue, the dreamer will soon be able to identify the wish because the day residue stimulated the wish. In this case, the psychoanalyst might ask: "What stood out from yesterday that might have affected you?" If there is a lot of anxiety, the dreamer may not immediately be able to identify anything because the dream work (condensation and displacement) are disguising it. Whatever the conflict(s) that have been stirred up in the day residue, these will appear in the dream in some form. This is how the dreamer and the psychoanalyst will be able to identify the upsetting conflict(s).

STUDENT: So are you saying that even a nightmare is a wish fulfillment?

DR. M: Yes, and I understand that this is counterintuitive, but as you work with patients in distress, you'll begin to see that these notions of Freud's are absolutely brilliant. Freud was the master of the negative correlation: what shows in consciousness is often negatively correlated with what is occurring in the unconscious.

STUDENT: What about lucid dreams, where you're stuck? Are those anxiety dreams?

DR. M: One can feel stuck in something, and you can't get out of it. This underscores the way Freud's psychoanalysis works: Freud might say that some part of the person doesn't want to remove themselves from the situation, but another part has found a creative way to reject this idea, so the person isn't aware that being stuck may be about wanting to be stuck. This is, by the way, an excellent example of how we understand the topographic conscious-ness and dynamic (or dynamic-conflict) aspects of Freud's metapsychology. It doesn't *feel* like you want to be stuck in it . . . it feels unpleasant and the trapped feeling is how the person disavows the part of themselves that wants to have exactly what they act like they don't want.

STUDENT: That goes back to my question earlier, then, about if you're supposed to know the dream. Is it supposed to make its way into awareness?

DR. M: These questions highlight the problems that Freud was struggling with, questions that were very hard to answer because Freud kept switching back and forth between biology and psychology. To answer your question on both levels: The person may or may not "supposed to be" conscious and therefore aware of the conflict, but the energy involved – energy that was stimulated the night before – that energy has got to be discharged. Freud was still a psychobiologist. As of now, Freud is telling us that the dream is our attempt to discharge powerful impulses that are trying to keep us awake so they can be gratified, but if we can understand them they become less conflictual and more easily gratified.

STUDENT: So his initial thought is that it's just energy, but later also there's this knowledge that getting into awareness is important. I mean, in the dream world you're feeling that you're stuck on something and you're saying that a psychoanalyst would say to you that you kind of *want* to be stuck there to work through it.

DR. M: Yes. What the psychoanalyst might say would concern such variables as: Where are the psychoanalyst and the patient in their relationship? In other words, how strong is the therapeutic alliance? Without knowing that, I can only tell you what the psychoanalyst would think. The psychoanalyst would think that they understand the basic meaning of the dream from the dreamer's associations as well as from the uncovering of the day residue. Whatever the psychoanalyst might say or not say, they would want to be empathic to where the dreamer is at that moment. For example, the psychoanalyst might think: *This person seems unable to get out of their own way; they keep putting them-selves in situations that are not gratifying and I don't know what this means, but I will begin to focus my questions on this.*

STUDENT: Right. So, in that scenario, the wish would be they want to master that?

DR. M: Yes, the worst human experience is the feeling of helplessness. By the way, that's a strategy of people who are in a relationship but say: "You can't fire me because I quit." While not helpful, for some people this strategy seems better than having to wait passively for the axe to fall on their relationship (at times with some people, they will "fire themselves" even if that it was *not* what was going to happen). A person who has had traumatic relationship experiences might decide that they are never again going to make themselves vulnerable.

As we'll see, Freud will talk about the infant's helplessness and conclude that it is the major source of human anxiety.

STUDENT: What about recurring dreams?

DR. M: A recurring dream in childhood is typically related to the child working on the mastery of some developmental process. A recurring dream in adolescence is typically connected to becoming a more separate person and consolidating one's own emotional and gender identity, both sexual and nonsexual. A recurring dream in young adulthood is about what most of you in this class are doing now, forging a career and beginning to make certain life decisions. One of the first things a psychoanalyst will ask in the initial sessions is: Can you tell me what is your earliest memory? Then the psychoanalyst might ask: Do you remember any dreams from your childhood? Then: Do you remember any recurring dreams that you had in your adolescence? Then: do you remember a recent dream and/or have you been having recurring dreams? Here the psychoanalyst will be looking for recurring life themes.

STUDENT: What would a psychoanalyst say about someone whose earliest memory isn't until they are, like, eleven, or someone who doesn't have a lot of early memories?

DR. M: The psychoanalyst would think that unless the person has had some kind of organic condition or injury, not being able to remember things suggests that the person had severe trauma. If you talk to a traumatized borderline patient and you ask the person about their history, what you will typically get is a lot of nothing:

> "What was your childhood like?" "A normal childhood." "How would you describe your mother?" "Oh, just a mother, I guess." "And your father?" "Just a father . . . he was mean." Here, the psychoanalyst will be thinking: *We're missing data here. This person is using avoidance and denial.*

I understand that to many of you this way of thinking is strange and exotic.

Now, to return to Student X's comment: What would a psychoanalyst think about if someone has blocked out all of the early childhood memories? Would this be considered to be an adaptive function? It might not be adaptive to this person *now*, but perhaps it was adaptive given the alternatives. If this person presents for treatment – a person who had a horrific history – and he or she wants to live in the present for now, that is OK. When this person is able to trust me, to trust themselves, and to trust the processes of therapy, we will revisit the past.

An example comes to me: Some years ago, a young woman presented herself for an intake interview. She was a student in a master's program in the mental health professions, and she came for an intake interview to assess whether she should be in therapy. The first thing that I found to be unusual was that she acted like she was in my office for a job interview, not an intake interview for psychotherapy. She was proper, formal, overly agreeable and solicitous. When I asked questions, she would give me many details and comments, but she presented these as if she was reading her CV to me. Then, however, I asked her about her earliest memory. This was her reply:

> "I guess I have an upsetting memory. My earliest memory is that my mother and father were fighting. And my father threw a dish at my mother and hit her in the head. I was three or four years old."

After this, she changed her tone, returning again to talking like she was reading her resume. What did I learn from this? I learned that all of her defenses centered on a very fragile self-structure and, in a certain way one could say that she presented as if she were two people. She was the person-presenting-a-resume-to-me and she was also the-person-who-had-a-horrific-childhood. It took the two of us approximately one year of therapy for this traumatized person to revisit her horrific childhood and those horrible memories.

Why am I telling you all of this at this point in our lectures? You ask: "How can one present an abstract concept such as 'love' or 'guilt' or 'chaos' in a dream?" I want to show you that the dreamer presents in a series of dream images just what the patient presents in words, and when words fail, they present in memories or even in enactments.[7]

STUDENT: I guess this is kind of connected to what you are saying: Why are we so bad at understanding our own latent content? Why do we find it so difficult? Even if we are interested, curious, it always seems like we need an outside source just [to] shed that light onto it.

DR. M: Dreams are connected to the most primitive and earliest parts of our selves. Unless the dreams are troubling us, they are continually interfering with our sleep and our functioning, it is rare for any of us to want to understand them. This is one of the things that is remarkable about Freud's courageous journey into the uncharted territory of the mind. If one is living their life and is happy, is loving and loved and productive, then of what use is it to know that we harbor envious, hateful, spiteful, cannibalistic, murderous and incestuous (to mention only a few) impulses? However, if one is suffering like the young woman we talked about (a very decent, caring, smart and dedicated person, I might add) and/or if one is treating this person in therapy, then both the clinician and the patient need to understand all about her so that we can help her to understand herself and change. When this young woman and I were able to make meaning out of the chaotic life she began to show me, she was able to make free choices about how she wanted to live; she began to possess more choices about how she was going to *be*. You might want to think about it this way: Troubled people are simply people who have the misfortune to have learned to rely on more-primitive defenses than less troubled people (what I am saying will become clearer in later lectures).

STUDENT: Can you give an example of a primitive defense versus a less primitive defense?

DR. M: Remember the man who was a disbarred attorney, who was now in another scheme to embezzle money through stock transactions? While he was using rationalization, which is a sophisticated, advanced defense, he was also using primitive defenses such as omnipotent control (believing that one can control fate via a kind of magical thinking. One believes, using a combination of skill and luck, they can get whatever they wish for) and denial (there is no problem with breaking the law if I am smart). If you remember, I suggested this to the patient when I told him, "If wishes could come true, your scheme could make you rich." And another defense, omnipotence: "I know better than everybody else and I can fool them." And denial: "The law is not going to affect me. It might affect you, but it won't affect me." And projection: "The world's a bad place, I'm going to get what I want because otherwise people will get what I want, and take it from me." These are primitive defenses.

A neurotic person might say, "I wish I could rob a bank, I'm in such bad shape financially," or, "You know, this money is lying right here, all I'd have to do is take it. But I can't. Then I'd be a bad person." These are more sophisticated defenses. Sophisticated defenses help one better recognize the constraints of reality. At the other extreme is a patient in a hospital. How would that person look? They might be staring off into space and be similar to a newborn in a dream state. In between both of these extremes is the young woman that we just discussed, as well as the disbarred attorney. They each employ primitive defenses, but much of the time they can recognize the difference between reality and nonreality. However, under stress/intense need/intense anxiety, each of them has access to primitive defenses.

STUDENT: But when you have a nightmare, one that is not working to keep you asleep, there's still meaning to it, right? How do you understand it? How do you analyze what the wish is?

DR. M: As I suggested, the easiest way is to go to the day residue. The residue is going to give clues to what was being stimulated. We took an easy one with the biological ones, like with the beer. Yet, easy or hard, when you ask about the day residue, you get some sense of what the dream is attempting to accomplish (what need/wish was attempting to discharge without producing so much anxiety that it wakes the dreamer). Think about it this way: Every dream is an attempt to solve a problem, the problem of partially discharging a need while keeping you asleep. With the biological example, the dream would be keeping you asleep because you are thirsty or hungry; with the psychological one, you are angry or longing for love or bewildered. Or, in the easiest one to understand, which Freud comes to later, you had a bad car accident, a trauma. You have dreams about this car accident over and over again. Later, Freud suggests the dreamer is trying to master the trauma of the accident. We'll see various ways one attempts to master trauma (such as in PTSD).

To continue with the material, the binding up of an unsettling idea and its accompanying feelings and anxiety is what occurs in the dream. The preconscious binds up the wish and then it's partially discharged. This is why Freud says that the dream actually guards sleep, by serving as a kind of safety valve for wishes. This is true even of anxiety dreams, lucid dreams and mastery dreams. These are dreams where the dream has not worked well enough to completely bind up the wish. The result is that the wish is partially discharged in a less hidden form and it stimulates anxiety, so the person awakens. The colloquial understanding of waking from a dream is in all of us: After having studied Freud and teaching this course for 40-plus years, I will still wake up and say, "Oh, I had an upsetting dream that woke me up." The dream didn't wake me up – technically – the dream was supposed to keep me sleeping. It partially failed and I woke up.

STUDENT: So anxiety dreams are when the preconscious doesn't censor.

DR. M: Well, let me stop you. You are close – the anxiety dream occurs when the preconscious censor can't bind the latent material *enough*, it doesn't totally bind the wish and keep the motor system blocked. The preconscious has not been effective enough in its use of condensation and displacement, and so the wish/latent content begins to emerge in a less disguised form (like the example of the patient's cannibal dream). This produces anxiety and the anxiety wakes you. If you wake up anxious but you hold your body still and keep your muscles bound, just as you had been doing while you were sleeping, you may be able to retrieve more of the content of the dream, and also be able to understand what made you anxious, as the wish will be less disguised in the available (manifest) content.

STUDENT: The preconscious is theoretically supposed to censor the wish, right?

DR. M: Yes, but keep in mind that a censor will not be able to keep out all incoming information. Even in a dictatorship, the government isn't going to be able to block out all of the news, no matter how it tries to. Instead, the government is going to present a redacted, transformed version of the news. Similarly, the censor of the preconscious is going to try to make the dream more palatable to the dreamer. By employing the dream work, the censor will alter the latent content so enough of the image can be acceptable to the person who is beginning to awaken. The goal is to alter the dream so that it is not so objectionable to the preconscious. This occurs via the mechanisms of condensation and displacement. At this point in Freud's work, this is still a biopsychological model. It's about how much energy gets through. We can talk about the dream's meaning, but that's only now about how the meaning has been altered to help the person discharge *some* of the powerful and upsetting feelings stimulated by the events of the previous day. In the Irma dream, Freud realizes that he harbors conflictual feelings toward some of his colleagues, that he is ruthlessly competitive and even small-minded. As I said in our first meeting, Freud is in a constant battle between the biological and the psychological. At this point he is trying to use his biological mind-model to explain something that, he thought at the time, is unique to humans.

From this understanding of dreams, Freud introduces the notions of the primary process and the secondary process. The primary process is the way of "thinking" that the dreamer uses, characterized by ways to discharge cathected energy. This primary process is aided by the dream work's use of condensation and displacement (what is now called associative reasoning). The secondary process is used by waking life and includes mechanisms like secondary revision and secondary elaboration, i.e., reasoning processes and concept formation.

The primary process is also the process that Freud says occurs in neurosis, and we can add, to deepen this understanding, the saying,

"While neurotics build castles in the air, psychotics live in them."

"Building castles in the air" is living in a way that you are dominated by day-dreams and wishes. Living in these castles is another matter altogether. So the primary process is seen in neurosis, and by understanding the normal phenomenon of dreams, Freud can begin to understand that these same processes are involved in psychopathology. We can see Freud moving away from an exclusively biological understanding of mental process to a psychological one.

Following this, Freud suggests that there are two kinds of unconscious: The (true) unconscious, and the preconscious. He suggests that the unconscious can never become conscious, while the preconscious can. Consciousness, then (the preconscious and the perceptual system), works by taking latent material and translating it, making it acceptable to our conscious self. Another way to say this is that the conscious system regulates pleasure and un-pleasure for all of us. We're in a constant conflict: How much can one be conscious of need states without becoming too anxious about them? Consciousness, as a system and censor, regulates pleasure and un-pleasure. That's what makes humans different from other species that simply discharge all of their wishes in motor activity.

As we've seen, Freud's dream theory is worked out with thoroughness and detail.

About 120 years' worth of clinical data suggest that dreams are not meaningless. Further, this data goes beyond self-report and clinical data: There is now dream research data (rapid eye movement and MRI). As I mentioned, another explanation is that these phenomena are only biological. In our discussion last time, I said that everything about living things has biological aspects. All mental processes are an interaction of the brain (neurological-biological) and the mind (psychological).

This appears in work that is combining psychoanalysis and neuroscience. One looks at human phenomena from a biological/psychological interaction. For example, Gallese et al. (2007) found that the neural circuits activated in a person who is carrying out actions, expressing emotions, experiencing sensations, are also activated automatically via a mirror neuron system in the observer of the actions, emotions and sensations. These authors propose that this finding of shared activation is a functional mechanism of "embodied simulation" consisting of automatic, unconscious and noninferential simulation in the observer and experienced by the observed. They also suggest that these shared neural activation patterns – and the accompanying embodied simulation – constitute a biological basis for understanding another's mind. The implication of this perspective for psychoanalysis, particularly regarding Freud's observations about the unconscious (including communication, projective identification, attunement, empathy, therapeutic action and transference-countertransference interactions) is that each of these functions has a biological/neurological basis. There is now a growing literature in the new field of neuropsychoanalysis.[8] One of the authors of this shared activation study (two of the authors are Italian research psychoanalysts) happens to be Dr. Morris Eagle, a psychologist and a retired member of our Derner doctoral faculty.

Modern psychological theory does not present as if something biological cannot also be psychological. That's why we study both the brain *and* the mind. The "Ebenezer Scrooge theory of dreaming" (*A Christmas Carol*, Desmond-Hurst, B., Director1951) is absolutely right, as I have indicated with regard to the findings of REM research, but it is more complicated than this. REM researchers have discovered some interesting things. They found that most people dream four times every night, and that during an emotional crisis or trauma the amount of dreaming is reduced. They suggest from a neuroscience point of view that such dreams are upsetting because the person is dreaming in an attempt to master the trauma. They are not psychoanalysts, they're neurologists and neuroscientists. They asked questions about the state of brain activity during dreaming versus nondreaming. In doing this research, they also began to have an understanding of dream content. Certainly that's a biological/psychological interactive process. Yet how do these mechanisms show themselves when one is neurotic? That is what we will be seeing this semester.

Freud's model provides us with a preliminary understanding of:

(1.) Consciousness
(2.) The unconscious
(3.) All mental processes

To summarize, *The Interpretation of Dreams* brought Freud to an understanding of the unconscious.

What is psychoanalytic theory? It's an understanding of the unconscious. Once we accept that there is an unconscious, we accept the main tenet of psychoanalysis. Psychoanalysts call this part of Freud's work *id psychology*: Freud's understanding of what he called wishes and how these wishes are important in human functioning. How do we process wishes, achieve pleasure, avoid un-pleasure and avoid danger? Freud will spend the rest of his career exploring the ways that human beings process, fear, avoid and deal with what we wish for and what we fear.

Summary of lecture 3

In Chapter 7 of *The Interpretation of Dreams*, Freud presented a highly sophisticated and evolved unconscious mental process that serves as a safety valve for sleep. The process Freud proposed is called regression. In waking life, psychological processes proceed from perceptual to motor, the reflex arc. A person who is hungry and spies a gratifying stimulus (say, a cookie) exerts motor activity and gratifies the need for nourishment by effecting a change in the environment (I am hungry; I spy a cookie; I eat it). What happens when I go to sleep but become hungry in the middle of the night? Or what if I go to sleep angry after an argument with my friend? I can wake myself up and gratify my need by exerting motor activity (by getting a cookie, in the first instance, or, in the latter situation, calling the friend and telling them off). Or I can stay asleep and dream of gratifying my need (say, eating a box full of delicious cookies, or dream that I am yelling at my friend). What processes occur to help me create a dream image to gratify my hunger or my anger or other needs, and therefore keep me sleeping? Freud suggests that the dream is a wish fulfillment. That is, a dream is a way of gratifying one's wishes. In infancy, when hungry, a baby cries, and a caretaker comes to bring the baby nourishment. The baby does not connect the nourishment with the cry. The baby experiences hunger and then pictures the gratifying scene of nourishment. Soon, whenever the baby is hungry, it simply pictures the gratifying image and feels soothed (the baby also cries so that it continues to be fed). Wish-fulfilling images (hallucinations) become associated with the baby's need for gratification. Over time, the young child no longer needs to hallucinate to gratify desires, as this has been replaced with a stimulus-response approach to the environment. But an earlier (regressed) method of gratifying needs remains in the unconscious of every one of us; this is the process that is called upon when we dream. In order to satisfy the need in a dream, we must reach into our vast storehouse of memories of need gratification to find a wish-fulfilling image that can be used to create a dream. Freud calls this regressive because by dreaming we are regressing back to an earlier form of thinking where our needs were gratified by hallucinations. The regressive thinking that the dreamer's mind uses is primary-process thinking, and Freud presents it in opposition to secondary-process thinking – the thinking of waking life, rational thought. Freud also suggests that this same primary-process thinking is seen in neurotics. However, when awake, primary-process thinking is upsetting, so the neurotic uses repression and/or creates symptoms to protect against this intolerable experience. In *The Interpretation of Dreams*, Freud expands the ideas he developed in working with neurotics to a model of the mind. *The Interpretation of Dreams* represents for Freud a transition from the study of psychopathology to a new theory of mind.

Notes

1 Epistemology aims to answer questions such as "What do we know?" "What does it mean to say that we know something? "What makes beliefs justified?" and "How do we know that we know something?" *Encyclopedia Britannica* (June 2020)
2 Embodied cognition (Vacharkulksemsuk & Fredrickson, 2012) suggests that many features of cognition, whether human or otherwise, are shaped by aspects of the entire body of the organism. The features of cognition include high-level mental constructs (such as concepts and categories) and performance on various cognitive tasks (such as reasoning

or judgment). The aspects of the body include the motor system, the perceptual system, bodily interactions with the environment, and the assumptions about the world that are built into the structure of the organism.

3 Explicit memory is one of the two main types of long-term human memory, the other of which is implicit memory. Explicit memory is the conscious, intentional recollection of factual information, previous experiences and concepts. Explicit memory can be divided into two categories: episodic memory, which stores specific personal experiences, and semantic memory, which stores factual information. Explicit memory requires gradual learning, with multiple presentations of a stimulus and response. Procedural memory, a type of implicit (or *nondeclarative*) memory, refers to unconscious memories such as skills (e.g., knowing how to get dressed, eat, drive, ride a bicycle without having to relearn the skill each time). Procedural memory learns rule-like relations, whereas explicit memory "learns" relations that are arbitrary. Unlike explicit memory, procedural memory learns rapidly, even from a single stimulus, and it is influenced by other mental systems. See Baker et al. (2005).

4 Sensory deprivation, or "perceptual isolation," is the deliberate reduction or removal of stimuli from one or more of the senses (Solomon et al., 1961). Simple devices such as blindfolds or hoods and earmuffs can cut off sight and hearing, while more complex devices can also cut off the sense of smell, touch, taste, heat-sense and the "feeling" of gravity. Sensory deprivation has been used in various alternative medicines and in psychological experiments. Short-term sessions of sensory deprivation are described as relaxing and conducive to meditation; however, extended or forced sensory deprivation can result in extreme anxiety, hallucinations, bizarre thoughts, temporary senselessness and depression.

5 A Ponzi scheme is a form of fraud that lures investors and pays profits to earlier investors with funds from more recent investors. The scheme leads victims to believe that profits are coming from product sales or other means, and they remain unaware that other investors are the source of funds. A Ponzi scheme can maintain the illusion of a sustainable business as long as new investors contribute new funds, and as long as most of the investors do not demand full repayment and still believe in the nonexistent assets they are purported to own.

6 Rapid eye movement sleep – REM sleep or REMS (Dement & Kleitman, 1957) – is a unique phase of sleep in mammals and birds, distinguishable by random/rapid movement of the eyes, and accompanied by low muscle tone throughout the body and the propensity of the sleeper to dream vividly. The REM phase is also known as paradoxical sleep, or PS, and sometimes as desynchronized sleep because of physiological similarities to waking states, including rapid, low-voltage desynchronized brain waves. Electrical and chemical activity regulating this phase seems to originate in the brain stem and is characterized most notably by an abundance of the neurotransmitter acetylcholine, combined with a nearly complete absence of the monoamine neurotransmitters histamine, serotonin and norepinephrine. REM sleep is physiologically different from the other phases of sleep, which are collectively referred to as non-REM sleep. REM sleep and non-REM sleep alternate within one sleep cycle, which lasts about 90 minutes in adult humans. As sleep cycles continue, they shift toward a higher proportion of REM sleep and the body abruptly loses muscle tone, a state known as REM atonia. Aserinsky and Kleitman (1953) defined rapid eye movement and linked it to dreams. Many experiments have involved awakening test subjects whenever they begin to enter the REM phase, thereby producing a state known as REM deprivation. Reports of dreamers upon waking have been used to study this phase of sleep.

7 "Enactment": While it has been used in a colloquial and rather imprecise way for some time, the term *enactment* probably emerged more clearly in psychoanalytic literature during the 1980s. In an enactment the psychoanalyst contributes, subject to their own

transferences and blind spots, being led by the relationship instead of accompanying it. Enactment implies a positive strength in treatment. See also Mendelsohn (2017).

8 Neuropsychoanalysis integrates neuroscience and psychoanalysis to create a balanced and equal study of the human mind. This approach began as advances in neuroscience led to breakthroughs in new information for psychoanalysis. Despite advantages for these fields to interconnect, there has been some concern that too much emphasis on the neurobiological physiology of the brain will undermine the importance of dialogue and exploration that is foundational to psychoanalysis. Critics will also point to the qualitative and subjective nature of the field of psychoanalysis, claiming it cannot be fully reconciled with the quantitative and objective nature of neuroscientific research. However, despite this critique, proponents of the field of neuropsychoanalysis remind critics that the father of psychoanalysis, Freud, began his career as a neuroanatomist, further arguing that research in this category proves that the psychodynamic effects of the mind are inextricably linked to neural activity in the brain. Neuroscientific progress has created a shared study of many of the same cognitive phenomena, and proponents for a distinct field under the heading of neuropsychoanalysis point to the ability for observation of the subjective mind and empirical evidence in neurobiology to provide greater understanding and greater curative methods. Neurospsychoanalysis aims to bring a field, often viewed as belonging more to the humanities than the sciences, into the scientific realm and under the umbrella of neuroscience, distinct from psychoanalysis, yet adding to the insight gained from it (see also Adolphs, 2003).

References

Adolphs, R. (2003). Cognitive neuroscience of human social behaviour. *Journal of Neuroscience, 4,* 165–178.

Aserinsky, E., & Kleitman, N. (1953). Regularly occurring periods of eye motility, and concomitant phenomena, during sleep. *Science, 118*(3062), 273–274.

Baker, D. G., Ekhator, N. N., Kasckow, J. W., Dashevsky, B., Horn, P. S., Bednarik, L., & Geracioti Jr, T. D. (2005). Higher levels of basal serial CSF cortisol in combat veterans with posttraumatic stress disorder. *American Journal of Psychiatry, 162*(5), 992–994.

Beebe, B. (2018). Comment on micro analysis of multimodal communication in therapy: A case of relational trauma in parent-infant psychoanalytic psychotherapy. *Journal of Infant, Child, Adolescent Psychotherapy, 17*(1), 14.

Bossis, A. (2015). Cited in Pollan, M. The trip treatment. *The New Yorker Magazine, 9.*

Dement, W., & Kleitman, N. (1957). The relation of eye movements during sleep to dream activity. *Journal of Experimental Psychology, 53*(5), 339–346.

Desmond-Hurst, B. (Director). (1951). *A Christmas carol* [Film]. George Minter Productions.

Freud, S. (1900). The interpretation of dreams. In J. Strachey et al. (Trans.), *The standard edition of the complete psychological works of Sigmund Freud, Volume IV.* London: Hogarth, ix–627.

Gallese, V., Eagle, M. N., & Migone, P. (2007). Intentional attunement: Mirror neurons and the neural underpinnings of interpersonal relations. *Journal of the American Psychoanalytic Association, 55,* 131–176.

Martinich, A. P., & Stroll, A. (2020). Epistemology. *Encyclopedia Britannica.* www.britannica.com/topic/epistemology

Mendelsohn, R. (2017). *A three-factor model of couples therapy.* Lanham, MD: Lexington Books/Rowman & Littlefield.

Rapaport, D. (1960). *The structure of psychoanalytic theory: A systematic attempt.* New York: International Universities Press.

Schacter, D. L. (1976). The hypnagogic state: A critical review of the literature. *Psychological Bulletin, 83*(3), 452–481.

Schulman, M. A. (1982). Intelligence and adaptation: An integration of psychoanalytic and Piagetian developmental psychology. *Psychoanalytic Review, 69*(3), 411–414.

Solomon, P. E., Kubzansky, P. E., Leiderman, P. H., Mendelson, J. H., Trumbull, R. E., & Wexler, D. E. (1961). *Sensory deprivation: A symposium held at the Harvard Medical School.* Cambridge, MA: Harvard University Press.

Spitz, R. A. (1945). Hospitalism: An inquiry into the genesis of psychiatric conditions in early childhood. *Psychoanalytic Study of the Child, 1*, 53–74.

Spitz, R. A. (1951). The psychogenic diseases in infancy: An attempt at their etiologic classification. *Psychoanalytic Study of the Child, 6*, 255–275.

Vacharkulksemsuk, T., & Fredrickson, B. L. (2012). Strangers in sync: Achieving embodied rapport through shared movements. *Journal of Experimental and Social Psychology, 48*(1), 399–402.

Chapter 4

Sexuality and the "stages of development" theory

Source: Three Essays on the Theory of Sexuality, 1905

From the 1940s into the 1970s, American psychoanalysis psychopathologized homosexuality and gender fluidity. Freud never psychopathologized it; this may surprise you. (See Freud's treatment of a gender-fluid woman, the poet H.D. (Doolittle, H. 2012),[1] and his "Letter to An American Mother" who wrote to Freud requesting he "treat" her son for homosexuality; Freud said homosexuality was not a neurotic condition (see Cheuvront, 2016).[2]

Three Essays was written in 1905, (Freud, 1905). As you can imagine, this work was received poorly by Freud's medical colleagues in early 20th-century Vienna. Freud was described as a libertine, his works as an "affront to religion," and one Viennese psychiatrist went so far as to say that the contents of the publication were "fit to be discussed only by the police" (Furst, 2003).

To continue, as someone who was trained as an American psychoanalyst, I went along regarding the pathologizing of homosexuality; I regret this. Some of the ideas that I gave up about sexuality – as I began to learn more about the full range of sexual function in humans – would probably sound as strange to you as the changes in our current understanding of sexuality originally sounded to me. As I have noted before, regarding Freud's misogyny – and the same is true regarding his understanding of sexuality and his lack of understanding of race and cultural difference – I ask you to walk in Freud's shoes. This can help us to see early psychoanalysis in the context of its time.

Three Essays on the Theory of Sexuality

Let me remind you that while Freud is credited with being the first dynamic psychologist, for much of his life he was a psychobiologist. Those who were to follow Freud were less connected to biology and more connected to psychology, (Cf, Darwin,1859). . As I've said: Although Freud was the first dynamic psychologist, he had a very ambivalent relationship to psychology.

In *Three Essays on the Theory of Sexuality*, Freud begins his understanding of human sexuality by discussing perversion. This is not unusual for a clinician.

DOI: 10.4324/9781003171393-5

One often begins a discussion about normality by contrasting it with abnormal examples and/or the reverse, by talking about the expectable. However, for Freud we see that his approach is a kind of sleight of hand: Freud believes that there is no normality when one studies sexuality – there is always a continuum, as opposed to an either/or. All of what we call perversion in the adult is normal to the child at some stage of their development.

When we look closely at Freud's work regarding sexual development, you'll see how advanced he was in understanding human sexuality. Later psychoanalysts, particularly American medically trained psychoanalysts of the 1950s, misunderstood Freud's theory of sexual development (had he been alive to see this, Freud would have been horrified by their conclusions and would have said so). That said, let's return to the subject of perversion.

Freud's work in *Three Essays* begins with a discussion of sexual abnormality. To do so, Freud looks to his contemporary, the psychiatrist/neurologist who, like Freud, had the courage to become an expert in this sensitive topic: sexuality. This was Dr. Richard von Krafft-Ebing. Freud reviews the ideas seen in Krafft-Ebing's book on perversions, *Psychopathia Sexualis* (1886).[3] Krafft-Ebing studied the pathology of sexuality when few clinicians would risk their reputations to do this. Freud views Krafft-Ebing's work from the Darwinian point of view. It is based on the goal of the preservation of the human species. From this lens, the aim of sex is the discharge of sexual products in intercourse and the object of sex is that member of the opposite sex who gratifies this aim.

Freud looks at Krafft-Ebing's (1886) description of the various perversions and he notes that all of these perversions are involved with some disconnection between aim and object. The result of these perversions is that none of them can produce offspring to continue the sexual procreation of our species. Let me remind you that Freud saw Darwin's theory of evolution as *the* driving force in adaptation to all life, including, of course, human life. By studying sexuality in the context of the Darwinian drive to preserve our species, Freud was presenting a biological description of abnormality. However, as we all know, sexuality is an emotionally charged and controversial topic that pulls for powerful emotional intensity. It is very difficult to be rational about sex.

The three categories of sexuality

For Freud, there are three categories of people with regard to their human sexuality: perverts, neurotics and normals. In this system, calling someone a "pervert" is not an insult. It is a judgment-free description of a person whose sexual preference is a disconnect between sexual aim and sexual object. It is a description focused on the preservation of the species via sexual procreation. With a so-called normal, one is describing a person with no disconnect between aim and object, and with a neurotic, Freud is describing a person who has a disconnect between aim and object but is attempting to flee from this disconnect by employing various defenses and/or creating symptoms and inhibitions, so as not to experience their own perverse sexual desires and wishes. If each of you can allow yourself, just for the moment, to withdraw the negative connotations of such terms as *pervert, neurotic* and *normal*, you will see that Freud is talking about a biopsychological process, not a value-judgment process. As an example of his thinking, I refer you to a very heartfelt letter, written by Freud, in English, in reply to an American woman, a mother, who wanted her son to be psychoanalyzed by Freud so that Freud could cure her son of his homosexuality. What this woman wanted Freud to do is what we now call "conversion therapy": "converting" a homosexual person into a heterosexual person. Freud said that he didn't treat homosexuality, as he did not understand it to be a neurotic condition (Grotjahn, 1951). True to his word, Freud viewed homosexuality as an orientation that doesn't fit the neurotic spectrum. However, he added, if the son had neurotic concerns about being homosexual or other neurotic conflicts not connected to his sexual orientation, Freud would be glad to work with this man. What we see in this letter is very different from what was portrayed by American psychoanalysis in the 1950s until the early 1980s.

To continue, Freud suggests in *Three Essays* that sexuality is present in all humans from the earliest time of infancy. However, it only shows itself directly in the form that we commonly understand sexuality to be when the person arrives at puberty. It is at puberty when, because of the biological/hormonal and psychological changes in the person, the aim and the object connect and each person is now capable of the procreation of our species via intercourse with an opposite-sex partner. Most importantly, Freud says that the common-sense view that at puberty every adult person wants intercourse with an opposite-sex partner is inaccurate. Further, Freud suggests (and clinical experience tells us) that this notion is false and that there is a connection between what is commonly called perversion and the sexual development of all humans. These notions did not make Freud very popular in Europe during the time that he wrote about them. They do not make him popular in some circles even now.

Freud next begins to follow the origin of the sexual/pleasure drive throughout the various erogenous zones of the body. He expands upon Darwin's theory of evolution and also on the work of Havelock Ellis, (Ellis, H., & Symonds, L. (1897).[4] to view evolution as the driving force in human adaptation to life. In doing this, Freud observes that the process of human development includes sexual development, both physical and psychological. The biological goal of life is its continuance and all humans are "biologically programmed" to create new offspring in order to protect our species from extinction. What causes human beings neurotic problems is that we are both blessed and cursed with consciousness. Freud suggests that if we weren't driven and directed by our consciousness, we'd be like every other creature: Sexual preference would not be so complex; it would only be about procreation, and this would be the extent of one's mating habits. With the human species, we have evolved, based upon a Darwinian understanding, so that we search for the best kind of sexual partner in our mind, in order to create the best kind of family environment in which to raise the children produced via sexual relations. Humans, fortunately and unfortunately, have tastes and develop preferences in our mating rituals, both physical preferences and psychological ones. As Freud reminds us, at one point in our history humans walked on all fours. At that point in our early history, our sense of smell was more developed. I have a dog, and when she sees another dog, she smells all their body parts; this is how she connects with the other dog. In the early history of our species, humans also did this. Our sense of smell was much more advanced. We retain this vague understanding of ourselves when we talk about the sexual attraction between two people by saying that the couple has good chemistry.

Freud adds that clinical experience has suggested to him that there exists a connection between perversion and sexual development, and that this connection is particularly strong in neurotics. That is, there's a particularly strong connection between perverse sexuality and the defenses against perverse sexuality. It is this defensive aspect that leads to neurosis. It is easier to see these same processes play out in the psychotic person, not the neurotic one. While in the neurotic symptoms may be hidden, in the psychotic person they are not. As an example, I once observed a young female receptionist in an all-male ward of a mental hospital. As she (I thought somewhat seductively/provocatively) walked from one office to another, passing by several male patients, several of these men would begin to rock back and forth in their chairs, and several times one man fell to the ground and made the sign of the cross. What was he telling us by this gesture? I intuit from this behavior that he viewed this young woman as a sexual object, and he was making a somewhat bizarre external effort to defend himself against internal sexual longings. Instead of doing all of this internally (in his head) or scrupulously washing his hands, or reading the Scriptures so that he could find a passage to calm himself and remove any dangerous sexual thoughts, this man defended himself externally. One could say he was metaphorically showing us his conflict, as psychotic people sometimes do, in a series of enactments in the environment. What neurotics might do more subtly, this man did openly – one of the comments I was taught to make to acutely psychotic hospitalized patients was a description of their confusion: ("'Inside' is 'outside' and 'outside' is 'inside'"). Those who write fiction intuitively understand this. For example, Shakespeare's portrayal of Hamlet includes many symbolic gestures that are metaphors for the expiation of unknowable and intolerable feelings, and, as seen in in the Bible, the washing away of guilt is a common ritual in religious practice.

Sexual development: Three Essays

With regard to Freud's model of sexual development, he notes that all young children experience pleasure with any bodily activity. If one observes a young child we know that they masturbate; they don't know they "shouldn't" do this until they are told not to. In order to help Freud describe his theory of sexual development, perversion and neurosis, he introduced something called libido theory. Libido is the force of sexual tensions.

Freud employs libido theory by presenting two formulas:

(1.) The neurosis is the negative of the perversion;
(2.) The child is polymorphously perverse.

With regard to these postulates, Freud is not using the term *perversion* polemically. By "perversion" Freud means only that there is a disconnection between aim and object; a perverse sexualized behavior does not serve the purpose of procreation.

For postulate 1, "The neurosis is the negative of perversion," what Freud means is that a person displays perversions, or instead, that person develops symptoms, and the intent of the symptom is to hide the perversion from the self – as well as from the rest of the world (an internal "making the sign of the cross"). Symptoms such as compulsive hand-washing or other compulsive rituals, or spells of anxiety or phobias, can each be understood as a series of defensive reactions to prevent one's perverse wishes from becoming conscious.

For postulate 2, "The child is polymorphously perverse," Freud means that young children get pleasure from any bodily activity, or I'll add that children don't know that there are certain bodily activities that adults believe they're *not* supposed to get pleasure from.

STUDENT: So do people get what is bad from society, or is it inherent?
DR. M: Over time children begin to learn the norms of their culture, and one of the Western cultural norms is that certain kinds of self-stimulation are allowable at any age, others are allowable in childhood but not in adolescence or adulthood, and others are never allowable at any age.
STUDENT: Is it the same when we talk about obsessions like OCD? The cognitive behavioral idea is that obsessions are not logical.
DR. M: It means that these obsessions are not logically true but they are psychologically true. That is, that they have psychological meaning and they perform some function. Of course it is better for a person to learn that they are struggling against perverse sexuality than to fall victim to compulsive counting or other rituals. We all know that when one writes an academic paper, it's required that we first clean our room – at least clean and straighten up the area in the vicinity of the writing, the desk. We need to straighten things out, right? By the way, that was said with sarcasm, but none of you got the sarcasm! In fact, what we are doing is a compulsive symptomatic act – attempting to deal with the feelings and anxiety being stirred within by the paper, attempting to order our internal chaos by first ordering our external chaos. This is metaphorically similar to – although drastically different psychologically from – the hospitalized man who dropped to the ground and made the sign of the cross as he watched a seductive woman pass by.
STUDENT: Symptoms . . . it seems interesting that in order to maintain our "normal" state we have to be symptomatic of something.

DR. M: In that sense, no one grows out of the developmental stages without some neurotic-like symptoms, inhibitions and/or compromises. Even if one has had perfect parents, came into the world with a perfect temperament, one's childhood temperament was completely in sync with the temperament of both parents . . . still, at the least, the person is going to develop compromises, somewhat less-than-debilitating symptoms. In our next lecture we discuss Freud's *The Psychopathology of Everyday Life*. Freud will be talking about blocks and inhibitions (and symptomatic acts) that temporarily interfere with one's routine functioning, even with those of us free of an actual neurosis.

STUDENT: When you described cleaning as a compulsive tendency, could it also be a form of procrastination? That's how I interpret it.

DR. M: Yes, we are saying the same thing: procrastination is also a compulsive (and obsessive) tendency. You're warding off, preparing yourself, but in some way also temporarily controlling time – by stalling. Now in the most nonneurotic people, the procrastinator is saying: "I really don't want to do this now. I'm going to clean my desk. I'm going to think of all the reasons not to do the paper, and then make a compromise in my head (this is called rationalization) I'm going to compromise in my head, then actually write the paper."

To return to libido theory: There are several postulates to libido theory. (1.) What is libido? Libido is a construction made by Freud: the energy fueling the mind. (2.) There's a developmental process where this libido attaches itself to various zones of the body. This is called the process of psychosexual/libidinal stages. You've all heard about this in other psychology courses, but I don't think that it made a lot of sense until you saw the connection between Freud's belief in the theory of evolution, including the belief that humans, like all other species, need to learn how to mate in order to perpetuate our species. The development of libido as a source of bodily pleasure is required so that enough humans develop a desire for heterosexual intercourse to procreate.

In other courses, you've heard about how the libido attaches to the oral, anal and phallic zones of the body and this is what is called the process of libidinal stages. These are survival functions for every human at each of these stages. If an infant is not deriving pleasure during the process of taking in nourishment, and he or she stops eating, that would be risky for the infant's survival – and in the metaphorical sense, for the survival of our species. Infants are pleasure-seeking, at first through the oral zone. At some point the human species learned to first suck, then bite and swallow, and, also metaphorically, we could say that in some of the disorders the adult who hasn't learned moderation "sucks" in everything, and this kind of person can be described as a certain kind of personality. Then there are people who "spit out everything." They are conceptualized as another kind of personality. Then there is a person with a kind of "lockjaw": takes nothing in, gives nothing back out; these people could be described as another kind of personality. What does personality mean? We would say that during the developmental stages, a certain amount of energy gets locked into (fixated at) a particular stage.

Why is this helpful? How are these metaphors useful for therapy? Let's take lockjaw. If you take little in and give little back out, you are deprived of the joy of love and intimacy. Such a person comes to the psychoanalyst, and what the clinician might say after hearing about this person's life is: "It must be cold and lonely to be you." As trust develops, the clinician might say "I guess you feel empty." Yet here's the good news, as this (schizoid) person feels understood and begins to realize that they won't swallow (or be swallowed) in the therapy (that is, the psychoanalyst is respectful of their boundaries in a way that their early objects were not), the person begins to feel safe and they grow. With regard to the anal stage, civilized adults in our culture are expected to walk around but not urinate on the floor; one begins to learn to control such processes. One learns because adults teach us to have bladder and sphincter control. In the battle for control over the young child's body, the battle for their autonomy also occurs. At this stage of human development, which one of my granddaughters is now going through, at two and a half, the battle is over who owns her body: Is it her or Mommy? A sensitive parent's going to put some pressure on the child to follow rules, but not so much pressure that the child feels it's a dictatorship. The next stage is the phallic stage. It is the period of time when children begin to discover their genitals as objects of pleasure. The phallic stage ends when the child begins to give up childhood sexuality, and begins to learn the rules of the larger culture. This is the period Freud calls latency: The child represses all of the memories of sexual pleasure that arose from each zone of the body. The young latency-age child is sexless in their approach to becoming a "mini-adult." The child learns to forgo interest in the self-stimulatory pleasures of the body, and learns the good works of becoming a learned, productive person via sports, school and social learning. These are relatively quiet times, particularly when one compares them to the turbulence of pleasure- seeking in infancy and the upheaval and return to the powerful drives experienced in puberty, when the adolescent becomes physically, but not yet emotionally, capable of having sexual connection. The job of puberty, then, is to help the adolescent learn about making the connection between aim and object for purposes of procreation. Later, we talk about this connection and how it has been misinterpreted by some psychoanalysts as a condemnation of homosexuality and of any sexuality that does not include procreation leading to the goal of species preservation. For now, I want to make an observation about love songs and their role in the adolescent's learning about Darwin's imperative: Love songs are never about soup.

An elderly man (my age), part of a heterosexual couple, is talking with his mate about their budding romance; she asks him if he wants "super sex." He replies: "I'll have the soup." What are love songs about? Who is the largest audience for love songs? Love songs are about finding a love object. Who buys the most music about love? Young adults do, because they are in the thrall of searching for an object . . . as in aim and object: Darwin's plan. Who buys music? Adolescents and young adults. Why? Because this is the period where libido is emerging into a more purely sexual form, becoming very powerful. Who is "in love" with a teen idol like Justin Bieber or Billie Eilish? Who buys music about love? Who thinks the most about love? Adolescents and young adults! This is the beginning of the connection between aim and object, and young people don't buy songs about soup.

(3.) The next postulate of the libido theory is that libido can be discharged, dealt with by reaction formation or sublimated.

STUDENT: Are those the reaction formations to the libido or you have a reaction formation to those feelings?

DR. M: Think of libido as an energy stream. How do we deal with it? You have a reaction formation to the feelings generated by the impulse of the libido. Reaction formation is composed of three types of feelings: shame, disgust and morality. Shame is about looking, or being looked at – hiding one's head from the imagined shaming eyes of the other. Disgust is an oral response – one feels almost sickened by an impulse. Morality is like waving a critical finger at another's behavior because that behavior triggers certain conflicts in you. Or the impulse can be repressed. Repression leads to neurosis (we'll see that too much reaction formation is another kind of neurosis, but for now, neurosis only means hysteria). Finally, libido may be sublimated. Freud means that the censor is taking the libido and discharging it via what we call higher-level defenses like intellectualization, rationalization, sarcasm, humor, writing a book, writing a play, dancing or lecturing about sex to a class about Freud. What I am doing right now, standing in front of our group and orating, is also in some way dealing with or sublimating voyeuristic/exhibitionistic conflicts.

STUDENT: I just had a question about the repression, is Freud saying something like: "I had these desires and I'm not going to acknowledge them or repression is in your unconscious"?

DR. M: Repression is like the censorship in a dream. You're not consciously saying: "I'm not thinking about this." That's a conscious suppression. You're not thinking about it: When repression works, it works well because you don't think it. However, the person pays a price for that. Think about holding a basketball in a bathtub full of water. At first it might not be difficult to hold it under water: You simply push the ball down into the tub. However, over time holding the ball under water becomes increasingly difficult. That is what happens when one part of the mind is pushing down an idea/feeling from another part of the mind.

STUDENT: What is shame?

DR. M: Shame is discomfort about seeing and being seen. We know that in certain cultures, the worst thing that can happen to you if you commit an offense is to be shamed. I believe that shame is an extremely powerful deterrent against breaking cultural norms in both the Japanese and the Indigenous cultures. Because shame is about looking and being looked at, it is an external process, while guilt is an internal process.

STUDENT: So a person that sublimates, are they otherwise asexual?

DR. M: They could be. If it's successful, one sublimation – this is *not* a value judgment – would be the calling of the [Catholic] priest, a man who is deeply committed to his calling and has found a way to deal with his urges by sublimating them to a greater good.

STUDENT: Do people tend to choose one of these?

DR. M: Do you mean choose purposely, or choose unconsciously?

STUDENT: Unconsciously. Not choose.

DR. M: No, choose is fine. . . . If we recognize that it's not free will, but one part of us is giving in to one process and not another process.

STUDENT: Whatever word it is, one of these over another . . . do they change based on the phase?

DR. M: We are going to find out later that these affects are connected to phases of libido development. The young child knows no shame but may experience disgust; shame, disgust, and morality are connected to toilet training. Further, these processes are connected to OCD, and in our culture everyone has some (typically vague) understanding of what it means when they say to someone "You're so anal." While many of us don't realize this has literally to do with toilet training, we do know that it has to do with cleanliness and orderliness. Of course, if one is a psychoanalyst, then we're thinking that the "anal" person had conflicts during toilet training, and therefore the person is struggling with feelings, that is, feelings are themselves dirty, messy and distasteful. The psychoanalyst also reasons that the person is employing the defense of reaction formation, and this is why one appears to be what a layperson calls "anal." Thus, to jump ahead briefly, we are going to see that the overuse of repression leads to hysteria, the overuse of reaction formation leads to OCD, and the overuse of the oral defenses – introjection (taking in) projection (spitting out) and withdrawal (a locked jaw) – lead to more serious personality problems. Using the model that Freud has presented to us, we see that the earlier these blockages occur, the more trouble one has going to the next stage of libido development.

STUDENT: I think I'm still a little confused by sublimation because I thought it was something that society regards as acceptable.

DR. M: While it could be this, the problem with that definition is that you're looking at a sublimation from the outside in, instead of from the inside out. Because some wish or feeling or behavior is acceptable, one is less likely to attempt to control it, suppress it or to repress it. That combination of behavior, feelings and wishes, such as being pious, sexually repressed and wanting (perhaps in reaction formation) to be overly good might lead the person to the choice of profession as a Catholic priest. This choice of profession is then reinforced by the person's reaction formations and repression (against sexuality and aggression). Thus the person is sublimating sexual and aggressive desires into a worthy profession. We haven't, by the way, gotten to the role of aggression. In this model a person who is sexually frustrated might be angry and the anger might encourage, instead of sublimation, a discharge in rage reactions.

STUDENT: Is marriage an example of sublimation?

DR. M: This might be a good time to distinguish between what Freud actually said about women and marriage and what I alluded to at the beginning of this lecture: psychoanalysis in mid-20th century America. Early second-wave feminists, including Simone de Beauvoir (1989), discredited Freud. They argued that Freudian theory worked to perpetuate sexual difference and reinforce the belief that inferiority was an inherent quality of the female. Freud's discussions on sexuality referred almost entirely to men, and he described women in negative terms, as lacking the "other" – that is, as having penis-envy – which reduced female development to a frustrated desire for masculinity. Freud's reputation was further diminished when his ideas were employed by conservative neo-Freudians to persuade unhappy women that their inferior social fate was biologically determined, cf. de Beauvoir (1989). However, just as in the case of homosexuality, Freud himself never said that. Feminist psychoanalysts (Benjamin, 1988, 1998) have attempted to reconcile Freud's patriarchal and somewhat naive understanding of gender and sexuality with his brilliant and valuable insights into the human condition. In this regard, I suggest Benjamin's work.

With this as our historical context, our task is to continue to understand Freud's history as well as how our personal/cultural history, attitudes, and biases may affect how we understand psychology. As a consequence, in studying Freud we seek to know the current theoretical and empirical knowledge base of psychoanalysis as it relates to addressing diversity in all of our work: research, treatment, supervision/consultation. With this in mind, one might say that a person who marries because they're so aware of every negative tendency in them, such as the tendency towards promiscuity, might marry for defensive reasons and this would be sublimation.

STUDENT: Well, it's unconscious, right?

DR. M: As I said about sublimation and the priesthood . . . for some people, yes, it would be the unconscious process of sublimating and the somewhat conscious process of rationalizing it. In this example, the priest is using certain kinds of what Freud will later call defenses. The priest would be saying, "I've given up sexual intercourse and sexual pleasure for a higher calling."

That's conscious. Now we might conclude that there are a lot of other things going on inside this particular priest, but those thoughts that are conscious are rationalized and intellectualized. Later we'll call these higher-level defenses. It is certainly better to employ higher-level ones than to fall to the ground and make the sign of the cross on a hospital ward. Similarly, a surgeon who is sublimating sadism has put these impulses to good use.

To continue with our discussion of this process of libidinal stages, imagine that the infant is a wild creature that needs to be fed (and there's an interplay between temperament and the environment), so a hyper and easily frustrated baby and a mother who is inhibited or depressed or overwhelmed, who has difficulty with emotion and is perhaps struggling with being a mother – any and all of this would lead to some trouble. So the child is going to be more frustrated. A sensitive mother will learn to satisfy the child, help them to transition from the bottle – or the breast – to solid food, and to deal with the child's frustrations about when to bite and not to bite. Soon the child will feel a certain safety in the environment; it can trust that the environment is going to be gratifying. Thus, with each stage, there needs to be a kind of optimal amount of frustration and an optimal amount of gratification. Too much gratification, and why should the child move on to the next developmental milestone? Too little and the outcome is the same, but here the child's stuck waiting to get what they never received. I'm not suggesting that every mother has to be perfect- but "a good enough mother" soon understands their child. We have all seen such a mother: the baby is fussing and the mother says: "Oh, he's hungry" or, "Oh, she needs a diaper change." How does the mother know this? The child, after all, doesn't speak. She doesn't really *know*, but she's beginning to read the subtle nuances of feeling in the child (like a good therapist; or the reverse: a good therapist is like a sensitive mother), and also beginning to project into the child. Sometimes the mother gets it right, sometimes not. One hopes that the mother (and therapist) get it right enough of the time, and what develops is a mutual loop. In fact, projection and projective identification actually start with the mother/child relationship whereby the mother is guessing/projecting into the child. This is the earliest origin of empathy; a loop gets created where a mother and newborn, then infant, then child, work out a relationship where they understand each other. Of course, like any system, this arrangement can go awry.

Fourth postulate: Personality is developed around the way that the child's libido is organized. Each of us develops oral characteristics, anal characteristics and phallic characteristics. An example might be that certain powerful leaders display phallic characteristics. By this I mean they push and shove, and make provocative statements. In its extreme, an oral character would be that the character style involves one or all of the following three possible activities that can be done with one's mouth during feeding: take in, spit out or lockjaw. (Please don't take this literally. I'm using these images metaphorically). To continue with this model, those who are always taking in might be understood to be passive dependent characters; those who spit out as having paranoid trends; and those who take in nothing and spit out nothing (lockjaw) as being in a schizoid withdrawal of contact from people. Each of these is a metaphor.

Freud's next postulate is: "Neurosis is a fixation on – or a regression to – some phase of infantile sexuality." What this means is the neurotic regresses to the stage of infantile sexuality where there is the most fixation, then the neurotic attempts to defend against the impulse (oral, anal, phallic) at that stage, and does so in their own particular way. For a simple example, if one has been anally fixated, under stress the person will regress to "anality." In order to become successful enough to be in a doctoral program, one has to be at least somewhat hardworking and obsessive-compulsive (we all can relate to the image that I mentioned previously: cleaning your desk/procrastinating before writing). The corollary to this postulate is: The earlier the fixation and/or the deeper the regression, the greater the psychopathology.

I also want to say more about libido being repressed, discharged or dealt with through reaction formation or sublimation. If libido is defended against by reaction formation, it's like setting up a series of dams on a river. The Libido River is meandering along, and then suddenly shame, disgust and/or morality block it. Because the libido has to go somewhere, it will soon get diverted. If the libido is sublimated, the energy of libido will be moved from sexual use to something more socially acceptable to the ego. Later this semester, Freud will expand on his understanding of the ways the psychological systems of the mind handle this libido. He's going to be more clear about the term *defense*. However, at this point in his work, Freud uses the term *defense* with a certain imprecision: sometimes as synonymous with repression, sometimes it stands on its own. Freud used the term *defense* even in his work with Josef Breuer. Freud will later expand on his notion of defense, and say there are many kinds of defenses. In 1936 his daughter, Anna, wrote a book, *The Ego and the Mechanisms of Defense*. In it she explored many defenses and how they work in handling internal *and* external demands. In doing this, she helped psychoanalysts study the ego and its functions. One of these functions is protection from danger. In this way we see that the ego is essentially an alarm system for the mind.

To remind you, we are in the part of our course called id psychology. When we study the defenses, we're studying the ego. We haven't gotten there yet. In fact, psychoanalysts who developed their work after Freud were less interested in studying a patient's impulses: it was common to work with a patient who had jealousy of siblings, conflicts over power and competition with the same-sex parent. In other words, there aren't so many variations on the theme of life's challenges. Instead the clinician looks at the defenses. The psychoanalyst assesses not only what is being defended against but also *how* the person is defending. The clinician examines the overuse of one defense or set of defenses versus other defenses. The overuse of a particular defense or pattern of defenses is what we will call character or personality. What psychoanalysts do now is they figure that there is a certain limited range of things that one longs for, that one fears, that one is angry about and that one is anxious/conflicted about. Once the clinician understands these things, the next step is to observe how the patient characteristically deals with conflict. For example, if a person tells the psychoanalyst a horrible story about their mother and then says, "but she's wonderful," the psychoanalyst thinks that this person is using the defense of idealization to protect them from other more negative feelings. The psychoanalyst also reasons that these other feelings are perceived as dangerous for some reason based on the patient's history. By the end of the lectures, we are going to get to what that "some reason" might be, why it might be dangerous for the patient if they did not idealize their mother. In current practice, psychoanalysts look at the defensive processes, and this postulate, that character structure, or personality, develops in the ways one handles libido, is an essential part of current psychoanalytic practice. We'll see that Freud was very interested in the processes that occur in the obsessive-compulsive. Freud had characteristics of both hysteria and obsessive-compulsive disorder, and he said this about himself. Via his self-analysis, Freud had the advantage of studying himself, and studying both of these characteristics. In the obsessive-compulsive, as we see particularly with the case of the "Rat Man," Freud noticed traits of orderliness, stinginess and stubbornness. He suggests these traits are related to struggles at the anal stage. As I said, all of us didn't get into a doctoral program without some obsessive-compulsive parts. We can relate to this.

In *Three Essays*, Freud says that neurosis is a fixation on, or a regression to, some phase of infantile sexuality. What we do know – and this is something Freud said for his entire life – is that if frustration is too great, humans have to do something about it. From Freud's earliest work on dreams, we've seen this. If asleep and frustrated, one can wake up, yell at the person lying next to them, or construct a dream that will temporarily solve the problems of both:

(1.) Keeping you asleep;
(2.) Discharging pent-up frustration.

With all of this background behind us, let's now have a detailed discussion of *Three Essays*. As indicated by the title, *Three Essays* is divided into three parts.

In the first section, Freud introduces the terms *aim* and *object*. Once he has established this duality, he can classify perversions and deviations using the idea that a perversion is a disconnection between aim and object, and therefore a deviation in Darwin's formula for evolution (any disconnection that does not lead to procreation won't lead to the continuation of our species; therefore it's a perversion).

Freud says that perverse feelings are present in all humans. That doesn't mean everyone enacts perversions, and/or that people with perversions are not also both capable and ready to procreate, only that perverse wishes are within each of us, because we've all experienced the childhood process of sexual development, with both fixations at and regressions to earlier stages.

Freud looks at the sexual instinct in neurotics, and he says that the sexual life of neurotics has perversions in it. Freud doesn't mean that neurotics perform perversions. Quite the contrary; he means that in neurotics, perverse wishes are strong enough so the neurotic must create defenses, symptoms and inhibitions to fend off their powerful drives. He says that in the unconscious mental life of every neurotic, we can trace neurotic sexual fantasies for each zone of the body. We know from child development (observing young children) that infants and young children get pleasure out of every zone of the body. We also know that what the culture labels as pornography are certain sex acts that include variations of the oral and anal openings. Freud says that there is nothing morally or psychologically wrong about this, as long as the person engages in intercourse and produces babies. As a Darwinian psychobiologist, Freud understands these other activities as "fore-pleasure" and "after pleasure," and each serves Darwin's function of the species' drive to survive. As we see with the entirety of Freud's theories, he employs Darwin's theory as the major adaptation of human life: the Darwinian adaptation. He understands everything that humans do as in some way or another related to what needs to happen in order to keep our species from becoming extinct.

Freud turns to an analysis of these instincts, and he says that both neurotics and perverts assign sexual significance to the oral and anal zones. This leads him to ask, "Why is this so?" Is it because neurotics are born perverted? No, he offers a biological explanation. Neurotics are constitutionally more easily frustrated, and/or more easily gratified in these "pregenital" zones of the body. Freud is not expressing a value judgment: This is a biological/evolutionary explanation. Neurotics are by birth more easily stimulated, gratified or frustrated through the oral zone and the anal zone. Now, Freud goes on to make a statement of logic (*psychologic*): *If* perversion is infantile sexuality, *and* neurotics suffer from perversions, *then* neurotics get stuck in an infantile state. Neurotics are those who have either remained in, or have regressed back to, a state of infantile sexuality.

STUDENT: Isn't that the same with perversion?
DR. M: No, a person who has perversions is also fixated or regressed back to an infantile state, but while a neurotic is in an infantile state, they're attempting to fight the impulse. A pervert has instead accepted the perverse impulses.
STUDENT: So if Freud is saying that each of these zones represents a certain stage of development, isn't it likely that all of us have different gratifications or frustrations in each area? So does that mean that everybody is neurotic?
DR. M: It means that everybody has made certain developmental compromises. However, there is a difference between a person with a severe obsessive-compulsive disorder, someone who is tortured by their rituals and conflicts, versus a person like one of us who might have some obsessive-compulsive processes. In the next lecture we will talk about what Freud calls the psychopathology of everyday life. His point in that work is that, just as with dreams, slips of the tongue, slips of the pen, false memories, symptomatic acts, forgetting, and one's earliest memories all follow an orderly process, but there are distortions that are evidence of conflict. If these issues don't typically interfere with one's regular life functions, then they're just processes of the mind. For example, Freud says that dreaming is a regression to an earlier form of thinking where thinking is hallucinating, but if one walks around hallucinating while awake, that's interference. All of us have inhibitions in our personalities, symptomatic acts, and certain defensive styles of dealing with libido. Some of us are profoundly troubled: I treated a young woman who took over an hour to get up the eleven stairs from the parking lot of my office to the waiting room. This person was so riddled with symptoms and inhibitions that she led a torturous life. The process is the same. It is the degree of impairment that's key.

STUDENT: Freud is making the claim that it was a biologically determined thing for someone. They were more easily frustrated or gratified at a stage . . .

DR. M: Yes.

STUDENT: What if it was their parents that made that experience at that stage more frustrating?

DR. M: Only later does Freud begin to talk about parental issues. The next generation of psychoanalysts (ego psychologists, object relations and self psychologists) talk about it more. I've made reference to situations of disconnection – for example, a hyperactive young child and a hyperactive mother, or an easily frustrated child and an easily frustrated mother, or a needy child and a withdrawn and depressed mother. I will later make some reference to the work of Mahler et al. (1973) and Kernberg et al. (1989); these clinicians work(ed) with people who suffer from Borderline personality disorder.[5] This means the patient finds it difficult to contain and appropriately deal with their feelings, which interferes with their living in the world. Kernberg applies Freud's (and Mahler's) understanding of the bodily zones. He suggests, by a sad twist of fate and genetics, people struggling with BPD had parents who were both disconnected and ineffective in parenting them. The combination was brutal and resulted in trauma. When you've become a good enough diagnostician to know that a person is troubled in that some of their more neurotic parts will show through, it's then your place to tell them. But the issue will always be about the degree of the disturbance. Do the symptoms and inhibitions interfere with routine functioning? The extreme might be the difference between someone who can't even get up my staircase, versus someone like one of us who feels the need to clean our desk before we write a paper.

In Part Two, Freud looks at infantile sexuality. He asks: "Why has the existence of childhood sexuality been overlooked?" Then, as he often does, Freud proceeds to answer his own question: He says that there is a kind of amnesia that takes over when the young child enters the latency period. Keep in mind that it was first Freud's self-analysis and later his analysis of his patients that brought memories from his own childhood (and his patients' childhoods) to him. With these memories also came examples of infantile sexuality. Freud began to discover his patients' – and his own – infantile sexuality. Using this data, Freud divides sexuality into three periods: infantile sexuality, latency and puberty. Freud believes the human species experiences latency while other species may not. That's his good news *and* his bad news. Having latency means that for our species we move from more primitive drives to at least two other kinds of mental processes and ultimately to abstract and logical thinking, to reasoning and to learning. In most human cultures, what happens to the child during latency? We go to school, where we learn reading, writing, arithmetic and reasoning. During this period, the latency-age child begins to learn sublimations. Because of sublimation during latency, the human child learns to discharge their impulses, but they also learn to push them down. The bad news is, for Freud, that this is one of the reasons that humans are prone to becoming neurotic, because while we discharge some, we also must push down (just like the basketball in the bathtub) most of our instinctual drives.

We will now focus on the infantile period. Freud says that this period is auto-erotic. By this he means that its focus is self-pleasure. Freud uses the young child's thumb-sucking to demonstrate this. What's the aim of thumb sucking? Oral satisfaction, whereas the aim of genital sexuality in the adult male is the discharge of semen, and in the adult female it is the reception of semen in the vagina. What's the object for the young child? There is no object as opposed to the male and the female objects in adult genital sexuality. The object is not a person of the opposite sex; the object is your thumb. Whether or not you want to believe in Freud's observations about the oral stage, when one observes the infant or young child, you see that everything goes through their mouth. That's the first place the world is discovered. Freud suggests that thumb-sucking is just like the masturbation that all children perform later. All infantile sexuality is autoerotic, and the child is polymorphously perverse. This means every child gets pleasure from any bodily activity, and until much later in development, there's no object, no interest in establishing a sexual relationship with a person of the opposite sex in order to procreate and produce the next generation of our species.

During early childhood, approximately ages three to five, all children begin sexual exploration. The child is curious and inquisitive about this issue as they're curious about everything. Children from farm families have an edge here. They see processes like intercourse (in nonhuman creatures), birth, death; they see many of the processes that urban/suburban children don't see. Without seeing these processes, all children have fantasies. Innocent children have fantasies that might not seem innocent to adults. One common fantasy in young children is that babies are born by eating, and they're delivered through the rectum. This makes some sense to a child – why not? You eat, your belly is filled up, mommy's pregnant, her belly is getting filled, right? These are "reasonable" attempts at understanding the basic processes of nature, given a child's limited database of human experience. There are also fantasies about the penis, or no penis. What Freud and early psychoanalysts neglected is the powerful feeling of loss that men have because we men can't conceive/carry babies. This is also a "lack." What's most important is not the specific content of children's sexual fantasies, but the fact that all children have fantasies about everything, including their bodies, reproduction and bodily functions. These might include: "Why does Mommy look like this and Daddy looks like that?" Or, "Why do both my daddies or both my mommies look like this? Why do my mommies look different than at that home?"

In Part Three of the book, Freud applies his findings about infantile sexuality to the changes that occur at puberty. Freud says now the real sexual aim, which is the discharge and exchange of sexual products in orgasm, and the adult object, that is, the human who is going to gratify that aim, are capable of being connected to produce the next generation of our species. Each person searches for an object. First in fantasy – that is, in worshiping, idealizing and falling in love with intimate friends and family members and then with famous people who are acceptable as objects for fantasy and idealization, such as actors, TV stars and musicians. These are people who are easily accessible to, and encouraging of, fantasy.

To continue, Freud goes on to say that finding the sexual object at puberty is a complicated process. What is the adult person's prototype? The first love object for all humans is mother. For any of you who have ever fallen in love, or known somebody who has fallen in love, what does that person feel when they fall in love? The person experiences an overwhelming feeling that they're part of something greater than themselves. The person can't get their lover out of their mind. They feel swallowed and consumed by the experience. That's the kind of prototype that researchers see in the earliest attachment of the baby to its mother. The prototype of this loved one's first love experience is suckling at the mother's breast. The earliest choice of object before the Oedipal experience is Mommy, and then Daddy. These are incestuous choices. Freud suggests that each person must resolve the issues involved in the incestuous choice of the parents when we begin to grow up and choose a mate of our own. Perhaps you have begun to notice the term *objects* here. We'll soon see that all of psychoanalytic theory begins with Freud, even the concepts discussed later as object relations theory. Others did not develop these notions and the terms that accompany them. Other theorists emphasized and elaborated these ideas. To expand on this, one of the things a psychoanalytic clinician looks for if somebody is having trouble finding a mate is:

> Is the person still maintaining a pathological attachment to parental (incestuous) objects?

From all of this, Freud now suggests that neurosis can be better understood. (I hope we've clarified what Freud actually said instead of what others may have told you he said).

Freud suggests: Every neurosis, every neurotic disorder, represents an inhibition in development. A neurotic has a disturbed sex life. But Freud isn't talking about adult sexuality. He is talking about an intermingling between the person's adult sexuality and their infantile sexuality.

When you hear:

> "Oh Freud, that's the person who wrote about sex," it's not entirely accurate, but it's also not inaccurate.

Freud meant that neurotics are stuck at infantile sexual conflicts and inhibitions that remain troubling to them. In the neurotic person's attempt to function within these conflicts, they develop inhibitions and symptoms that interfere with their functioning.

STUDENT: When you say "neurosis," are you still referring to just the neurosis or more than that?

DR. M: I'm talking about what Freud called the neuroses, which really meant, ultimately, all psychopathology – perhaps with the exclusion of psychotic conditions, but even that is unclear as the diagnostic system of Freud's time was extensive in categories but limited in understanding (and imprecise regarding diagnostic indicators). We see this in more detail when we discuss Freud's case histories. For now Freud uses the terms *hysteria* and *neurosis* interchangeably, but they're not the same. Later he'll become more specific, but hysteria is the most common neurosis at this point in his work. Hysterical patients had very dramatic symptoms; they were showy, and this is where Freud's training was, with Charcot, Janet and Breuer, who were treating patients diagnosed with hysteria.

STUDENT: In the book *Trauma and Recovery*, Judith Herman criticizes Freud's theory of hysteria. She also says that Freud abandoned the idea that hysteria is caused by sexual abuse in childhood.

DR. M: This is a very important question. Herman and others Jeffrey Masson, 1986)[6] are critical about the way Freud first presented, then discounted his sexual theory: that the etiology of hysteria is the result of sexual molestation, particularly of girls by members of their own family. Some of these critics even suggest that Freud changed his theory because he was afraid of the controversy the theory might cause. However, this controversy highlights both reasonable concerns – about Freud and about the era during which he worked – and it highlights a subtle misunderstanding of Freud's shift from a total reliance on a trauma-only model of the etiology of neurosis to a second model of psychic determinism in etiology. While Freud's second model did include the environmental factor of the inappropriate stimulation of a child by an adult, that factor is clearly no longer the major causative factor, nor is it the only causative factor, because the new model emphasizes the primacy of developmental factors in etiology. As I mentioned, Freud was very ambivalent about acknowledging any change in his views. As you'll see as our lectures continue, there are some circumstances where trauma, particularly sexual trauma, is the only true explanation for a neurosis. While in these cases one also sees psychological sequelae that's related to the aftereffects of the traumatic events, they're not causative of it. However, *if* the trauma explanation were the only etiological explanation for all neurosis, since the occurrence of neurosis is so widespread, *then* everyone who has neurotic symptomatology would have to have been sexually molested in childhood. This seems numerically impossible! Freud began to believe that neurosis in most cases is the result of a developmental process that is part of the human condition and, like most of our behavior as Freud understood it, is related to Darwin's concept of evolution as the driving force in adaptation to life. In this case, the Darwinian component would be a process of sexual development for the ultimate purpose of adult sexual relations in order for an orderly continuation of the human race. Yet, that said, to make things even more complex, it is also possible to have been prematurely sexually stimulated in childhood without actually having been physically molested. There are sexualized families and sexualized relationships between parents and children that can and do stimulate a child prematurely and can lead to neurotic resolutions (this is why one studies not only the patient's conscious experiences but also infers unconscious experiences). Thus, psychoanalysts focus on the patient's development as well as on the historical family in order to see all of the variables that have brought a particular person to a particular level of development, fixation or neurosis at a particular time.

The following case might help us understand the difficult questions involved:

A case of traumatic memories

Her physician sent a young woman to me. She was a high school senior (18 years old) and was applying to and visiting colleges. She had recently been plagued by a recurring image: staring at a small flashing light in a dark room. The image seemed to have come out of nowhere. This was becoming disruptive to her: She was having trouble studying; sometimes she was having trouble driving as the image flashed in her head, and she was increasingly upset by it. As I said, a colleague had sent her for a consultation. (I happen to have heard from this young woman a few years after our sessions. After she saw me, she had been accepted at, and was attending, an excellent college, was very involved in a sports team. She was also in a serious relationship with a young man. I believe that she wrote to reassure me.) I didn't do much – I saw her four or five times – and at first I thought the obvious: that this symptom was about leaving home (that is, about what it might mean to be going off to college, to be independent. In part this was true but not the main part of her story).

Finally, I did what I should have done in the first place. I asked:

"Has anything different happened to you recently?"

She replied: "No nothing at all, just that I got my license and my parents are letting me use the car to drive to school, instead of taking the bus."

She continued to associate: "When I take the bus to go to school, the bus goes the long way . . . (*now she paused*) but when I drive now (the shorter way) I drive past my old neighborhood" (*at this point, her narrative began to seem like a detective story*).

I asked: "Your old neighborhood? "She replied: "Yeah . . . we moved when I was seven . . . *wait* . . . the old man (neighbor) used to take me to the basement and penetrate me with his fingers. I stared at the dark wall and imagined a flashing light."

I asked a few more questions and learned that this neighbor had died (from natural causes) two years before this young woman's symptoms began to manifest themselves.

I think that while we spent only a couple of sessions processing this experience (during which I made a remark, in passing, that this was very difficult for many reasons, followed by, "You lost some of your innocence"), what I didn't say at the time was that she had, in a certain way, also lost some of the trust that she had in all adults, even in her parents, because she wouldn't/couldn't tell them what happened to her. Why did she tell me? I don't know. What did it mean that she couldn't tell them, that she lived with this terrible trauma alone until she remembered it and confided it to me?

To be clear, I do believe that getting ready to go off to college, driving a car, and thus being more independent, we're all involved in the dynamics of this young woman's remembering her trauma at the time she did. But what is the point of this story? The point is that this young woman put herself into a state of self-hypnosis. She put herself into a dissociative state where a person self-hypnotizes so they don't see, feel or hear an experience that is intolerable. She did this first as a young child and it was now coming back as a flashback. Perhaps the flashing light in the dark was some hope to be rescued. I know that she trusted her doctor enough that she took his recommendation to come to me for sessions and to tolerate my questions. Perhaps he, and now I, were the flashing light. Her experience had been intolerable at the time it occurred. It had remained in a dissociated state since that time. I will remind you to ask me this question again throughout these lectures to see if any of our (new) explanation of this complex/controversial issue begins to make sense to you. It is a symptom of hysteria.

STUDENT: Is hysteria a less common thing today than in Freud's time? I feel like it was focused on a lot then, but we don't hear so much about it now.

DR. M: An hysterical character style is not less common, but hysterical physical symptoms are less common (not including the physical symptoms associated with anxiety) because people know enough to not present themselves to a physician, for example, with paralysis of an entire hand but no other paralysis (this is called "glove anesthesia"). Internists and neurologists know this is anatomically impossible without also having paralysis of the entire arm on that side of that body. Doctors now know to send somebody to a psychologist (although they will often use code words like, "You have a problem with your nerves," or "You need to do something about your stress"). In other words, the culture has become more sophisticated, so that people ask their doctor for a psychologist referral, or they keep their hysteria to themselves. Feinstein (2011)[7] says there are fewer examples now of conversion hysteria than were seen in the time that Freud practiced, but there are many examples of hysterical anxiety and many examples of hysterical components to one's personality. We'll highlight this in later lectures.

STUDENT: What does Freud think happens in latency?

DR. M: Freud thought that latency is an essential part of human development; that it is phylogenetic.[8] That means that it gets passed down to each generation in the DNA of the human species. We have latency because we possess consciousness. Because of our consciousness, we have the ability, as well as the need, to make choices. One of those choices is that in order for our species to intellectually advance, we need to give up our infantile sexuality and learn abstract concepts that require delaying gratifications and impulsivity. These sacrifices have helped the human species to advance in the control of our destiny by learning, and then teaching, each successive generation how to live productively in the world, as well as to learn how to pass down our legacy of knowledge by teaching reading, writing and other communication skills. One requirement for this learning is that our species needs to replace wish fulfillment with sublimation. If instead we give in to our infantile wishes and desires, and we don't find appropriate sublimations, we become impulsive creatures who clash with others. An unfortunate result here is that if we don't find enough sublimation, we will then hold back the full expression of impulses and desires by substituting neurotic inhibitions and symptoms.

STUDENT: Would it really be latency if it were not that we don't have sexuality, it's just that we repress it during this one period?

DR. M: We are saying the same thing. What we have is a repressive barrier that comes over the person as a latency-aged child. A little boy during the Oedipal period, that is, before latency, might say that he loves his mommy and that he also loves the girl down the street. What does he say when he's six or seven when that same young girl wants to join his boys-only club? "Yuck, girls!" What does he say about her at 14 years old? He says nothing because he's too shy, but he watches her and thinks about her. What does he say about her when he is 20 years of age? "I'm in love with her."

STUDENT: Okay. This whole thing where children have sexuality but they don't have, like, the mechanism . . .

DR. M: The physical abilities that come with puberty make it possible to connect the aim to the object.

STUDENT: Yeah, because they don't have the ability to physically do that. Does he have some understanding of why nature would have created it this way? Like why didn't sexual urges just come up at puberty, wouldn't that make more sense?

DR. M: I think if pressed he would say that our species just developed so we have more sophisticated defenses, and because of that we have preferences. You know, you put down the dog food, and usually the dog eats what you give it or, if not hungry, leaves the food alone. The dog doesn't say, "Yesterday you gave me steak and I want that today. Don't you understand that I don't like food from a can?"

Other creatures don't have the kind of sophisticated preferences that we have. Because of our consciousness, we have fantasies. Darwin suggested that our sophistication helped to make our species better survivors, more able to adapt to any environment. As an example, a heterosexual man and woman get introduced, and they are attracted to each other. The man says to his friends, "She's really beautiful . . . and smart." The woman says, "He's really interesting . . . with great eyes." Where did they learn these categories? Dogs don't have these categories; they sniff at each other's behinds. I don't know if I am capturing the spirit of what I mean, what Freud was saying. Humans are both blessed and cursed with consciousness. The blessing is we have created certain very sophisticated mechanisms where we can protect ourselves from other predatory creatures, alter our environment to make it more hospitable, heal our species (and other species) from illness, understand our own mind, and to some extent, understand the minds of our friends, neighbors and even our enemies. However, the disadvantage of our sophisticated minds is that we have to struggle with consciousness and preferences and doubts. We are desperate to develop a sense of identity and sense of meaning. Once we develop a sense of identity, it is both precious, and, for some, precarious. Imagine a person who struggles with schizophrenia. This kind of person feels a tenuous sense of identity from the moment that they awaken to the moment they go to sleep.

STUDENT: So you brought up the age range of three to five when there's some exploration that's going on. Obviously puberty is biologically determined, so that age varies based on your gender and the individual –

DR. M: There is some data that both in terms of the food we are giving our children (too much fat) and amount of exposure to sexual content in the media, puberty is occurring in humans at an earlier age. The long-term implications of this are not clear, but at some point each child begins to want what their parents have. The child wants to possess both parents as love objects, then has the realization that that's not possible. In later lectures, we will see that the child's sense of disappointment (that they can't possess Mommy and they can't possess Daddy) forces upon the child the need to form their own *sense of identity*.

The two major notions in Freud's theory that we will study throughout this course are the following:

(1.) Neurosis is a defense against intolerable experience;
(2.) Human beings require and crave a sense of identity and achieve it by seeking out and taking in our closest (loved and hated) objects.

As we understand more about these formulas, you'll learn what psychoanalysts actually do.

I want to conclude with some final thoughts about Freud's *Three Essays*:

As Fine (1987) suggests to us, the essence of *Three Essays* can be defined by two propositions:

(1.) The importance of sexuality as a force in mental life;
(2.) The childhood roots of sexuality.

Both of these propositions make sense to me. As Block Lewis[9] reminds us (1986), Freud wrote *Three Essays* before researchers had discovered the chromosomal differences between the sexes, and that was a long time ago. Freud's biology might be primitive, and the idea of libido as something quantifiable that one can accurately measure seems unnecessary, yet another example of Freud's ambivalence about psychology: his drive to put psychological processes into biological terms. Yet here are some things to think about with regard to the power of sexuality as a force in our lives:

How many of you remember when you were 13, 14 years old?

As a male, I can say a bit about the horror of getting an erection without wanting to, and wondering: *How am I going to stand up when the school bell rings and I have to change classes?*

In other words, I felt that my body had been taken over by demons. Those of you who have watched pornography know about the fascination people have with various kinds of sex, and it is sex that is not always about sexual intercourse, but about taboo sexuality of other bodily parts – not typically aim and object in sexual contact. Throughout all of Freud's writing he maintained one basic idea, from his earliest work with *Studies on Hysteria* to all of his later work about identification and the development of the defenses of the ego. That is: much of human behavior and a good deal of our mind, conscious and unconscious, is concerned with bodily gratification in some form. This basic idea has a corollary: If the frustration of our bodily needs is too great, all other human needs become irrelevant. When undergoing frustration, the issues become in part quantitative (this is where Freud was correct that all human behavior is an interaction of the biological and the psychological factors): How much frustration can one tolerate before becoming a neurotic?

Summary of lecture 4

Freud expanded his understanding of the unconscious that he presented in *The Interpretation of Dreams* in several other works, including *Three Essays on the Theory of Sexuality* (1905). In *The Interpretation of Dreams*, Freud had suggested that the unconscious of the dreamer contains infantile, wish-gratifying memories. In *Three Essays on the Theory of Sexuality*, Freud explored the nature of these infantile memories, suggesting that they consist of pleasurable desires developed in infancy and early childhood centered on the stimulation of bodily zones, each of which is required for human adaptation and survival. Problems in this development lead to neurosis. The first bodily zone is the mucous membranes of the mouth. The baby is required to gratify the need to suckle and then renounce suckling when weaned. The next bodily zone is the anus, which requires that the young child learn to control its bowels and urethra. The task for the young child at the phallic stage is to gain control over self-stimulatory (masturbatory) genital desires. What is the reason for this developmental process? Why do we need this shifting of pleasure from one zone of the body to another? Freud saw Darwin's theory of evolution as the driving force in human adaptation to life. In *Three Essays* Freud suggests that because we have self-consciousness, we seek pleasurable experiences that gratify both our bodily needs and our psychological needs (for a human carnivore, this might mean a preference for steak versus lamb). The goal of this developmental process is to help one to mature the childish pleasurable sensations in bodily zones and mind to prepare for the adult pleasurable sensations of sexual union. This will result in procreation and the continuation of our species. The model of sexual development is designed so that one will, someday, choose a member of the opposite sex with whom to procreate. Not *all* humans need to have orgasm as their aim and to have an opposite-sex partner as their object, with procreation as their goal. But, Freud suggests, there is a relationship between sexual development and neurosis. Freud proposes that neurotics are particularly susceptible to blockages/fixations in their sexual development; this makes them more prone to developing neurosis. Freud also proposes that what is fantasized by the neurotic is normal to the young child at some phase of the child's development.

Notes

1 While Freud was a cis-gendered white male, his analysis of H.D. (née Hilda Doolittle), lasting approximately 20 weeks during 1934–1935, and her autobiographical account of this time in *Tribute to Freud* (1956/2012) is informative. Not only was H.D. openly bisexual in a period of widespread homophobia, she came to understand gender as androgynous or nonbinary through the analysis. Gender and sexual orientation were themes that H.D. was intensely interested in; she challenged Freud on these themes in their work together, rejecting Freud's first assertion that her bisexuality was a result of mother-fixation (DuPlessis & Friedman, 1981). It appears the two came to collaborative understanding of H.D.'s gender and sexuality, evidenced in one (delighted) letter she wrote to her partner Bryher (née Winifred Ellerman) in 1934: ". . . I have gone terribly deep with Papa [Freud]. He says, "You had two things to hide, one that you were a girl, the other that you were a boy." It appears that I am that all-but-extinct phenomena, the perfect bi . . ." (Freedman, 2005, pp. 499–500).
2 Cheuvront, J. P. Jr. (2016). Henry Abelove's "Freud, Male Homosexuality, and the Americans". *Studies in Gender and Sexuality*, *17*(2), 80–85.
3 Richard von Krafft-Ebing (1840–1902) was an Austrian psychiatrist and author of *Psychopathia Sexualis*. This was a forensic reference book for physicians and judges that was written in an academic style to discourage lay readers. The author deliberately chose a scientific term for the title of the book and wrote parts in Latin for the same purpose. *Psychopathia Sexualis* was one of the first books about sexual practice that studied homosexuality and bisexuality. During its time, it became the leading medical-legal text on sexual pathology.
4 Henry Havelock Ellis (1859–1939) was an English physician, eugenicist, writer and social reformer who studied human sexuality. He cowrote the first English medical textbook on homosexuality (Ellis & Symonds, 1897) and also published works on a variety of sexual practices and inclinations, as well as on transgender psychology. Freud credited him for introducing the psychoanalytic ideas of narcissism and autoeroticism

5 These clinicians worked with people who suffer from borderline personality organization.
6 Jeffrey Masson (1941) is an American author best known for his book, *The Assault on Truth* (1984), where he argues that Freud abandoned his seduction theory because he feared that acknowledging the truth of his female patients' claims that they had been sexually abused would hinder the acceptance of psychoanalysis.
7 According to Feinstein (2011) estimates of 20–25% of patients in a general hospital setting have individual symptoms of conversion and 5% of patients in this setting meet the criteria for the full syndrome.
8 Phylogenetic: In biology, phylogenetic is part of a system that addresses the inference of the evolutionary history and relationships among or within groups of organisms (e.g., species, or more inclusive taxa; Forster & Renfrew, 2006). These relationships are hypothesized by phylogenetic inference methods that evaluate observed heritable traits, such as DNA sequences or morphology, often under a specified model of evolution of these traits.
9 Helen Block Lewis' (1913–1987) research on shame, guilt, and gender within psychoanalysis led to her publishing over 50 articles and several books. In our course, we refer to her classic article, Block-Lewis (1988) *Freudian theory and new information in modern psychology*. Interestingly, she was the mother of Dr. Judith Herman.

References

Benjamin, J. (1988). *The bonds of love*. New York: Pantheon Books.

Benjamin, J. (1998). *Like subjects, love objects*. New Haven: Yale University Press.

Block-Lewis, H. B. (1988). Freudian theory and new information in modern psychology. *Psychoanalytic Psychology, 5*(1), 7.

Cheuvront, J. P. Jr. (2016). Henry Abelove's "Freud, Male Homosexuality, and the Americans". *Studies in Gender and Sexuality, 17*(2), 80–85.

Darwin, C. (1859). *On the origin of species by means of natural selection, or the preservation of favoured races in the struggle for life*. London: John Murray.

de Beauvoir, S. (1989). *The second sex* (H. M. Parshley, Trans.). New York: Vintage Books (1953).

Doolittle, H. (2012). *Tribute to Freud* (2nd ed.). New Directions Publishing (1956, Pantheon).

DuPlessis, R. B., & Friedman, S. S. (1981). "Woman is perfect": Freud's debate with H.D. *Feminist Studies, 7*(3), 417–430.

Ellis, H., & Symonds, L. (1897). *Sexual inversions*. London: Wilson & MacMillan.

Feinstein, A. (2011). Conversion disorder: Advances in our understanding. *Canadian Medical Association Journal, 183*(8), 915–920.

Fine, R. (1987). *The development of Freud's thought: From the beginnings (1886–1900) through id psychology (1900–1914) to ego psychology (1914–1939)* (2nd ed.). Lanham, MD: Rowman & Littlefield.

Forster, P., & Renfrew, C. (Eds.). (2006). *Phylogenetic methods and the prehistory of languages*. Cambridge: McDonald Institute Press, University of Cambridge.

Freedman, A. (2005). Gifts, goods and gods: H.D., Freud and trauma. *English Studies Canada, 29*(3–4), 184–199.

Freud, A. (1966). *The ego and the mechanisms of defense*. New York: International Universities Press.

Freud, S. (1895). Studies on hysteria. In J. Strachey et al. (Trans.), *The standard edition of the complete psychological works of Sigmund Freud, Volume II*. London: Hogarth, 1–307.

Freud, S. (1900). The interpretation of dreams. In J. Strachey et al. (Trans.), *The standard edition of the complete psychological works of Sigmund Freud, Volume IV*. London: Hogarth, ix–627.

Freud, S. (1905). Three essays on the theory of sexuality. In J. Strachey et al. (Trans.), *The standard edition of the complete psychological works of Sigmund Freud, Volume VII*, London: Hogarth, 123–246.

Furst, L. (2003). Freud and Vienna. *Virginia Quarterly Review*, *77* (Winter 2001). www.vqronline.org/essay/freud-and-vienna

Grotjahn, M. (1951). Historical notes: A letter from Freud. *International Journal of Psychoanalysis*, *32*, 331.

Herman, J. (1992). *Trauma and recovery*. New York: Basic Books.

Kernberg, O. F., Selzer, M. A., Koenigsberg, H. W., Carr, A. C., & Appelbaum, A. H. (1989). *Psychodynamic psychotherapy of borderline patients*. New York: Basic Books.

Mahler, S., Pine, M., & Bergman, A. (1973). *The psychological birth of the human infant*. New York: Basic Books.

Masson, J. (1984). *The assault on truth: Freud's suppression of the seduction theory*. New York: Farrar Straus & Giroux.

Von Krafft-Ebing, R. (1886). *Psychopathia sexualis*. New York: Rebmam and Company.

Chapter 5

Psychoanalysis and the beginnings of a "theory of mind"

Source: The Psychopathology of Everyday Life, 1901

Today we discuss the topic that receives the most interest from the general public, often referred to as the "Freudian slip." Freud called it "the psychopathology of everyday life."

A joke:

Two twenty-something men are talking and one says:

> "Hey, I had a Freudian slip last night . . . I was at dinner at my parents' house and I wanted to say to my father: 'Dad, please pass the salt.'"
> However, instead I said, 'Dad, you son of a bitch, you ruined my life.'"

What we see here is that the Freudian slip is so common that when hearing this, one understands the humor: There's no hiding the hostility toward the father, so it's not a Freudian slip. Knowing this is what makes the joke absurd, and funny. It's clear that the general public (at least in the Western Hemisphere) has some vague understanding that the purpose of a Freudian slip is to hide *nonconscious* (unconscious) content from the self in order to be able to say one has made a Freudian slip. This is in contrast to dreams; some people believe that dreams are random, some believe that dreams are religious or mystical messages. This is probably because in waking life a "slip" is typically a minor blip in conversation. There is very little working over by the mind; a slip has temporarily converted one to primary-process thinking. That's in contrast to dreams, where much of a dream as it initially appears upon awakening has been worked over, converted from latent to manifest content.

To review

What we have seen so far in Freud's writings is that he's more a psychobiologist than a psychologist. I understand that this is quite confusing to you. This is a question that comes up a lot about Freud from students of psychoanalytic theory.

DOI: 10.4324/9781003171393-6

What Freud means is that the first pleasurable sensations for all human beings are the pleasurable feelings of the mother's touch, the pleasurable sensations of the mucous membranes of the mouth, sucking at the breast or bottle. With time and development, we become more sophisticated in our aesthetic discrimination of pleasure. We still get pleasure from holding in our bowels and from touching, kissing and being touched and kissed. However, after puberty, in sexual situations, it's now also called "fore-pleasure," the pleasure that comes before and in preparation for sexual intercourse as it propels the participants to continue from one kind of sexual stimulation to another, with the ultimate goal of preparing the sexual partners physically and emotionally for sexual intercourse by sexual penetration of the female by the male. So, yes, Freud meant that this is sexual pleasure, and no, he also didn't mean that it is adult sexual pleasure! That's why this is all so confusing that a child experiences powerful pleasurable sensations. In a chemical/physiological way, this pleasure originates as pleasure at different zones of the body; over time the human becomes discriminating by turning the pleasure from self-stimulation into purposeful preparation of a heterosexual couple for intercourse. Freud as a Darwinian biopsychologist (Freud, 1905) says this is motivated by the evolutionary (instinctual) drive to procreate/maintain our species (what every species needs to do); it is just that humans do this in a somewhat more complex way. That said, I hope today's lecture will be both educational and fun.

Perhaps I have a somewhat strange idea about fun. For example, one of the bits of fun in this lecture is I'll show you how I publicly humiliated myself by making a Freudian slip at the podium in front of a hundred psychoanalysts. My slip occurred years ago at a conference where I was the moderator and program chairman: I introduced the speakers. By the way, I hope some of you have brought slips of your own. I have a few slips here from a number of sources, slips from over the many years that I have taught, from former students. And I will present public comments of famous politicians that are slips and then, hopefully, slips from you.

In our exploration of Freud's early works, *Studies on Hysteria*, *The Interpretation of Dreams* and *Three Essays on the Theory of Sexuality*, he suggests that repression is a protective process, that its purpose is to ward off unpleasant experiences. Freud argues that this process of protection comes from his original observations studying neurosis. Neurosis is a defensive process designed to protect humans against intolerable experience. Repression fulfills a protective function by blocking intolerable experience from us. All humans search for pleasure, and Freud says that pleasurable desires are called wishes, while un-pleasurable desires are called fears (because they produce anxiety – Freud later expands on anxiety, but for now it is the same as fear). In this model, Freud says that the purpose of repression is to maintain a balance so we can seek pleasure and yet also avoid the sometimes intolerably painful experience of anxiety. In both *The Interpretation of Dreams* and now in *The Psychopathology of Everyday Life*, Freud makes a transition from exclusive focus on the study of neurology and psychopathology to the study of so-called normal behavior. While all of us dream and all of us make slips, most of us also function with a reasonable amount of normalcy. By presenting both works in this way, Freud again shows his brilliance: these works give the reader a chance to see unconscious processes in action without labeling the processes as psychopathological.

By the "psychopathology of everyday life," Freud means slips of the tongue, errors of omission and commission (omission means not doing something, commission means doing something you weren't supposed to do – turning lights on and off because you're not sure whether you've done this correctly), or failures to carry out certain actions, as well as all other minor mistakes that only temporarily interfere with functioning. These are the various phenomena that we now call Freudian slips. Freud's belief is that every slip should be taken seriously; the slip has a psychological meaning, even if the meaning is currently obscured.

Later we see that Freud presents three factors, suggesting that any slip that fulfills all three is a true Freudian (unconscious) slip. If the slip does not fulfill these three conditions, then the slip might be a momentary, meaningless cognitive error, or it might be a sign of a temporary (or even permanent) brain injury or a symptom of some other problem affecting one's cognition. For one example of the latter, if you were interviewing someone and asked the simple addition question: "What's one plus one?" and, their reply was, "One plus one equals 50 million," this answer would be of concern: the person might be joking, or they might be undergoing cognitive deterioration due to brain trauma/injury/disease, or they might be suffering from a functional psychotic disorder, but they would probably not be demonstrating a Freudian slip because nothing in their answer is effectively hiding behind this mistaken response. It sounds bizarre (like the young man's cannibal dream sounded to me). The need for wish fulfillment and the defense against this need struggle; these same processes that Freud described in the mechanisms of dream creation also produce what Freud calls a compromise: a Freudian slip. We're beginning to see that this same need/wish/defense formula that produces slips and dreams also produces psychological symptoms.

Does anyone have a slip that they can later share? Great!

Now, let's start with the slips.

Background: Richard Nixon and his self-destruction from the Watergate scandal.[1]

Nixon won the 1968 presidential election. He also did what no U.S. president had done since the communists wrested control over mainland China: visited that nation and began diplomatic relations with it. Nixon won his second election of 1972 in a landslide. Thus, Nixon had no apparent reason to do anything criminal, but one theory is that Nixon had always been a petty criminal who surrounded himself with loyal thugs. His closest advisors, H. R. "Bob" Haldeman and John Ehrlichman, arranged to have a small group of men break into the Democratic National Committee Headquarters, located at the Watergate complex of buildings in Washington, D.C. After the five burglars were caught and the conspiracy was discovered – chiefly through the work of a few journalists, congressional staffers and an election-finance watchdog official – the incident was investigated by the U.S. Congress. During this investigation it was discovered that Nixon had an audiotaping system in the Oval Office. An audiotape was discovered with a recording of Nixon considering offering hush money to the burglars.

As his presidency was failing, people closest to him were being indicted – men who had been with him through his days as congressman and vice president. On the day before his top two advisors, Haldeman and Ehrlichman, were to be indicted, Nixon was asked about both men (keep in mind the possibility of Nixon being impeached was becoming more likely; in fact, Nixon would soon resign before facing this impeachment scenario). At this time of impending doom, when asked about the two men, here's what Nixon seems to have wanted to say: "These two men, Haldeman and Erlichman, are men of impeccable character."

Instead, here is what he did say: "These two men are men of *impeachable* character."

Of course we have no way of knowing this, but was Nixon saying: "Impeach them, not *me* . . ." (Johnson, 1979)?

Here is another one about politics. The slip occurred when George W. Bush was running for president:

In 2000, George W. Bush was running for president against Al Gore; he called himself a "compassionate conservative"[2] (some liberals feel it's not possible to be both compassionate and conservative because of the structure of the economics involved in conservatism, but that's a discussion for another time). While campaigning in New Hampshire, he arrived to give a speech to a group of single mothers who were struggling financially, and in other ways as well. In an attempt to portray himself as a compassionate conservative, and to show these women (and the TV cameras) how empathic he was to their situation, Bush wanted to say:

"I understand how hard it is [for you] to put food on the table . . ."

Instead Bush said:

"I understand how hard it is [for you] to put *food on your family*."

What does it mean to "put food on your family"? One could speculate that Bush was saying that poor people *eat sloppily*.

What we understand from Freud is that each of these slips represents a struggle between a wish and a defense; the slip emerges as a compromise between the two. Thus, "impeccable" becomes "impeachable." "Food on your plate" becomes "food on your family." Freud has taught us that the person who made the slip had been trying not to make conscious a disavowed, preconscious wish, but then said something that actually made it clear that some other content was hidden underneath. In each case, the person who made the slip had been ambivalent. Ambivalence does not mean "negative"; it means both positive and negative in a dynamic struggle.

Now, closer to home: Derner School of Psychology slips and then, my slip:

Here's a wonderful slip by a Derner doctoral student of a few years ago. This young woman, as self-reported, had come from a "proper Bostonian" background. I'm giving this background because the slip she made actually horrified her, but it makes sense in the context of her background: I was talking to her class about Freud's *Three Essays*, and making the point about Freud's belief that neurosis is a fixation on, or a regression to, some earlier period of infantile sexual development. At this point, she raised her hand:

"Dr. Mendelsohn, about . . ."

Now what she wanted to ask about was *fixation*. Instead, she said:

"Dr. Mendelsohn, about *fuckstation* . . ."

Given her background, one could speculate that she was filled with both wonder and anxiety with respect to the words she was hearing. Therefore, a conflict between both impulses broke through as a slip.

I hope that some of you are prepared to tell the class about your experiences with these phenomena. To break the ice, I will now tell you about one of mine.

Many years ago, I was program chair of our Adelphi Psychoanalytic Society as part of the postgraduate/postdoctoral programs in psychoanalysis. This meant I'd poll the membership about who they wanted to make presentations at meetings. I'd then contact the speaker and make the arrangements. This was before email, so the work occurred by phone and letter and was labor intensive. In the backstory to my slip (I said it occurred in front of a group of psychoanalysts), I got a request from several members who wanted to hear about working psychodynamically with oppositional children. While this wasn't my clinical interest, it was what the society membership wanted; it was my job to get it for them. I looked at the literature, made phone inquiries to colleagues and, on these recommendations, wrote to an expert in this area, Dr. David Smith (not his real name). My friends and colleagues had told me, by the way, that Smith was a difficult person but a fine speaker. After what seemed like an endless back-and-forth correspondence, I secured a date and I asked him during the course of a phone call to send me his CV, as this is what I used for my introduction. He sent the CV, and on the night of his presentation, he arrived on time to a full house. As I said, I wasn't particularly interested in his topic, but one thing I did like to do was to introduce the speaker, and, lord knows, I had worked hard enough to get him – I felt I deserved to be able to do that! When Dr. S. arrived, I introduced myself, said I was honored to meet him, told him a bit about our group and showed him what I'd taken from his CV. He read what I had written and then he asked me a question that no one had ever (before or since) has asked me:

"Are you a child psychoanalyst?" he asked.
    I replied: "No."

Then he shocked me by (brusquely) saying the following:

"Perhaps someone who works with children could introduce me."

My reply was also brusque:

"No, that won't be possible."

Then I got up, walked to the podium, took the microphone and after a few pleasantries spoken into our (unfortunately) well-functioning sound system:

"Ladies and gentlemen, we are honored to have with us today Dr. David Smith. Dr. Smith is professor of psychiatry at XXX University, consultant at XXX and supervising psychoanalyst at XXX."

What I wanted to say next was:

"His talk today will be psychotherapy with oppositional children and other resistant conditions."

Instead, I said:

"His talk today will be psychotherapy with oppositional children and other resistant *physicians*."

There was a pause, then the crowd roared with laughter. Only two people weren't amused: Dr. Smith and I.

What does this slip mean? This man's disdainful behavior toward me (this was his reputation) put me in a dilemma. I wanted to act professional and felt that I had to praise someone who had just insulted me. Consciously, I wanted to do so, but unconsciously I felt otherwise. My censor resolved the conflict by making a compromise; instead of going on a public rant about Dr. S. and directly displaying my own disdain and contempt, it broke through in the form of the slip.

Does anybody in class have a slip for us?

STUDENT: My slip took place last year. I was breaking up with my ex-girlfriend – I mean, I should say that she was becoming my ex and we were fighting and I said: "Listen, Alyssa," but her name is Ashley. Alyssa was my *other* ex-girlfriend.

DR. M: That's great! I mean, as you listen to it. It's wonderful because what you're doing is saying to her: "Listen, you are already on that *other* list, the ex- list. You're on the list of the exes, why don't you get it? Also, I think we can understand your introduction when you said: "I was breaking up with my ex-girlfriend." She was an ex *already*. She was now "an Alyssa."

Thanks! Does anyone else have one?

STUDENT: Here's one. I was talking to somebody else who is also biracial, and we were talking about our experiences and specifically we were talking about high school. And she said: "Yeah, I was the only white girl there." When she caught herself, she was embarrassed.

DR. M: Perhaps she was embarrassed because she was caught showing a preference? This is wonderful, because there are several issues that may have contributed to this slip. We talked about the principle of overdetermination.[3] I suggest that the slip is not only about race but also about preferences for one parent versus another. This person is the product of parents of two races. As you begin to work with diverse patients, you'll find that a person's issues might not only be about what we consider to be the most common issues of diversity – race, sex and gender orientation – but may also include preferences for one parent over another and/or character differences between the parents, birth order of the person and other things that we might not immediately understand from the demographic data: what was occurring in the life of this person's parents – and in their relationship – when they were conceived, et cetera. Of course, there is the most obvious issue, race. Unfortunately in American culture, whiteness can be valued over blackness. Psychologists Drs. Kenneth Clark (1958) and Mamie Clark[4] highlighted this in research on internalized racism, using concepts derived from Freud's original work on projection and unconscious identification. The Clark data was used in the landmark Supreme Court decision overturning the use of "separate but equal" laws employed to maintain segregated school systems.

Thank you for your examples!

During the years that Freud wrote, *The Psychopathology of Everyday Life* was his most popular work; he said that it was written for a popular audience. However, this work can also help us apply Freud's ideas, not just to psychopathology and dreams, but also to other so-called ordinary phenomena.

Freud is applying the same psychoanalytic theory that he presented in *The Interpretation of Dreams;* now he is using this to understand other ordinary phenomena that were previously thought to be accidental. The major idea of this book is that some errors (the Latin word for this is *parapraxis*) are unconsciously motivated. Remember the formula that Freud had in decoding the dream: the wish versus the defense against the wish results in a compromise. The unconscious motivation for a slip is the same as the unconscious motivation for a dream: it is a wish.

Freud isn't saying that all errors are unconsciously motivated. He lists the conditions under which unconscious motives for a slip exist. What Freud is doing is he's adding another variable to the psychology of memory and forgetting. Freud is not trying to replace the cognitive-psychology explanations of memory and forgetting, only to add to them. In order to distinguish between forgetting that results from normal psychological process as opposed to a severe organic or functional disorder – or a third possibility, a mistake motivated by repression (a slip) – Freud presents three conditions:

(1.) The error is within normal limits, not an outlandish error, because an outrageous error would never be able to sneak past the censor (which is what a Freudian slip is created to do). For example, if asked to solve an addition problem, "How much is one plus one?" and you answered: "50 million," either the censorship has failed as a result of psychosis or brain impairment, or you weren't paying attention, or you purposely decided to not cooperate, or you're of limited intelligence;

(2.) The error is also something that is considered temporary. Every time I want to call Ashley's name, I shouldn't be mistakenly calling her Alyssa, because this slip is no longer a slip; it's now a symptomatic act;

(3.) Once a person realizes they're in error, they don't perceive any motivation for it, otherwise it has not served its function: making a compromise between a wish and a defense against that wish.

Because many of Freud's ideas have now become part of the culture, without understanding what a slip actually means, a person might say: "That's a Freudian slip of the tongue." Just like one might say: "You're so anal." The person who has made a slip knows what it's called, although no motivation is perceived for the error.

When these conditions have been fulfilled, we have a parapraxis[5]

The screen memory

As we're beginning to see, our unconscious system is creative. I will soon present an early (screen) memory. However, before I do, an early memory comes to mind that I recently had in a group therapy session that I lead. This memory had me thinking about the creative power of the unconscious and how it can be used clinically.

Here is the context, and then the memory: During a group session last week, a memory returned to me I hadn't thought about in many years. It was wonderful because it's so obvious when you hear it. The context is that in the group there are two male group members who were talking about an old group conflict between them that I naively thought had been resolved. I said something about the resolution and, next thing I knew, both of them were enraged (at first at each other, then at the group, and then, finally, at me). They were both threatening to quit the group, even threatening violence against each other (given each man's history and psychological dynamics, violence, while not impossible, is unlikely).

Here's the memory

My mother is talking to a neighbor on the first floor of our apartment building (I'm about three or four years old). We're at the top of a long flight of stairs that leads down to the basement. The basement door is open because the basement is where the washers and the dryers are. I'm sitting on my tricycle, perched at the very edge of the stairway (I believe that my mother was just about to take me outside to ride, but this could be a secondary elaboration – remember this term from *The Interpretation of Dreams*?).

I see nothing else in this memory, although the story I was told later was that the superintendent of the building saw me flying down the stairs, and witnessed helplessly as I smacked into a basement wall and broke my nose in three places. I hadn't had this memory in a long time, but it came back to me when I was thinking about this class and about what happened in the therapy group. Early memories come back to us at times, and it is as if the unconscious wants to remind us of something, teach us something. Maybe I had been feeling too arrogant, a bit too reckless in the group, or even in this class. In that case, the memory serves as a warning: stop flying around, get back to earth! Perhaps also it says something about my mother's care or her inattention; it's a reminder to me: *Don't be as inattentive as she was on that day.* This comes home now that I have two young grandchildren and I am reminded about how much attention a young child requires just to protect them from danger. Thus, this might also be a reprimand to myself: you did not protect these group members from themselves and protect the group from the sudden explosion in the room, as expressed by these two members. That is, *by being inattentive, preoccupied, perhaps too interested in some other conversation(s), you failed in your protective function.*

Screen memory continued

With the concept of the screen memory, Freud presents another opening into the mind of the child: how one develops a life narrative. A screen memory is called a "screen" because it's like a strainer. If you pour just-washed fruit into a strainer, the fluids go through and what's left over, stuck to the screen, is the actual fruit.

A screen memory is composed of three components of the person's memories: earlier, contiguous and later memories condensed into a single memory image. One can also think of a screen memory the way one thinks of a myth. Myths are fantasies that attempt to provide a solution to basic psychological dilemmas shared by large groups of people. Myths are culturally shared stories passed down through generations orally or in written form. Freud (1913) suggests that when asked for an earliest memory, some people present a myth or fairy tale as if it had actually been part of their own history. The myth has become a part of the person's life narrative. Keep in mind that this same condensation is the process that we observe in the dream work.

I will now tell you one of my earliest memories, which dates to somewhere in my two-and-a-half-year-old range.

I am in my grandmother and grandfather's apartment in Manhattan (the apartment that I have mentioned before). My grandfather, who I adored for the very brief time that I knew him, is sitting in his big chair at the other end of the living room. I am little; the world is very big and the living room seems the size that a football field would appear to me now. I'm running toward my grandpa, who's sitting in his "Papa's chair" (I too have a Papa's chair, and my granddaughters, now two and a half and five years old, have been calling my chair "Papa's chair" since they were two).

Back to my screen memory:

I was the first grandchild on my maternal grandparents' side of the family, a boy in a nonreligious but culturally Jewish family.

In the memory,

I'm running toward my grandpa, toward his chair, and he scoops me up in his arms. However, then I look around the room and what I see is confusing: people are sitting on funny beanbag-type chairs, looking somber, and some on little stools, and some are crying.

That is the memory.

The fact, and therefore the context, is that my grandpa died when I was two years and five months old. (When I discuss this memory, I often feel a chill.) Here is what I now understand about this memory: My two-years-and-five-months-old self must have gone into my grandparents' living room and looked at grandpa's chair and said some version of:

"What the f . . .? Where's grandpa? And, moreover" (I had a very sophisticated vocabulary at two years and five months),"Why are all these people sitting around looking somber and/or crying?"

As in many families at that time, nothing related to this was being talked about. My two-years-and-five-months-old mind was bewildered. Thus, the memory is the result of the manifest content and latent content mixed together: it is a series of past, contiguous and later memories strung together. With this information, we can now ask: What is our reconstruction?[6]

I wished for my grandpa, not these people who were sitting around somber and crying. Yet when asked my earliest memory, this is the memory that comes to mind, as if it happened just the way I remember it now. My preconscious had taken an earlier memory (my grandpa's greetings and hugs) and a later memory (the shiva[7] and mourning period), and condensed them.

In this instance, while it matters how accurate the actual experience was, it's also important to keep in mind that the screen memory is conveying a psychological truth about me and my development, as important as the actual experience had been.

A screen memory is thought by Freud to be a conscious memory of a long chain of memories that have been repressed. When we think about it, this idea makes perfect sense, since of the millions of events that have occurred (the millions of blips of perception that happened throughout our lifetime), why do we ordinarily remember only a few of them? We only remember a few because these few are portraying and symbolizing experiences that are important to us. They are conveying conflicts – perhaps problems that we solved, often conflicts that we are still seeking to have mastery over.

There are times over my years of clinical work when a person began to present a memory and then stopped and said, "Wait. That's not a memory. That's part of a storybook that my mother/father/grandparent read to me when I was a child." In other words, this person took the story and made it into a memory. Keep in mind that those who write fairy tales and stories for children also have an unconscious, like the rest of us do.

One story that is particularly relevant to children, especially as a narrative about family history, is *Sleeping Beauty*. Do you know the story of *Sleeping Beauty?*[8] *Sleeping Beauty* was born to a king and queen (she was a princess). When she was born, the king was supposed to invite all of the 13 witches of the kingdom to her birthday party, but he forgot one; he only invited 12. All 12 came to the baby's party and each presented a gift: "I wish her beauty." "I wish her intelligence." "She's going to be talented." Suddenly, while witch 11 was presenting her gift, the mean 13th witch appeared; she was angry. She announced: "When she turns 21, she's going to be weaving and she's going to prick her finger, and she's going to die." Thank goodness, witch number 12 hadn't given *her* wish yet. She chimed in: "Yes, she will prick her finger, but, *no!* The princess will not die. She's going to sleep for 100 years. The whole kingdom is going to go to sleep until Prince Charming finds her; he will admire her beauty, he will kiss her, and the kiss will awaken the whole kingdom." The story proceeds, and the king and queen – try as they might to protect the princess by hiding all needles and sewing implements – are unable to stop fate. The princess finds an old room in the castle; there is a sewing kit. She pricks her finger and goes into a deep sleep for a hundred years. The whole kingdom goes to sleep and cobwebs develop everywhere. Why am I telling you this fairy tale? I would suggest that the story line is modeled after being frozen to death, a deep sleep that mirrors the reactions that occur when a mother goes into postpartum depression, or when a fetus dies during delivery, or when a young child dies; that is, when there's a death in a family, the actual death of a child or a mother – or the psychological death of a postpartum depression. When people come to you and they remember this particular story as a prominent memory or theme of their childhood, the story has appealed to them because they and their family of origin have become – in some ways – frozen in time, unable to grieve or mourn their loss.

In this regard, I refer you to the Disney movies *Frozen I* (2013) and *Frozen II* (2019).[9]

The first time I heard about the importance of this fairy tale, the fairy tale came from a young woman in an early therapy session; her answer to my query had me almost falling off my chair. I had asked questions about her history and, in fact, one of her siblings, prior to this woman's birth, had died (one could make the point that the woman in front of me was a replacement for the never-met, deceased sibling). This patient then described one room in her childhood home as "preserved as if my sister was still alive and would be coming home any minute." In this example, the earliest memory told me something important about this person, her family, her earliest psychological development. The earliest memory, by telling us about one's earliest relationships, tells us about the early seeds of what kinds of transference the person is going to have with you. There will be clues to how, in the transference, the therapist may soon become a chaotic parent, or a violent parent, or a disinterested parent, or a savior parent or a frozen-in-time/ deadened parent.

In *The Psychopathology of Everyday Life*, Freud makes a contribution to understanding normal human behavior. This understanding is invaluable as a tool for clinicians in their work, as it gives us an understanding of what's to come. Perhaps you can now see that I suddenly remembered a childhood memory in my therapy group that helped me to understand and remind myself that I might have been reckless at an important moment in the group's life. Perhaps something made me distracted so I missed an important group theme. What I got from my memory was a message from inside myself that I had not seen something. This process is called working with the counter-transference; we'll be talking about it in later lectures. It is a process that Freud gave thought to but did not fully develop. It was left to future generations of psychoanalysts to do so.

To summarize, Freud's theory can be formulated in the following way: We're all motivated by a variety of wishes. Under certain circumstances, these wishes can break through into consciousness and interfere with our routine functioning. An important clinical question in this regard is: Is this interference a permanent attack on one's functioning or a temporary one? A serious and permanent interference in functioning is not a slip/parapraxis or symptomatic act. We all have slips and symptomatic acts. You are positive that your appointment is at three o'clock, and show up at three for your one o'clock appointment. That's a symptomatic act. Unless you're always chronically going to an appointment at the wrong time, something about this mistake itself is particularly meaningful, but temporary. Under certain circumstances one's wishes temporarily break through and interfere with routine functioning. It's possible to specify the conditions where such breakthroughs occur; Freud calls them parapraxis. As you become familiar with the projective processes in psychological interviewing and psychological testing (such as in the Rorschach test), you'll begin to see in the conversations that the subject has with you how easily wishes emerge. As an example, the subject is shown an inkblot card and they have a look of fear in their eyes, and say: "Oh, that's weird. Really weird." Psychologists call this an avoidant style. What does an avoidant style mean? It is typical of those who have phobic anxiety. If one has a phobia about airplanes, you avoid them. If you have phobic anxiety you might also show your phobic anxiety by using distancing and avoidant words like "weird" and "strange."

The reason for these examples is to show how an understanding of the preconscious transactions (the psychopathology of everyday life) between clinician and patient has value in making meaning out of the experience.

Summary of lecture 5

In *The Psychopathology of Everyday Life*, Freud continues extending his understanding of the unconscious mind. He does so using the insights gained from the psychoanalysis of neurotic patients. Starting with the observation that neurosis is an unconscious defense against intolerable experience, Freud looks at a variety of normal phenomena, such as slips of the tongue, which had previously been thought to be accidental. Freudian slips, like dreaming and neurotic symptoms, follow an orderly process where there is a blocking (repression) of thoughts and emotion followed by a failure of the repression. However, in these phenomena, the failure of repression is temporary and the interference with the person's functioning is minor and brief.

Notes

1 Watergate was a political scandal in the United States involving the administration of US President Richard Nixon from 1972 to 1974 that led to Nixon's resignation.
2 Compassionate conservatism" is an American political philosophy that stresses using conservative techniques and concepts in order to improve the general welfare of society. In recent times it has been strongly associated with former US President George W. Bush, who commonly used the term to describe his personal views. Bush said, "I know how hard it is for you to put food on your family," at a campaign event at the Greater Nashua, New Hampshire, Chamber of Commerce, on January 27, 2000. In Weissberg (2009) *Slate.com*
3 Overdetermination occurs when a single observed effect is determined by multiple causes, any one of which alone would be sufficient to account for ("determine") the effect. In the philosophy of science, this means that more evidence is available than is necessary to justify a conclusion. Overdetermination is in contrast to underdetermination, when the number or strength of causes is insufficient. The term *overdetermination* is used by Freud as a key method to gather data in psychoanalysis.
4 Kenneth and Mamie Clark (1958) were African-American psychologists who conducted research with children (they were also active in the civil rights movement). The Clarks were known for their 1940s experiments using dolls to study children's attitudes about race; they testified as expert witnesses in one of five cases combined into the U.S. Supreme Court case *Brown v. Board of Education* (1954). Their studies found contrasts between African-American children attending segregated schools in Washington, D.C., and those attending integrated schools in New York. The doll experiment involved a child being presented with two dolls. Both of these dolls were identical except for the skin and hair color. One doll was white with yellow hair, while the other was brown with black hair. The child was asked questions inquiring which doll they would play with, which one is the nice doll, which one looks bad, which has the nicer color, etc. The experiment showed a clear preference for the white doll among all children in the study. One of the conclusions from the study is that "a Negro child" by the age of five is aware that to be "colored in . . . American society is a mark of inferior status." This study was titled "Emotional Factors in Racial Identification and Preference in Negro

Children" and was not created with public policy or the Supreme Court in mind, lending credibility to its objectiveness. Their findings exposed internalized racism in African-American children, self-hatred that was more acute among children attending segregated schools. The research paved the way for an increase in psychological research into areas of self-esteem and self-concept. The use of the understanding of unconscious identification stems directly from Freud's work on the identification processes in the formation of the ego (see lecture 6).

5 Freudian slip, also called parapraxis, is an error in speech, memory or physical action that occurs due to the interference of an unconscious wish or internal train of thought. Examples involve slips of the tongue, but psychoanalytic theory also embraces misreading, and mishearing, as well as temporary forgetting and the losing of objects.

6 In *reconstruction* the psychoanalyst assesses the current symptoms and forms some hypotheses about what the person's childhood family must have been like to influence what they are like now.

7 Shiva (literally "seven" in Hebrew) is the weeklong mourning period for relatives in Judaism. The ritual is referred to as "sitting shiva" in English. The shiva period lasts for seven days after the burial. Following the initial period of despair and lamentation immediately after the death, shiva is a time when people discuss their loss and accept comfort from others.

8 *Sleeping Beauty* is a classic fairy tale about a princess who is cursed by an evil witch to sleep for 100 years. A handsome prince awakens Sleeping Beauty. The story has been adapted many times throughout history and has continued to be retold by modern storytellers and various media.

9 *Frozen* is an American computer-animated musical fantasy film produced by Walt Disney and released by Walt Disney Pictures. It's inspired by Hans Christian Andersen's 1844 fairy tale *The Snow Queen* (2002). It tells the story of a fearless princess who sets off on a journey alongside a rugged iceman, his loyal reindeer and a naive snowman to find her estranged sister, whose icy powers have inadvertently trapped their kingdom in eternal winter and whose parents had mysteriously disappeared (perished) years before. *Frozen II*, set three years after the events of the first film, follows them as they embark on a journey beyond their kingdom (Arendelle). They want to discover the origin of the sister's magical powers and save their kingdom after a mysterious voice calls out to this sister.

References

Andersen, H. C. (1844). The snow queen. In *New fairy tales. First volume. Second collection.* Denmark: Nye Eventyr. Første Bind. Anden Samling.

Buck, C., & Lee, J. (2013). *Frozen* [Film]. Walt Disney Animation Studios, Walt Disney Pictures.

Buck, C., & Lee, J. (2019). *Frozen 2* [Film]. Walt Disney Animation Studios, Walt Disney Pictures.

Clark, K. B., & Clark, M. P. (1958). Racial identification and preference among Negro children. In E. L. Hartley (Ed.), *Readings in social psychology*. New York: Holt, Rinehart, and Winston.

Freud, S. (1895). Studies on hysteria. In J. Strachey et al. (Trans.), *The standard edition of the complete psychological works of Sigmund Freud, Volume II*. London: Hogarth, 1–307.

Freud, S. (1900). The interpretation of dreams. In J. Strachey et al. (Trans.), *The standard edition of the complete psychological works of Sigmund Freud, Volume IV*. London: Hogarth, ix–627.

Freud, S. (1901). The psychopathology of everyday life. In J. Strachey et al. (Trans.), *The standard edition of the complete psychological works of Sigmund Freud*. London: Hogarth, vii–296.

Freud, S. (1905). Three essays on the theory of sexuality. In J. Strachey et al. (Trans.), *The standard edition of the complete psychological works of Sigmund Freud, Volume VII*. London: Hogarth, 145–243.

Geronimi, C., & Clark, L. (1959). *Sleeping beauty* [Film]. Walt Disney Animation Studios, Walt Disney Pictures.

Johnson, J. P. (1979). Nixon's use of metaphor: The real Nixon tapes. *Psychoanalytic Review*, *66*(2), 263–274.

Weissberg, J. (2009, January 12). *Top 25 Bushisms of all time*. slate.com/1/12/2009/the-top-25-bushisms-of-all-time.html 01/12/2009.

Wu, D. (2002). *The snow queen* [Film]. Hallmark Entertainment.

Chapter 6

The beginning of ego psychology

The process of identification

Sources: On Narcissism, 1914, and Mourning and Melancholia, 1917

We begin discussion of ego psychology with a review of Freud's works *On Narcissism* (1914) and *Mourning and Melancholia* (1917).

Around the time of World War I, Freud began to revisit his basic ideas. Psychoanalysis began with observations from *Studies on Hysteria*; neurosis is a defense against intolerable experience. At first, Freud explored the nature of "the intolerable" (he called it the longed-for and feared wish). During this early period, Freud ignored the defenses (he typically used the terms *repression* and *defense* interchangeably). Yet Freud's later interest in the defensive processes, what we now call ego psychology, may be his greatest contribution. Id psychology was focused on the wishes/impulses, while ego psychology focuses on how the person defends against these wishes/impulses. In much of the psychoanalysis that Freud performed, a patient came to him with symptoms. Freud suggested the presence of a wish (he believed the wish was a bit of fixated infantile sexuality; this sexuality had been modified in a compromise with the person's defensive structure and he called this defensive structure repression). Freud believed the compromise between the wish and the repression typically emerged as a symptom. When he presented the correlation *infantile sexuality/conflict/compromise = symptom* to the patient, their symptom disappeared. Thus, Freud's treatment model was to remove the patient's symptoms by discovering and labeling these unacceptable wishes (and their childhood origin) that conflicted with the patient's adult mind.

In this model, which Freud employed for a long time, he essentially ignored the issue of the defenses until these defenses appeared in the therapy as a resistance to the treatment. Then the goal was to eliminate them. We'll see this when Freud's patient Dora abruptly left her treatment with Freud. One speculation is that she left suddenly because Freud's understanding of her was wrong, or she left suddenly because his manner with her was disrespectful or because he was controlling her. One could make a case for any or all of these explanations. Yet Dora's symptoms were abating. Therefore, one might also make the case that she left because of her resistance to the uncovering of even more conflictual material connected to her forbidden wishes, such as longings for the love of both of her parents.

DOI: 10.4324/9781003171393-7

In the years that Freud worked with what we call id psychology, he had often made reference to an ego but had typically done so as if the ego was synonymous with the self. This was confusing because he would sometimes also talk about the ego as a group of independent psychological processes controlling consciousness. Thus, Freud understood the ego both as the self *and* as a system that can block upsetting wishes from becoming directly conscious. Yet until Freud had clarified the nature of wishes, that is, clarified the nature of the id, he wasn't ready to clarify the nature of the defenses – of the ego. Further, just as Freud believed that the wishes connected to infantile sexuality are the key to understanding the neurosis, *he began to believe that the ego and the ego defenses are key to understanding psychosis.*

Thus, in Freud's earliest work, he was interested in the intolerable experience. The wish that becomes the intolerable experience is what he focused on. He believed it was the "blunting" of this wish that produced the patient's symptoms, such as a conversion or a phobia or an inhibition.

As I have mentioned to you throughout these lectures, we study Freud as the founding theorist of our current psychoanalytic system. I have also mentioned that in the current day, when a clinician works with troubled people, we typically categorize our patients into two clinical types depending on the nature of their suffering:

One kind of person comes to treatment because they have an interest in being closer, more intimate, with others, and also feels that they want to be more genuinely authentic and autonomous. Such people often worry that wanting one (intimacy) might mean that they will have to give up the other (authenticity/autonomy). These people are neurotic and/or have a neurotic character.

A second type of person, clearly more disturbed than the first, comes to treatment so that they can find a way to achieve psychological survival as a separate functioning person, and perhaps become connected to another person. These people are what we now call those with severe character disorders, borderlines and psychotics. If you want to work with this second group of patients about issues such as intimacy and about being authentic, you're not empathic to their basic survival needs.

STUDENT: The term *psychotic* that you're using . . . I think of someone who's really ill.

DR. M: This will get clearer today. To continue, just as Freud felt the nature of the wish is important in understanding neurosis, he felt that the ego and its structure is important in order to understand more-disturbed people. One implication of this is that the original psychoanalytic treatment goal – to remove the patient's repressions (defenses) so they can understand their wishes – may not always be what's best for the patient; we're going to see that having defenses is in fact a good thing. To remind you about the man who had a cannibalism dream, we might think he'd have been better off with stronger or different defenses. Freud continued to look at the oral, anal and phallic stages. But the issue became a kind of figure-ground switch. He moved from looking at what wishes are fixated at each stage to how the ego handles each wish at each stage. All humans are going to have somewhat of a rough time with the oral, anal and phallic stages. However, only a few of us are going to hallucinate and be delusional because of childhood fixations.

On Narcissism

Ego psychology formally begins with Freud's 1914 work *On Narcissism*. This work involves an extension and elaboration of what Freud had called libido theory. In ithe looks at both the aim (as before) and also at an in-depth study of the choice of object. He describes how important the object is going to become for later work in psychoanalysis. This will lead psychoanalysis into an intensive study of what we now call object-relations theory and its offshoot, relational psychoanalysis. Many people with some familiarity with current psychoanalysis but little familiarity with Freud are shocked to find that object-relations theory didn't start with British psychoanalysts of the 1940s; it started with Freud in 1914.

The major points in *On Narcissism* are:

(1.) Freud describes libido as psychic energy of variable force;
(2.) He finally describes the development of object choice, how we choose others to love/connect with;
(3.) He describes the meaning of the term *narcissism*.

Until this work, narcissism was typically discussed as an issue connected to the relationship of the patient to the psychoanalyst, as in the difference between the transference neurosis, where the patient can establish a relationship to the analyst, in contrast to the narcissistic neurosis, where the patient cannot establish a relationship because they're too narcissistic/self-absorbed. In *On Narcissism*, Freud introduces the concept of the ego ideal. This ego ideal is what Freud later develops into the superego. This ego-ideal concept is going to help us understand *why* psychoanalysis works. It works by creating a new ego ideal, helping a person to take in (identify with) the psychoanalyst and thus help the person to understand their "self" and the influence of previous object relations on the formation of their sense of "self."

The title *On Narcissism* indicates Freud's reason for writing this work. Freud hoped that understanding this concept of narcissism could give him a better understanding of psychosis, the most primitive process of withdrawal into the self. For example, when we observe the schizophrenic patient on a hospital ward, we notice two things that are happening in the patient:

(1.) They have withdrawn from the external world, staring into space;
(2.) When one talks to this withdrawn patient, what you are going to hear is something called megalomania 1, an overinflated sense of the patient's self.

This megalomania takes the form of "I'm great" or "They're out to get me." In the first instance, "I'm great," the megalomania is easy to see. In "The world is out to get me," it's harder to see this process, but it's still there. Why would the whole world be out to get this particular person? The whole world is out to get them because they are the focus of acclaim (I'm great) or hatred (I'm an important enemy). A common megalomaniacal delusion in psychotic patients is that they're God or Jesus. Let's think about being a schizophrenic in a hospital. You don't feel very significant. So the idea that you are one of the most, or the most, powerful being that has ever existed would be attractive. All of us have a little bit of omnipotence and mega-lomania inside of ourselves; it gives us hope and confidence that we can overcome adversity. However, with the hospitalized psychotic person, this becomes their delusional belief. So we can observe these two things with this psychotic patient on the hospital ward:

(1.) The patient withdraws their interest – libido – from the external world (sitting silently and staring into space on the ward of the hospital would be an example of this);
(2.) The patient turns all of that withdrawn energy (libido) toward (into) the self; we call this megalomania.

As we begin to develop an understanding of object relations, we'll see that the newborn/infant begins "being in the world" with an inability to differentiate between self and other. Later, this infant begins to notice others, in particular the parents, because of their role in nurturing this child. However, for some unfor-tunate souls – for reasons that are both genetic and environmental – this interest is short-lived; their interest comes crashing back into the self. The person loses interest in others and in the world around them. This is the process that occurs in what Freud calls the narcissistic disorders. The most vulnerable, most common age when people suffer a breakdown, by the way, is between 16 and 20. Yet one can have a breakdown and be hospitalized, but have the right meds and the right talk therapy. In that scenario, their reaction to a question from the doctor is, hope-fully, going to be:

DOCTOR: "You know, three weeks ago you were saying you were Jesus."
PATIENTR: "I don't remember that at all . . . that is very weird."

In *On Narcissism*, there is a shift from a focus on the id, thus on the wishes, to a focus on the ego, thus on the defenses. It also involves an extension and elabora-tion of what Freud previously called libido theory. Freud will soon look at both the aim (as he had done before) and begin an in-depth study of the choice of the object. We are also going to see how important the object will become for later work in psychoanalysis. This is going to lead psychoanalysis to an intensive study of what we now call object-relations theory.

Psychosis, the most primitive process of withdrawal a person makes, is now understood as a fleeing back into the self. In other words, Freud says that the person may have had interest in others, but they've withdrawn that interest back into the self. We're going to see how Freud describes this happening. If this happens, then the self is now filled with psychosis. That is, when you see somebody on a hospital ward who's not interested in anybody else, they are filled with delusional material; thus, you assume that an interest in others was there once, but it's now gone. Instead of filling the self with mother and father, and having images of these objects with love, energy and interests [the psychotic says,] "I've given up on them. I'm only about me, and my delusions."

STUDENT: Narcissists don't care about anyone?[1]

DR. M: Like every kind of psychopathology, there's a range. I've worked with a number of couples where at least one member can absolutely love and be loved, but only on their terms. That love is typically about, "I need total control." Can such a person *love*? Can they *be* loved? It's going to be hard for such a person who has been so traumatized by loss/abandonment as a child that their thinking processes are rigid, and at times even delusional. I have said to you that I hope that each of us can become increasingly curious; unfortunately, with this kind of person, they are often so wounded and rigid that they are not able to be curious about why it is that they have left a trail of lovers and friends. Sometimes what this kind of person needs is a wake-up call.

STUDENT: Can the narcissist be woken up?

DR. M: Yes. By being loved and not exploited, loved though imperfect enough to want love. These are difficult concepts for a narcissist.

STUDENT: What if there's no kind of life-altering event, then a narcissist would have no motivation?

DR. M: Less motivation. The other thing that helps narcissists, and even helps psychopaths, is getting old. When you get old, you have less energy, and the world doesn't easily forgive you because you're not as attractive. That's why I believe older media stars become more self-reflective. They start getting fewer parts while they also start to more become human. They do charity, express gratitude.

Now to the key part of this work: in the third section, Freud considers the changes that occur in the narcissism we develop.

Freud suggests that we set up a kind of ideal in ourselves by which we measure our actual self. You're getting to know the people in my early life, my Aunt Mildred, Theodore Reik, the jazz trumpeter Miles Davis, the jazz drummer Philly Joe Jones, my mentor at Adelphi Gordon Derner and, of course, my mother, father and sister (in no particular order); these are some of the objects (persons) in *my* ego ideal, the objects by which I measure my actual self against my ideal.

Freud says that this ego ideal contains the narcissism that had previously been in us, that we abandoned in childhood. We gave it over to our parents and others, because one thing about being a child is you can't do anything. You start by thinking that you're the center of the universe, but it doesn't take long before you realize that you are *not* the center of the universe: you still can't even crawl, you can't walk; other people have to do stuff for you . . . maybe you are *not* so great? You move from being the center of the universe to believing that Mommy's the center of the universe. There are daily narcissistic wounds where you're reminded that you're just a powerless child, that you don't even have control over yourself. These narcissistic wounds make us give up our omnipotence. Where does the omnipotence/narcissism go? It goes to the powerful people in our life. I like to call these first objects Mom and Dad. They become the first center of our universe.

Freud says, once we recognize the difference between the ego and the ego ideal, we are faced with the following question: How does one form opinions about oneself?

How do I know I've reached my ideal? Freud reasons that there's a special process in us, a structure that is constantly evaluating whether we're reaching this ideal, constantly monitoring our current actions with the standards set by the ideal. This structure's job is to guarantee that narcissistic satisfaction from the ego ideal is received. This structure is called the conscience. You might be noticing what's happening here? It's not going to happen at this lecture, but this structure will later be called the superego. As you know, because each of you went to college, took courses, did well, studied, got research experience, got clinical experience, applied and was accepted to this program, you've been motivated by a desire to reach your ego ideal.

STUDENT: I understand primary narcissism and the way that I understand it is the saying, "In order to love others you must love yourself."

DR. M: Actually, we don't even know that there *are* others when we have primary narcissism.

STUDENT: I guess I'm having trouble with primary narcissism.

DR. M: Of course, these are very difficult, counterintuitive notions. Primary narcissism is when you think you're the center of the universe, before you know that others exist. Then you slowly begin to see that there are others. To understand this process, what do we commonly say? If you've had any clinical experience before you came here, you know what they say about psychopaths; they say that they don't have a conscience. That's not true. They have a conscience. They just don't want it. Loving oneself first is what we all do. It's actually the opposite. In order to love one's self, one first needs to love (an) other: the caretaking, mothering one. Once you love others, you test them. Then, when you love another person, your internal objects say "good," you are in love with another person. Further, loving yourself exclusively is actually a bad way to start the world, but that's what we've got. One needs to develop one's self out of this before we can actually love anyone else. When you are an infant, nobody exists and you're omnipotent. In this regard, here is a question, Why do people have such powerful reactions when, for instance, somebody like Ruth Bader Ginsburg dies? This is because the dead person has taken a symbolic place in our ego ideal.

STUDENT: So we all have some narcissistic tendencies. Is part of it that there's some level of disappointment playing that into your "self"?

DR. M: Yes. There's always a little bit of secondary narcissism in all of us.

STUDENT: And that happens later?

DR. M: Disappointment happens throughout our lives, but if in the earliest time we don't establish basic trust (Erikson, 1963) in our environment, that's going to start us on a bad process through the oral, anal and each stage after. There's always going to be residue, because with human beings relationships are ambivalent, and no human being is perfect. No mother is perfect, no father is perfect and no child is perfect.

To continue, a person judges whether or not they are living up to the standards that they set for themselves. The mechanism used for this purpose is called the conscience. The conscience derives first from the parents and then from society. We see here that Freud is laying the groundwork for the superego.

Mourning and Melancholia (1917) is another of the foundational works of ego psychology. Mourning is the process of grieving an *actual loss*, while *melancholia* is the term that Freud uses for depression.

The book is important in three ways:

(1.) Freud devotes a section to depression (melancholia);
(2.) Freud presents an in-depth discussion of the concept of identification. I've been promising this discussion to you throughout these lectures. This is a very important concept;
(3.) Through the process of identification, Freud changes the idea of what can be taken into our unconscious. Previously, Freud had only talked about unconscious ideas or feelings. Now he begins to talk about the "taking in" of unconscious persons. That is, objects can be taken into the unconscious, not just feelings and ideas. When we understand that persons can be taken into our unconscious, we're also able to understand much more about the earliest psychological development of human beings. We're going to change our understanding of what the ego is, what the ego ideal is and what psychoanalysis actually does.

Prior to this work, Freud tasked Karl Abraham[2] with unraveling the psychodynamics of depression. Abraham had written some papers about it, and had suggested that depression seems connected to difficulty at the oral stage. Abraham couldn't do much more than this. So Freud started looking more closely at depression and began to reason that perhaps depression is not an illness in its own right: perhaps it is a symptom. This was revolutionary. By the way, much of the medical/psychological community still treats depression as an illness as opposed to a symptom.

One current understanding is that depression is both a symptom and that there are biological components and vulnerabilities that make it an illness.

In this paper, Freud compares melancholia to mourning. Mourning occurs when somebody who you love, or somebody who's a substitute for those that you love, dies. A substitute for one's love objects might be in a different generations) Abraham Lincoln, Franklin Delano Roosevelt, John F. Kennedy, Martin Luther King Jr., Princess Diana, the musician Prince, George H. W. Bush or Ruth Bader Ginsburg – all cultural figures from various eras, from the political and/or entertainment fields, who lived prominent lives and whose deaths became cultural events.

In melancholia/depression, no actual loved one (or substitute) has died. However, in both melancholia and mourning, the person has similar reactions, such as sadness. This is interesting to Freud:

> In mourning, somebody actually dies, the mourner is sad.
> In melancholia, nobody dies, but the melancholic is also sad.
> How can we understand this? Yet there *is* a major difference between these
> two states.

In depression, one also develops self-reproaches. We attack ourselves. That doesn't happen in pure mourning. (By the way, we now know that there's no such thing as a "pure" mourning. There's always some ambivalence and we do have a little bit of self-reproach in normal mourning as well, but the primary feature is sadness.) However, mourning decreases in the mourner after some duration (Rhee, 2017).

In a depression, one is not only sad but also hating oneself and reproaching oneself, and that doesn't happen in pure mourning. This whole situation doesn't make sense to Freud. Perhaps, Freud suggests, in mourning there's an actual loss, but in the depressive, the person is reacting to a loss, but it is an internal loss.

Freud reconstructs the process as follows:

> Person A is attached to B. There's some disappointment; that is, Person A disappoints Person B. Their relationship is shattered. Person B emotionally falls down; however, soon they pick themselves up, dust themselves off and move on.

However, it is not the same for Person B Prime.

Person A Prime is attached to Person B Prime. There's some disappointment; that is, Person A Prime disappoints Person B Prime. Their relationship is shattered.

Freud says the melancholic/depressive is reacting to some internalized loss in the same way as the mourner is reacting to a real loss. In some breakups, one person might mourn a little and go on. But another person might go into a depression.

He reasons that the depressed person maintains the attachment even though they can't maintain the relationship. How do they do this? They regress. Depressive people are oral. We've all observed that infants put everything in the mouth.

The first relationship we have, our relationship to the world, is through the mouth. The depressed person can't maintain the relationship, but at least they can maintain the attachment. Person B Prime emotionally swallows Person A Prime (see Figure 6.1).

In this regard, can you remember the dream of the young man, the cannibal dream? By the way, as I said, this man shouldn't have "known" this about himself. You guys in this course can know it. Not him. His stronger (secondary) defenses weren't working; this person ought not to have had such a clear dream with the latent content revealed, content about cannibalizing. This was a very regressed image of what the experience of the depressive process is, a primitive process like the man on the hospital ward who kneeled and made the sign of the cross. So, the person can't maintain the relationship, but instead maintains an attachment by identifying, that is, by swallowing the "other" who has disappointed them.

Next, Freud wonders: What about the self-reproaches observed in the depressive? Perhaps these people become hateful towards the rejecting other. Perhaps what they couldn't express to the person in reality, they now do so internally. The depressive attacks the object unconsciously in a way that they couldn't attack the object in reality. When you attack this object, since it is inside of you, you're actually attacking the internal object in your self. Freud's suggesting that if one could consciously do this, they wouldn't become depressed. What would happen is that they'd be disappointed and angry with the person who dumped them. They'd be conscious of it. They'd get over it. But in the depressive, the sadism is now unconsciously turned on the substituted internal object (Person A Prime) and the rejected one is abusing that object, making it suffer, deriving sadistic gratification from its suffering. By self-punishment, the depressive patient gets revenge on the object that denied them love.

STUDENT: In the essay, it seems like Freud is saying that instead of attacking the outside person, you're attacking yourself, so you've internalized that about one person. In a way that it makes more sense to me.

DR. M: Yes. What Freud is also saying (implicitly) is that this internalizing is a way to preserve that object.

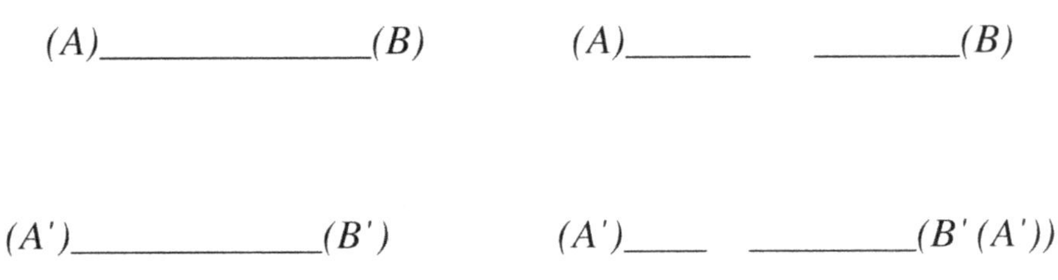

$(A)_____(B)$ $(A)_____ \quad _____(B)$

$(A')_____(B')$ $(A')\_\_\_\_ \quad _____(B'(A'))$

Figure 6.1 The process of identification

STUDENT: Right. It also seems to be what the person has really done, like in the breakup situation, is that they've internalized the rejection that the other person did to you. So I'm confused. Which one is it?

DR. M: It's both. Maintaining the relationship and doing things in the relationship you wouldn't have dared to do outwardly – such as be angry, because you've learned in your history that when you break up with somebody or when they hurt you, it's your fault. You're going to be angry, but be angry with yourself instead of the other person. This is now called the defense of identification or introjection. Even though Freud had already written *On Narcissism*, he wasn't ready to fully understand that this is about the superego attacking the ego. In this work he's pointing out that something is happening. People get depressed. They internalize objects, and this comes from their historically ambivalent relationships where they learned to take in (introject) anger instead of push it out (project it). Freud is going to say (in our next lecture) that every relationship is ambivalent. What I just described is what everybody does. That's how we all form a superego.

STUDENT: What about the concept of depression after a breakup being not attacking oneself, but . . .

DR. M: Normal grieving.

STUDENT: What if it's just like, "I'm depressed because this person doesn't love me anymore, I'm not good enough"?

DR. M: You mean that the person is conscious of it?

STUDENT: Right.

DR. M: That's normal mourning, therefore short-term. The problem is what happens when it's not conscious. The person comes to you and says:

"I've been depressed for months."

"Do you know why?"

"No."

"Were you depressed as a kid?"

"I would have bouts of depression. My mother was depressed. It must be chemical."

"Oh, your mother was depressed. Was she available to you when she was depressed?"

"No, we had a housekeeper who was nice to me. She was fired. When I was nine."

"Do you know why?"

"No."

"Oh. So nothing's happened in your life recently? No losses?"

"Well, my best friend's father died."

"Oh, when?"

"Six months ago. And that's when I started getting depressed."

"Oh. How come?"

"Gee, actually, he was like a second father to me."

(I'm thinking, he was also like a first mother to you and like the housekeeper and a first father, and other comforting figures, who you weren't able to acknowledge as your true nurturers because that would have been too frightening.) This new loss had repercussions; it set off a chain of unconscious memories of loss. So the chemical theorists are right that these processes typically occur in somebody who is vulnerable, but there are many ways to be vulnerable. One can be chemically vulnerable; one could also have had a series of unmourned losses. What he'd done with those unmourned losses is that he turned them against the "self," instead of being able to fully grieve.

Identification

Freud next explores the concept of *identification*. Identification is the earliest type of relationship. The process occurs in the oral stage first (remember the patient's cannibal dream). In this earliest process, the ego wants to take the object into itself and to devour it. Keep in mind such phrases as "You're eating me up alive." In *On Narcissism* (Freud will later modify this view), he says that "normal people" outgrow this kind of identification. They move on to different kinds of object relationships, to more mature kinds of relationships. But as in any regression, when object love is frustrated, some people regress to this earlier kind of identification.

At the beginning of these lectures, I said there were two important formulas that we learn about in this course. We saw the first one in our first lecture. It is: Neurosis is a defense against intolerable experience.

Here is the second: Object cathexes regress to identification.

The identifications seen in depressives are the result of frustration in love with a significant other. We regress from emotional connection to swallowing.

Next, Freud relates all this to the contents of the unconscious. Until now, what had been thought to be in the unconscious were intolerable wishes. Now Freud reasons: if an object can be incorporated (identified) in the ego, then we should expand the whole conceptualization of the contents of the unconscious. We thought the unconscious was filled only with tolerable and intolerable wishes. Now, he reasons, it's also filled with tolerable/intolerable objects. Like wishes, these objects are filled with cathexes that we want, and cathexes that we fear. Freud later uses this observation for the concept of the superego, which is the incorporated representation of the swallowing of objects. The superego is made up in large part by our first objects, our mom and dad. These objects are then the incorporated representation of the mom and dad, taken into the unconscious by an unconscious identification (but also consciously, so that one can see a person who walks the same way that their dad or mom walks; that's called imitation).

STUDENT: So having the superego is a good thing?
DR. M: It sure is. Later, Freud develops a formula more commonly used today: that in depression, the superego attacks the ego in the same the way that the parent(s) attacked the child in childhood; with the obsessive-compulsive

disorder, the ego fights back. "You're bad." "No, I'm not." "Do this ritual and you won't be bad." We'll talk about this in more detail next lecture.

Summary of lecture 6

Around the time of World War I, Freud began to reevaluate his ideas. He'd started his work by observing that neurotics flee from intolerable experience. In his writings prior to the war, Freud had focused on the nature of this intolerable experience. He had concerned himself with the contents of the unconscious mind that, if not allowed to become conscious, can cause neurosis. Now Freud looks at the nature of the defensive processes that block experience. He's fascinated by two clinical phenomena: psychosis (narcissistic neurosis) and depression (melancholia). Just as he felt that the nature of the wish is important in understanding neurosis, he's beginning to believe that the structure of the ego is important to understand more disturbed persons. One implication of this is that the original treatment goal of psychoanalysis (to remove the patient's repressions – defenses – so they understand their wishes) may not always be what's best. In *On Narcissism* (1914) and *Mourning and Melancholia* (1917) Freud extends his understanding to the processes that occur in severe psychopathology and introduces the concept of identification: a key concept in psychoanalytic theory.

Notes

1 Narcissists want adoration. Each mate is supposed to be the other one's self object Kohut (1971).
2 Karl Abraham (1877–1925) (Falzeder, 2002) was an influential German psychoanalyst and collaborator of Freud. Freud called Abraham his "best pupil."

References

Erikson, E. (1963). *Childhood and society* (2nd ed.). New York: W. W. Norton & Company.
Falzeder, E. (Ed.). (2002). *The complete correspondence between Sigmund Freud and Karl Abraham (1907–1925)*. London: Karmac Books.
Freud, S. (1914). On narcissism. In J. Strachey et al. (Trans.), *The standard edition of the complete psychological works of Sigmund Freud, Volume XIV: On the history of the psycho analytic movement, papers on metapsychology and other works*. London: Hogarth, 67–102.
Freud, S. (1917). Mourning and melancholia. In J. Strachey et al. (Trans.), *The standard edition of the complete psychological works of Sigmund Freud, Volume XIV: On the history of the psycho analytic movement, papers on metapsychology and other works*. London: Hogarth, 237–258.
Kohut, H. (1971). *The analysis of the self: A systematic approach to the psychoanalytic treatment of narcissistic personality disorders*. New York: International Universities Press.
Rhee, S. L. (2017). Structural determinist aspects of depression in Freud's "Mourning and Melancholia". *Psychoanalytic Social Work, 24*(2), 96–113.

Chapter 7

Further explorations in ego psychology "Beyond the pleasure principle" and the ego, the id and the superego

Sources: Beyond the Pleasure Principle, 1920, and The Ego and the Id, 1923

As we've seen, Freud's works are intellectually and emotionally complex and difficult to read (he wrote in a Germanic style). If you're struggling with the material, that is expected – don't be discouraged. Today, we first discuss Freud's final look at his metapsychological view of instincts (id). Then we continue with ego psychology.

The aggressive drives

Up to now, Freud had attributed most human behavior to the sexual instinct ("Eros" or libido). With this essay, *Beyond the Pleasure Principle* (1920) Freud goes beyond the simple pleasure principle, further developing his drive theory with the addition of a death drive, Thanatos (the Greek personification of death).

The book describes humans as struggling between two opposing drives: Eros, which produces creativity, harmony, sexual connection, reproduction and self-preservation; and a "death drive," which brings destruction, repetition, aggression, compulsion and self-destruction. Freud posits that the process of creating living cells binds energy and creates an imbalance. It's the pressure of matter to return to its original state, which gives cells their quality of living. This pressure for molecular diffusion can be called a "death wish." The compulsion of the matter in cells to return to an inanimate state extends to the whole living organism. The psychological death wish is a manifestation of an underlying physical compulsion present in every cell. He argues that dreams where one relives trauma serve a binding function in the mind, and are connected to a compulsion to repeat. Freud now admits that such dreams are an exception to the rule that the dream is the fulfillment of a wish. Asserting that the first task of the mind is to bind excitations to prevent trauma (so that the pleasure principle does not begin to dominate mental activities until the excitations are bound), he reiterates the clinical fact that for a person in psychoanalysis there is a compulsion to repeat the events of childhood in the transference; this disregards the pleasure principle. The idea of the repetition in dreams as an attempt at mastery of trauma, as well as the idea of the

DOI: 10.4324/9781003171393-8

patient's compulsion to repeat trauma in psychoanalysis (also for the purpose of trauma mastery) both continue to be important concepts in psychoanalytic theory and practice. However, the cellular metaphor of Freud's might be the one that just doesn't work, particularly when we compare it with his structural model of dreams (See lectures 1 and 2).

This new model reminds me of the following joke:

> A man is carrying a violin case on Seventh Avenue and 55th Street in Manhattan, and he stops to ask another passerby: "Excuse me, how do I get to Carnegie Hall?"[1]
>
> The other man replies: "Practice, practice, practice."

The metaphor of a death drive seems like a stretch of logic to me that doesn't answer the question(s) that Freud was asking. This seems to be an attempt to explain his brilliant observations in quasi-medical terms. All the rest of the brilliant observations – and theorizing about trauma – might be best understood in other ways. That is, the concept of a death drive as used to explain human aggression might be better discarded. Aggression is more likely a response to the organism's reaction to frustration, terror or a searching for mastery. To dare to attempt to "psychoanalyze" the master: It's not a great leap to connect Freud's fascination with cells with his struggle over cancer of the jaw . . . perhaps an attempt at mastery?

Yet, students and even many clinicians who currently practice with psychoanalytic therapy – such as object relations or relational clinicians – are often surprised when they learn that they've been working with concepts like projective identification and inducement and enactment as if these were relatively new concepts. However, often these concepts are not new. As an example, in 1911, Freud wrote to Ferenczi talking about an "induced countertransference not uncommon with patients that have suffered trauma."[2] Thus, many of Freud's trauma concepts were groundbreaking. In my opinion – and not every psychoanalyst agrees with me (Klein, 1963) – this does not seem to be one of Freud's best concepts.

In *Beyond the Pleasure Principle* we can see Freud's conflict between two etiologies. One etiology is trauma-based, that is, it is based on the power of a single or a few events to change the course of one's psychology. The other is developmentally based, that is, it is based on the understanding of psychopathology as the result of complications in sexual and emotional development. There is a misconception with some, the mistaken belief that Freud abandoned one for the other. Freud focused on one instead of the other, but never abandoned either trauma or development as etiological factors. This matters to certain people who feel that Freud abandoned the understanding of trauma as a causative factor in the neurosis because he began focusing on the sufferer's unconscious motivation(s). These critics will sometimes suggest that Freud was blaming the suffering person for their traumatic experiences. If you work with a trauma victim who was abused, for example, a young child who was sexually abused, and in the abuse certain longings were stimulated, a discussion of these longings can sometimes be mis-understood. For some it's possible to mistakenly hear, "They asked for it, wanted it." Clearly, this is *not* what the psychodynamic clinician would say or think. Yet avoiding such a discussion may also be doing the child a disservice, because (through no fault of their own) the child may now have certain feelings that are not helpful and they are being encouraged to *not* express them. They may be unable to have these feelings validated, understood and put in their proper place for use at a more appropriate time in life. In this regard, perhaps the young woman that I mentioned whom a neighbor had abused wasn't able to tell her parents about her abuse because of the feelings that the abuse had generated. If someone is prematurely stimulated by a traumatic experience, and later wants help with it, in order to fully help the victim we need to understand them. For example, such a victim of abuse may unfortunately associate love/longing with guilt/shame.

What Freud actually wanted to do was to deepen our understanding of trauma by adding an understanding of developmental process to it. This means the clini-cian needs to work with and understand the victim's needs, longings and wishes so we can help them find ways to integrate these needs and longings into their current personality. The victim's trauma has complicated and interfered with a developmental process. But it doesn't only interfere with the process by connect-ing traumatic experience with what should be an innocent childhood – it may also stimulate certain longings that can later become guilt, self-hatred and shame.

Beyond the Pleasure Principle is Freud's attempt to more fully understand trauma. Freud had a very difficult problem with World War I. It was particularly difficult for him to understand the brutality and violence, because he had reasoned that positivism was going to cure all human problems; human violence made little sense in that context. Science was supposed to make things better for the human species. Yet science had produced biplanes, mustard gas, and bombs that were even better at destroying people than the guns and artillery created before. Freud witnessed the carnage and horror of the war, and this made him wonder:

"How does this fit into the idea of pleasurable wishes as the primary motiva-tor of all human activity?"

How do hate, murder and the thrill of killing fit into that?

Freud also began to realize he had an intellectual problem, a problem many of you already identified when I first introduced dreams. Many of you asked,

"How could a dream be a wish if it scares me?"

At the time that you asked, I explained that a day residue had stimulated a wish and that this residue had stimulated the dream and that's why the dream was working to keep you asleep, so that you didn't have to gratify every wish by wak-ing up. But what about people who have dreams after a trauma, like after a war experience?

Let me remind you that I also said that after a traumatic loss I encourage a person to dream. Such dreams often contain the same aspects of a horrific traumatic experience happening over and over again.

For example, I want you to imagine a battlefield scene:

> Two soldiers are in a foxhole, and they're talking about how they're going to get some time off from the war. You get time off in every job. While you don't get weekends off in a war, you get a leave. They're talking about the leave each will take. These are two Austro-Hungarian soldiers talking about where they will each be going, not just back to their base, but back to Vienna, or Budapest for a week. Other soldiers are going to replace them, and they're talking about this in their trench and sharing a cigarette. Meanwhile, the war is going on around them. They're having a pleasant conversation in the middle of a war. Suddenly there's an explosion, and afterward only one man wakes up, to find his partner dead. The survivor is injured, and they take him to a field hospital for treatment. That night he starts having a dream – the same dream over and over again – of his traumatic experience in the trench. So, it would make sense for you to ask (as Freud did) what kind of wish is this? "He can't be wishing for the explosion?" Of course not! However, in Freud's brilliance, he now recognizes something isn't quite right about these traumatic dreams: What this person has dreamt is not actually what happened to both of these soldiers at the explosion. It was similar but not the same.

This is the dream, and it differs from the actual experience. The differences are both subtle and important:

> The soldier is sitting in the foxhole with his friend, sharing a cigarette. "I am sharing the cigarette with my friend, we're talking about how he's going to be in Vienna and I'm going to be in Budapest. Suddenly, I hear a whirring sound and a flash of light from far away. It's getting louder and louder and then I'm out."
>
> That's not what happened to them during the actual trauma. What happened is slightly different (you'll see why this matters). In the actual traumatic experience, the soldier was talking to his buddy, and then he fainted. He fainted! What is different in the dream? In the dream he's adding images that produce preparatory anxiety.

Here's the dream again (with additions):

> "I was talking to my buddy. I saw a flash of light in the distance (*patient tenses up in his stomach, then muscles over his entire body tighten*). Now I see a bigger flash of light, (*his body is crouching for cover*). Next, I hear a whirring sound. It gets louder, and then I see and hear an explosion (*he braces himself*), then I faint." The dreamer is introducing warnings.

Freud asks us: What's the most horrible thing for humans? Helplessness.

The dreamer, by adding preparatory anxiety, is slowly attempting to master the dream's experience of helplessness. If one has the misfortune to have a car accident, one dreams and daydreams about the accident over and over again:

> "Your car was going to XX place. You thought you had a green light. The light changed in the middle, and a guy hit you.
>
> "You're going through this over and over. Now you're seeing the light change. You're also seeing him from the side of your window (which didn't actually happen during the accident, because you would've gotten out of the way). Now you're tensing up."

These traumatic dreams/daydreams are an attempt to add mastery anxiety or preparatory anxiety to master the trauma. That's the takeaway, the wish that's gratified.

STUDENT: Do you think in the case of the war dream it could also be sort of like also mastering other feelings?

DR.M: Yes, it would still be mastery. For example, perhaps this soldier is mastering guilt: *I'm alive and he is not.*

STUDENT: Doesn't dreaming make the anxiety worse? Like, there's so much I could have done and I didn't?

DR.M: Yes at first, but it also eliminates helplessness; this is the traumatic dream's main feature. Freud believes the feeling of helplessness is the worst feeling that humans can feel because it reminds us of when we were helpless infants. As I've asked, have you ever seen a helpless newborn, screaming and crying? It is a terrifying sight. The traumatic dream as a need for mastery is the takeaway from *Beyond the Pleasure Principle*.

Freud goes on to speculate about this, but for our purposes what comes out of this work is the wish for mastery of trauma and that there are probably two drives:

(1.) Sex: in other words, love, pleasure and connection;
(2.) Mastery: in other words aggression, power and control.

There are also probably two kinds of aggression:

(1.) Aggression that arises out of a frustrated need;
(2.) Aggression as a search for mastery, control and power.

The ego

We now discuss the next aspect of Freud's ego psychology: the development of character or personality.

What is personality? It's the frequent use of certain defenses. What are defenses? We're going to find out in the next few lectures. For now, if a person comes to see you and is continually contemptuous and demeaning – that is, someone who's characteristically contemptuous – I'd be thinking that the person uses narcissistic defenses like idealization versus devaluation (in other words, idealizing themselves and devaluing others). The person is acting like they are better than others, because better is all they can have, since their childhood was empty. They didn't get love. What they got instead was either idealization or devaluation (contempt). This would be my speculation, and as I have said repeatedly, a clinician speculates *and* continues to be curious. However, one might soon replace this speculation. Even in an ongoing case, one might reformulate their understanding of dynamics based on the ongoing sessions as well as on the changes that occur in both the patient's transference to the therapist and the therapist's feelings (transferential and nontransferential) about the patient.

This may all sound very complex to you, but as these lectures continue and clinical examples emerge, it will become clearer to you.

With these ideas in mind, we'll begin: *The Ego and the Id* (1923).

As Brenner (1974) suggests, in *Beyond the Pleasure Principle*, Freud took a last look at what he'll soon be calling the id (the instincts-impulses-wishes). In this current work, *The Ego and The Id* (1923), Freud presents his definition of the ego. Given the title of the book and its beginning, it would seem like the ego is what the book will be about. However, Freud doesn't continue to explore the nature of this ego until his next work, *Inhibitions, Symptoms and Anxiety* (1926). In this work, Freud moves from a somewhat cursory discussion of the ego to a more in-depth discussion of a new concept: the superego.

The ego and the id are actually about the superego. To summarize: *Beyond the Pleasure Principle* clarifies the id/drives; inhibitions, symptoms and anxiety clarifies the ego; the ego and the id clarifies the superego. I hope that Freud is becoming more understandable.

The superego

The superego is a new concept for Freud and it's a key concept for what is now ego psychology. There had been plenty of discussion throughout Freud's writings about the ego – he often spoke of it as synonymous with the self – but the superego appears here for the first time.

As we know from the last lecture, Freud is struggling with the concept of guilt – remember his work on the ego ideal and the conscience. Freud wonders: How do we deal with criticism?

What do we do when somebody disappoints us? We take them into the self. In *The Ego and the Id*, through the concept of the superego, Freud is going to look more closely at the Oedipus complex. He will systematically deal with two concepts that we're going to spend the rest of our lectures talking about: object relations and identifications.

We've seen that beginning with *On Narcissism* (1914) Freud had postulated an ego ideal. He developed this further in *Mourning and Melancholia*, where he talked about the taking in of or identifying with objects that you are ambivalent about, who have hurt and disappointed you. Today, these mechanisms/functions are renamed the superego.

The ego develops out of the id. The id is a group of instincts, needs and wishes, a cauldron of powerful needs and wants. Over time a kind of crust develops over the newborn's id. If you've seen a newborn, when it wakes up, light is painful and noises disturb it. In Freud's new model, the newborn is extremely sensitive to all sorts of stimulation (internal and external). In the early days of life, it sleeps a lot, it eats, sleeps some more, urinates, and defecates. It opens its eyes for only a little while. Over time a "crust" develops over this organism to screen out powerful external (and internal) stimulation. The crust gets more and more sophisticated, begins to process internal needs as well as reality, and begins to slowly deal with both of these states with more cognitive sophistication. This crust will soon be called the ego.

Later, in young childhood, the superego develops, and it develops out of this ego. Because the young child has to deal with both inner-need states and reality, they also have to figure out what aspects of reality can be used in their best interests, and what reality is good/what reality isn't good. This is because of what I like to call "the great imperial eyebrow." You know: the mother's (and later in development, the father's) eyebrow? The use of mother's lifted eyebrow teaches the child that mother is not happy about something. If mother's not happy, that's not a good thing.

The superego is the result of the resolution of the Oedipus complex. Some may have noted that other courses about Freud spend a lot of time on this Oedipus complex much earlier on in their presentation of Freud, but I didn't do so until today. You'll see why. Prior to this, Freud's idea of the Oedipus complex might have made no sense to you because he didn't present the mechanisms that one employs to take in others who determine our good and bad. Only now, as Freud introduces the notion of identification, can he say that one begins to determine what's going to please one's mommy, what's going to please one's daddy and what's going to displease each. The superego rises out of the resolution of the Oedipus complex by taking parental images into it. To define the superego, Freud has to go deeper into the concept of identification.

Identification

For Freud, the earliest identification (for now) comes out of a wish to be like one's father; this is true for both sexes. Freud's society was patriarchal. The father was the head of the family and the mother's job was to do the day-to-day caretaking and nurturing of the child. Freud once said that every human relationship is ambivalent, except for the relationship a mother has with her son.[3] In Freud's time, the mother's job was to nurture and adore the child. The earliest identification starts with the wish to be like the father (Freud should have said to be like the parents). The mother actually has a more crucial role in the development of conscience (rights and wrongs), particularly in the early years of development, than the father. We'll see in next lecture that the most important job for the father of a newborn is to take care of the mothering one.

For now, Freud says all children try to be like the father, but when frustrated in this, the child regresses (as Freud said in *Mourning and Melancholia*, this is what also occurs in depression). That is, the child takes the father into their personality. So, instead of being *like* the father, the child falls back on the earliest identifications (like a metaphoric swallowing of the father). In this way, the wish is not to be like the father. The wish is to *be* the father.

The formula is: *Object Cathexes Regress to Identifications*

Guilt, which is a superego punishment, results from this taking in of a harsh, critical and controlling father. But guilt's a funny thing. When we symbolically take our father in, we don't only take in the times when father was literally critical or abandoning, as well as the times when he was loving and nurturing. We also take in our own anger toward him, the anger that we projected into him. Thus this "father" is not the actual father. He's the father as well as all of our complex and ambivalent feelings about him. Some are the result of projection and therefore irrational. This is one reason why clinicians can't make snap judgments about the person's early objects when they give their historical narrative; we have to more deeply understand their experiences. To understand them from the context, we have to understand them from the history, which the person sometimes is not fully aware of. Thus, the superego is always harsher than the actual parents. If one doesn't have a strong enough ego – somebody for example, who is depressed and who comes with a weakened ego – there's a lot of guilt and hate (the ego is not protecting the person from an overly harsh conscience, harsher than their actual childhood objects).

With this background: *The Ego and the Id* is the first systematic presentation of Freud's three-part theory of personality: the id, the ego and the superego. Many survey courses of psychoanalytic theory start with this work. Can you now see the absurdity of that?

The Ego and the Id is about the superego. In his next work, *Inhibitions, Symptoms and Anxiety* (1926), Freud talks in more depth about the ego.

Freud begins by looking back at his metapsychology. While he had first reasoned that the unconscious and the repressed are the same (remember the dream lectures), there's the preconscious, the unconscious and the conscious. He thought that the unconscious and the repressed material were the same.

Now, Freud realizes that when he's working with patients and making interpretations, the person sometimes doesn't hear the interpretation. And, the patient may be unconscious (unaware) of what Freud had just said: they do not realize that their mind is "blocking" the interpretation. That is, Freud says something that the ego of the patient is supposed to look at, but the patient doesn't hear it.

Up to now (with his work on dreams), Freud thought the unconscious is the repressed material from childhood, and all the stuff that's repressed, it's not conscious. It's the person's unconscious wishes. Now he thinks:

> I have people in analysis and I make an interpretation, and I ask if they have any reaction to what I said." They say: "What did you just say?"

Further, they're unaware of the fact that "they're not hearing it."

In this instance, the resistance to Freud's comments can't be coming from the unconscious because Freud's comments are supposed to be stimulating the perceptual system. Freud realizes the resistance must be in the ego. But this means that a part of the ego is unconscious. This is confusing. So Freud begins to substitute something called an organized ego. He suggests that the ego is composed of the perceptual system and the preconscious, working together. The perceptual system deals with the outside, while the preconscious deals with the inside. This will also help Freud to explain the defenses in his metapsychology. You heard about this from dreams, but now Freud thinks this also happens, in some way, while we're *awake*.

In the next chapter, Freud asks the question: "How does the unconscious become conscious?" He goes back to his dream theory and says the unconscious becomes conscious through the intermediary of the preconscious. The preconscious and perceptual system are now renamed "the ego."

Next, Freud quotes a Hungarian psychiatrist, Georg Groddeck, who had written a book the year before this work. Groddeck's book is called *The Book of the It* (1919). In *The Book of the It*, Groddeck attempts to differentiate between the self and a second process, a "place" where there are deep, powerful internal forces – the place of each human's irrational passions. Freud takes this agency, Groddeck's *It*, and renames it the *id*. All the arguments that now happen instantly on Twitter, by the way, used to happen via letters and books. In that context, Groddeck wrote Freud a nasty letter after *The Ego and the Id* was published in which he said, "You stole my *It*." Coincidentally, Freud and Groddeck shared the same birthday, May 6. On Groddeck's and Freud's next birthday, Freud wrote: "I hope your *It* and my *id* have a very happy birthday."

STUDENT: So, the superego develops through the ego.
DR. M: Let me do this with more detail. I promise you'll get a sense of it. The ego develops out of the id's experiences with the "external world." It does so by acting first through perception, later through consciousness. When one is a newborn, the world is just a blur. Then we begin to become conscious, as we know with early memories. The ego's job is to substitute the reality principle for the pleasure principle of the id, so our early memories are wishes and they slowly begin to include more bits of reality. In the ego, perception does the same thing that the instincts do in the id: it drives the mind's system. If you're crossing the street and a car comes toward you, your perceptual system sees

danger and you jump onto the curb. The ego has the job of substituting the reality principle for the pleasure principle of the id. In other words, in the ego, perception does what the instincts do in the id. The ego represents reason and sanity, while the id represents our passions.

STUDENT: Got it!

DR. M: In the next chapter on the ego and the superego, Freud takes up his old concept of the ego ideal; he renames it "the superego." He also says that the superego is less closely connected to consciousness than the rest of the ego. Next, Freud returns to some of the ideas that he had considered in depression. There he suggested that object cathexes (attachments to objects) regress to identifications. He now feels that this process is more general – applicable to all humans, not just to people with depression. He says that when any young child's attachments are frustrated, which often happens when one is a child, the child takes that frustrating object into the ego. It follows that the ego is a storehouse of prior object choices. You may remember that I talked about my ego ideal and I mentioned my Aunt Mildred, my musician heroes, my parents, Gordon Derner and some other teachers. We take in those who influenced us, frustrated us and gratified us. We take these "objects" into our "old attic warehouse."

STUDENT: Is this only with the father?

DR. M: He says it's more likely to happen with the father, but all relationships are frustrating.

STUDENT: The frustration is key?

DR. M: Yes, he says you're more likely to take in an object when you're disappointed, as disappointment/frustration lead to regression, just as we saw in last week's lecture on depression. There's going to be continual frustration with reality. If the frustration with reality is too much, and the newborn/young child is not equipped, they're going to retreat into themselves and that's not good. For all the rest of us as young children, while life is frustrating, we deal with the frustration by taking the object in and preserving it. That's how we preserve our relationship to the object, as Freud originally thought happens only in depression. Otherwise, the first time your mother didn't give you a bottle on time, you wouldn't have a relationship with her anymore:

> "That's it, I'm done with you! The bottle was three seconds late, do you know what three seconds is to me, a newborn? It's a long time, huh? I'm done. I'm going elsewhere. (Where?) That's a good question."

Freud says the superego, is the storehouse of old object choices, but keep in mind that the superego is at first just a part of the ego and only becomes a separate "structure" after the resolution of the Oedipus complex. Freud could have been more precise, and less confusing, if he had said the following: "The superego part of the ego is a storehouse of old object choices." Every person who influenced you – the younger you are, the more powerful the influence, as some of the influencers were in your life before you had words, and these objects, with the associated images and feelings, are therefore more influential. Thus, a very powerful negative force will have even more power over you because you can't explain and rationalize it away and/or soothe yourself from that force.

STUDENT: So it's a form of a defense when we protect ourselves?
DR. M: Yes, it is the defense of identification. Its purpose is to protect the relationship from being destroyed. Remember that in *Mourning and Melancholia* (1917) what Freud said was that the relationship is shattered, but the attachment remains. In some ways, being depressed after a breakup means you're still in love with the relationship, but you can't have the relationship, so you make a second choice: you maintain the attachment. That's why we have the formula that depression is incomplete grieving and incomplete mourning. Most of us, if we're fortunate, have had enough experience dealing with loss, so if we have an unfortunate breakup or a disappointment, we find a way to preserve the relationship in reality or, if we have fallen down, we get up, dust ourselves off and move on. If we can't, and we've maintained this attachment, what are we going to do? We're going to attack ourselves. If a person comes to me and says they're having trouble in a relationship, marriage, business relationship or friendship, I'm looking for the disappointment. If a person comes and tells me they're depressed, we have more work to do. First, we have to identify what relationship disappointed them, and how bad the disappointment was. If the person says simply, "Well, I lost so-and-so. They died." I'm going to ask myself, why did this person who I'm now seeing not grieve and mourn this loss properly? There are mechanisms (they're a little better now than they used to be). In my childhood, family members died, disappeared, never heard from again, and when I asked my mother about some relative (I couldn't ask my father; he'd get annoyed), she'd say: "Oh, they're 'gone.'" If somebody comes to you and they are clearly depressed and they can't point to something but they point to a loss, I'm going to say this loss was not adequately mourned. There was ambivalence, hurt. No relationship is without some ambivalence, but even with the most ambivalent relationship there are processes involved with the funeral that can help with the mourning. With a mourner who is also depressed, there must be something we're missing here, that the patient's missing, something they're not able to talk about, and something they're unaware of.

To continue, Freud now begins to believe this process of identification is a much more general process, applicable not just to people with depression. Because of this process of identification, the effects of the earliest identifications in childhood must be very strong. When these identifications are studied, Freud begins to discard his original idea about the Oedipus complex.

He says that it's much more complicated than just that all children want their father. He suggests that we compete with our mother because we want our father *and* we compete with our father because we want our mother. Freud now believes that there are both positive and negative feelings within each of us toward both parents.

Do you want to know something Freud didn't talk about? Because I'm also a couples therapist, we know that other relationships are in this mix. Our parents marriage! Freud didn't talk about that. Siblings! He didn't talk about that much either!

To go on, the superego is the higher nature of humanity. The power of authority becomes invested in the superego and the tension between the superego and the actual attainments of the ego is experienced as guilt. You all know that, you're in a doctoral program, so you've got guilt and high standards. Social feelings that are shared by a group suggest that this group shares common aspects in each of their superegos. Sometimes we share the same superego, and it's not always a good one. With the internalization of the Third Reich (Nazi Germany), which was around more than a decade, young children were raised with the same superego, and the same symbols of a common superego, such as the swastika.

In the final chapter of the book, Freud looks more closely at the superego itself. The superego is not only in touch with the ego; it's also in touch with the id.

We now have a whole new model. It is called Freud's structural model of the mind (see Figure 7.1).

It contains:

(1.) The ego, which has two parts (a.) a perceptual system and (b.) a preconscious;
(2.) The id;
(3.) The superego (with identified objects in the storehouse of this superego). The superego has two functions: one is called the ego ideal and other is called the conscience.

The ego is constantly measuring itself against this ego ideal. If it doesn't match the ideal, then the conscience attacks. The conscience and ego ideal, through the process of identification, had, in childhood, swallowed images of powerful people who originally helped to determine who each of us *is*.

With these new concepts, Freud can begin to explain things that made no sense to him before.

Freud noticed that there were certain patients who have a negative therapeutic reaction. This means that even though they understand everything, every explanation that ties their symptom(s) to a childhood wish, these patients actually get worse in psychoanalysis instead of better. Freud wonders: *How is this possible?*

In his original model, the more you "un-repress" the wishes the better. With this new superego model, what he sees is that there's often a sense of guilt that is finding atonement in the illness. Every time a person releases id material, the superego attacks harder. This leads Freud to a new understanding of guilt. This is interesting, because Freud was a proper and uptight man, raised in the Victorian tradition, so he had plenty of guilt. Freud now says guilt can be explained by the

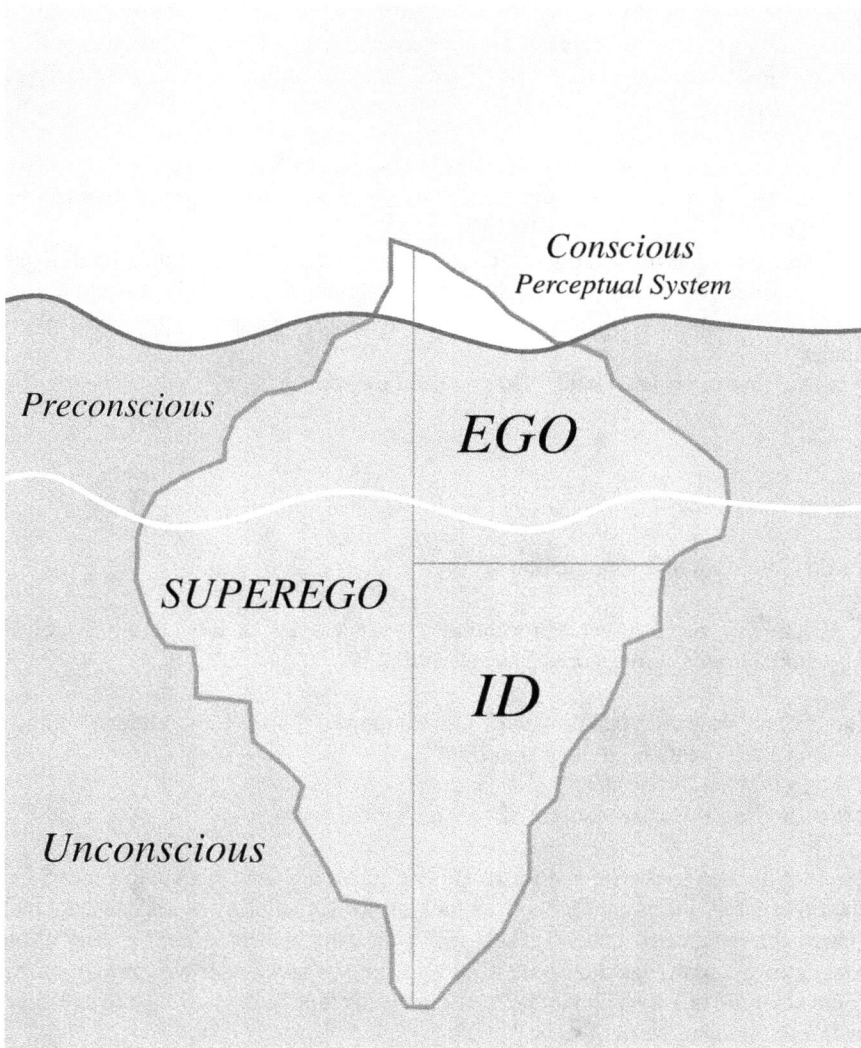

Figure 7.1 Freud's structural model of the mind

tension between the ego and the ego ideal. In the obsessional neurosis and in the depressive, this tension – and thus the guilt – is very strong.

By the way, knowing this formula helps us understand something else. Why is it that a hard-driving, ambitious person who retires is in danger of depression? Because if you're hard-driving and ambitious it means you have a very strong and demanding ego ideal. How have you pleased it? You've worked very hard: you're obsessional. You've stopped the superego by appeasing it via hard work. You're the best, the emperor/empress of your universe; you're having great success. You're able to fend off your high ego-ideal standards, to satisfy them, by obsessional behavior. Now, you retire. What's happening now may not be good.

Further, guilt may be related to crime. Some people have an exaggerated sense of guilt, and they may even commit crimes in order to be caught so they can be punished.

I once worked with a surgeon who was convicted of shoplifting. His defense lawyer asked me to see him and write him a letter so they might make the sentence more lenient ("If there's no further stealing, he's a valuable member of society.").

In the first interview I said, "Do you need the money?"

HE: "No."
ME: "Why'd you do it?"
HE: "I don't know."

I said (sounding like a magic man):

"Did you recently get a promotion at your hospital or have another professional honor before you did the shoplifting?"

HE: "Yeah. How did you know that? Did someone tell you? I don't understand . . . but I felt great about the promotion."
STUDENT: What did he steal?
DR. M: It wasn't even something of value, a knickknack.

He said he was looking for a thrill. He had also done this as an adolescent. On the other hand, I thought that he was looking for something else, because he had tipped the balance to make himself feel guilty for his success. The shoplifting and getting caught was punishment for his crime of success. If we had more time today, I would talk a bit about the dynamics of his family, but suffice it to say there was a family context to this.

Also, some people even admit to crimes they didn't commit.

Here are some examples of the new formula: id, ego and superego.

(1.) The superego and the ego attack the id; what we get is a neurosis;
(2.) The id and the superego join forces against the ego; the ego offers us information about the constraints of reality. The superego is our morality, pride and righteousness and the id is our instincts. If the id and superego merge against reality, we call that hypomania. What one sees here is some version of the following: "There's no bad in me, I'm the greatest, but the outside world . . . that's all bad."

Patients hospitalized with episodes of bipolar I (manic) and/or Adolf Hitler, Joseph Stalin and other tyrants might be examples of this kind of problem.

The meanness of the superego in the cases that we're now talking about suggests to Freud that the superego is connected to our angry and sadistic parts. Freud created the negative correlation. The more you see something on the outside (consciousness and behavior), the more you assume that the opposite is true on the inside (the preconscious defenses and symptoms). The bureaucratic, uptight, rigid person who is polite to a fault and controlling of self and others may actually have a lot of hate in them and a very powerful superego that they're using to defend against their hate. They may actually have a strong desire to explode, and that's what makes them even more rigid and controlling of themselves.

Our next lecture concerns Freud's last major theoretical work, *Inhibitions, Symptoms and Anxiety* (1927).

Summary of lecture 7

Originally, Freud attributed most human behavior to the sexual instinct (Eros or libido). In *Beyond the Pleasure Principle* (1920) Freud goes beyond the simple pleasure principle, further developing his drive theory with the addition of a death drive, as well as focusing interest on a drive for mastery as an adaptive process in the person suffering from trauma. Freud's focus on the importance of psychological defenses was a new (figure/ground shift) approach to psychoanalysis, and led to his final theoretical works. In *The Ego and the Id* (1923) Freud proposes a three-part system of personality: the id, the ego and the superego. To do this, Freud returns to his model of the mind. He asks, how does the unconscious become conscious? Through the intermediary of the preconscious, this preconscious and the perceptual system form the ego. In the same year, psychiatrist Georg Groddeck wrote *The Book of the It* where Groddeck suggested that we're propelled by unknown instinctual forces. Freud adopts Groddeck's terminology to differentiate between these unconscious instinctual forces (the id) and another system, (the ego). The ego is that part of the id which has been modified by the influence of the external world acting through perception and consciousness. The ego's task is to substitute the pleasure principle of the id, (i.e., the primary process) for the reality principle of the ego (i.e., the secondary process). For the ego, perception does what instincts do in the id, that is, it's the driving force for mental activity. The superego is also introduced in this paper. In a previous work, *On Narcissism* (1914), Freud had suggested that each person sets up a kind of unconscious ideal in themselves. Now Freud suggests that this ego ideal is constantly being measured against the actual attainments of the ego by another mechanism, commonly called the conscience. The conscience and the ego ideal together form the superego. The superego is a kind of storehouse of old memories of parental praise and criticism. While the id represents passion, and the instincts and the ego represents reason and sanity, the superego represents morality and pride. With this new concept of the superego, phenomena that had previously been inextricable can be understood. For example, instead of celebrating successes, certain people create situations where they are punished for them. How can this be if we're pleasure-seekers? Employing the new concept of the superego, Freud says, such people suffer atonement for success due to guilt from an overly harsh superego. Psychoanalysts now apply these observations to also understand certain kinds of criminal behavior.

Notes

1 Carnegie Hall is a world-famous concert venue in Midtown Manhattan, New York City, located at 881 Seventh Avenue occupying the east side of Seventh Avenue between West 56th Street and West 57th Street
2 In 1911, Freud talked about "being induced" by the patient (Brabant et al., 1992)
3 "Every human relationship is ambivalent, except for the relationship a mother has with her son." Freud (1926), *Inhibitions, Symptoms and Anxiety*

References

Brabant, E., Falzeder, E., & Giampieri-Deutsch, P. (Eds.). (1992). *The correspondence of Sigmund Freud and Sandor Ferenczi, Vol. 1, 1908–1914*. Cambridge, MA: Harvard University Press.
Brenner, C. (1974). *An elementary textbook of psychoanalysis*. Garden City, NY: Anchor Books.
Freud, S. (1914). On narcissism. In J. Strachey et al. (Trans.), *The standard edition of the complete psychological works of Sigmund Freud, Volume XIV: On the history of the psycho analytic movement, papers on metapsychology and other works*. London: Hogarth, 67–102.
Freud, S. (1917). Mourning and melancholia. In J. Strachey et al. (Trans.), *The standard edition of the complete psychological works of Sigmund Freud, Volume XIV: On the history of the psycho analytic movement, papers on metapsychology and other works*. London: Hogarth, 237–258.
Freud, S. (1920). Beyond the pleasure principle. In J. Strachey et al. (Trans.), *The standard edition of the complete psychological works of Sigmund Freud, Volume XVIII*. London: Hogarth, 1–6.
Freud, S. (1923). Inhibitions, symptoms and anxiety. In J. Strachey et al. (Trans.), *The standard edition of the complete psychological works of Sigmund Freud, Volume XX*. London: Hogarth, 77–174.
Freud, S. (1926). The ego and the id. In J. Strachey et al. (Trans.), *The standard edition of the complete psychological works of Sigmund Freud, Volume XIX*. London: Hogarth, 3–66.
Freud, S. (1927). The future of an illusion. In J. Strachey et al. (Trans.), *The standard edition of the complete psychological works of Sigmund Freud, Volume XXI*. London: Hogarth, 1–56.
Groddeck, G. (1949). *The book of the it*. New York: Vintage Books (1919).
Klein, M. (1963). *Envy and gratitude, and other works, 1946–1963*. London: Hogarth Press.

Chapter 8

Anxiety and the Ego

A new theory of anxiety, a new theory of defense and a new theory of object relations

Source: Inhibitions, Symptoms and Anxiety, 1926

STUDENT: "So, the ego and the superego walk into a bar. The bartender says I'm going to need to see some *ID* . . ."[1]
DR. M: Great! Where did you hear it?
STUDENT: Random stuff that came onto my website.
DR. M: That's great! We can see again that Freud is part of the cultural heart of Western civilization.

With today's lecture, we complete our discussion of Freud's major theoretical works. After *Inhibitions, Symptoms and Anxiety* (1926), all major theoretical breakthroughs in psychoanalysis were made by other theorists.

The first group of people who wrote about psychoanalytic theory after Freud is called the post-Freudian ego psychologists. These people extended Freud's concepts, and their intention was to solve the several (theoretical and technical) problems that had arisen when one closely followed Freud's innovations in treating emotional distress. For example, if defenses only arise out of conflict, does that mean defenses are bad? If defenses are bad, does that mean that we have to eliminate them via psychoanalysis?

In Freud's original model of treatment, the goal was to remove a patient's repressions. But very early on in our lectures, I talked about a young man who had a cannibalistic dream. With this kind of person, one might not want to eliminate certain defenses, because when the clinician strips away certain protections, then the person is walking around with some very primitive ideation. Also, if you remember, we talked about a young man who I hypothesized had previously had a psychotic breakdown and later performed on the Rorschach inkblot test in an unusual way. That is, he remembered none of his inkblot responses soon after he made them. In this example, I suggested that it was a good thing that he had forgotten his earlier responses. That meant that much of the primitive material was starting to be repressed. It wasn't suppressed, which would mean that he'd be conscious of it and be trying to hold it down. It was repressed, meaning it was, for all intents and purposes, "gone." With this person, we wouldn't want him to have

DOI: 10.4324/9781003171393-9

a treatment that "analyzes his defenses away." It's actually a very good sign, if you're going to have a breakdown in your twenties, to not remember anything that happened soon after that. It means it's been "sealed over" (that's the colloquial term) and the person has moved on to a better-functioning system of defenses. The post-Freudian ego psychologists wondered: what are the implications of all this? If you extend Freud's theory – and theory of technique – outward, what are the implications?

We begin now with a discussion of the concept of anxiety. Anxiety is at the root of all psychopathology. In some of the neurotic disorders, anxiety is obvious. This describes the people who we might see and say: "He/she is nervous" or "That person looks anxious." However, there are also other neuroses where you wouldn't know that the person is suffering from anxiety. This confusion is what led Freud to talk about repression; the anxiety is there, but hidden because it is repressed. In other words, the layperson's definition of a neurotic person as one who is nervous is incorrect. It doesn't capture what the process is because not all anxiety is conscious, and since it is not conscious it doesn't always show itself directly. As a corollary, the amount of anxiety can't always be immediately determined, because the amount of anxiety is related to the kinds of defenses that the person employs.

Freud's first theory of anxiety dates to the 1890s. We talked about this early in our lectures (Breuer & Freud, 1895; Freud, 1900). At that time, Freud suggested that anxiety is the result of blocked-up libido, i.e., a blockage in the flow of sexual/psychic energy. In other words, Freud had speculated that each of us has sexual or psychic energy and that the energy is attempting to be discharged into consciousness. But with a neurotic there are blockages, and somehow the energy is prevented from being discharged, so it converts into anxiety. That is, it turns to anxiety the way wine turns into vinegar. Freud called this the toxic theory of anxiety. Thus, his first theory of anxiety is that a blockage (repression of libido) leads to anxiety (the libido, which is unable to find expression in normal sexual and emotional ways, converts into anxiety). This toxic theory of anxiety is what he presented and believed in until *Inhibitions, Symptoms and Anxiety*. As I said to you in the last lecture, his previous work, *The Ego and the Id*, is not really an in-depth look at the ego or the id – it's about the superego. But this new work is about the ego. In it, Freud focuses more closely on the ego and revises his ideas of anxiety, suggesting that it doesn't come from sexuality, i.e., from the id, but instead that anxiety comes from the ego. Freud reasons that while fears are a biological response to danger, anxiety differs from fear: with anxiety the danger isn't real – it's subjective.

When Freud revisits the origin of anxiety, he begins to believe that his original theory – that is, the theory that suggested that the instinctual impulses from the id have been somehow transformed from libido into anxiety (i.e., blocked from discharge) – can't always be true because the same anxiety seems to come from several different impulses. That is, the same anxiety comes from sexual longing, hunger and thirst, fear of castration, fear of attack, fear of rage and fear of internal attack/superego, not just fear of external attack.

Freud starts thinking: *Maybe this whole model that I have been using is wrong, or at the least, it's incomplete.*

He now suggests that anxiety is not only a response to internal pressure and blockage, but that anxiety is also a signal given by the ego that there is an internal danger. It took a lot of time for Freud to do this – he wrote *The Interpretation of Dreams* in the 1890s and he wrote *Inhibitions, Symptoms and Anxiety* in the late 1920s. But this is what he arrives at: Just as fear is a response from the perceptual system, anxiety must be a response to danger from the preconscious.

STUDENT: So, you're hiking in the mountains and you hear a rustle in the bushes . . . and you think it might be a bear.

DR. M: Yes, and you run. But what do you do if it's an internal danger? You *also* run. You run internally. You set up defenses and inhibitions and symptoms. That's the way to internally run, just as you would run from external danger by using your feet.

STUDENT: I get it.

DR. M: To continue, Freud begins to pull these observations together in his second theory of anxiety. Repression doesn't lead to anxiety. Anxiety leads to repression.

Anxiety is a signal given by the ego that danger threatens. Freud begins to explore the nature of this danger. He comes to the conclusion that the danger has as its prototype the helpless feeling that we have as newborns and infants. What's the danger there? Freud begins to realize that without the mothering one, we're doomed. The danger in infancy is a separation anxiety. It is the terror of separation from the mothering one. Freud (finally) discovers the importance of mothers: If you're going to talk about separation anxiety, you need to look back to the earliest times of infancy. Father comes into the picture later.

In the early days, weeks and months of the baby's life, the important action is with mommy. The fear is the loss of this mothering one, that is, the fear of the loss of that creature who is keeping the baby alive.[2] The prototype of this separation anxiety is the birth experience. Freud gives lip service to Rank's "birth trauma" theory: from the moment of birth, a birth trauma is stamped into us, so that we're frightened of the loss of the mothering one. However, Freud now reasons that our psychological development starts more likely after birth as a simple S/R (stimulus-to-response) process. That is, the newborn creature begins to (metaphorically) see that it needs the mother. Then, over time, the mother becomes increasingly important. Freud does talk about Otto Rank as the first to look at the actual separation from the mother. Rank[3] had discovered that one of our basic influences is that from the moment of our birth we're suddenly ripped out of a safe and cozy environment of the womb and into danger.

What we now know is that from the time we're born, there is also an experience of helplessness. We don't know what a newborn experiences, but if you look at a newborn, they look pretty unhappy when they're born. As I've told you, having seen newborns and young children, they don't do much. They're awake very briefly and they sleep most of the time. They defecate and urinate, eat and sleep. But when the newborn is hungry, or distressed for some other reason, it's a scary thing to look at. One of the sounds that I think is probably ingrained into humans is hearing a crying human baby, which is very distressing for our species.

STUDENT: So in his new theory of anxiety and the newborn experience, what structure is actually causing the anxiety?

DR. M: This is the profound question that Freud struggled with. We can only guess: it is the id, but there is a primitive "membrane" that begins to grow over the id to protect the newborn from being overwhelmed by stimulation. This is what will later be called the ego, and its first job is to give off a signal of anxiety.

In other words, the id's gratification has been blocked and it's converting/producing a powerful arousal of need in some way. This thin membrane between the id and newly forming ego sets off an alarm. Because the new creature hasn't naturally discharged their feelings, tensions, or impulses, these sensations turn into anxiety.

This question moves us to our next point: In Freud's first theory, when he worked with adults, Freud was seeing people in his practice who were anxious. He started asking them about their sexual practices. What he found is that they had a history of coitus interruptus, impotence, frigidity or abstinence, et cetera, and he began to believe that the person was anxious because they were sexually frustrated. Although he'll now change his theory, with some cases Freud's original observation is actually correct. With others, however, they're sexually frustrated because they have anxiety instead of the reverse: sexual arousal signals anxiety. That is, sex has become the danger, so the person avoids sex. On the other hand, in the second model it's just as he saw with dreams. (Remember that in an anxiety dream, the dream contains upsetting content, thus you wake up.) One has a need, but it has upsetting content, so we awaken. We'll soon see that you get anxious because some impulse has been associated with separation anxiety. If I wish this or I feel that, my mother's not going to love me; she will leave me. I know this may seem like a kind of stretch of logic, but what Freud will soon say is that some need/wish has become associated with danger.

To continue, while Freud jumps from one point to another point, then back to the first, the nature of anxiety is the focus of *Inhibitions, Symptoms and Anxiety*. In the first part, Freud looks at the difference between an inhibition and a symptom, and he says an inhibition is in the ego. A symptom is not. Here is an example of what he means:

You have three people: one has nothing, one has an inhibition, one has a symptom. Where do people go to meet? Besides online.

STUDENT: A bar?

DR. M: Okay, a bar. You've got 3 combinations of pairs of friends, and each combination is experiencing the same thing differently.

(1.) Friend A goes to Friend B's house, because they agreed they're going to go out to a bar, to socialize. Friend A says to Friend B, "You want to go out and socialize? Friend B says, "Absolutely." They go to a bar.

(2.) In the second combination, one person is inhibited. Friend C says to Friend D, "You remember when we said we're going to go to the bar? But Friend D says, "I just don't feel like it." And they don't go.

(3.) Now we've got the third combination: one poor man has *hysteria*. Friend E says to Friend F, "Let's go to the bar." And friend F says, "Yeah, wait, I would love to go to the bar, but suddenly I can't . . . I have lost the use of my foot. My foot is paralyzed, just like what used to happen to people like me in Vienna."

Do you hear the differences? "I don't feel like it" is an inhibition. This inhibition is in the entirety of the self, owned by the self. However, a symptom is outside of the self: "It's not my fault that my foot doesn't work, I would really like to go, but it's my foot's fault."

When we see Freud's case histories we'll see that some of what he talked about is rather remote from what psychoanalysts do now. Some is not. Yet Freud founded and developed talk therapy. We maintain certain principles, which, while modified, can be applied to today's patients.

In the past, Freud was asking:

"What is the nature of our psychosexual wishes?"

He has now created a figure/ground shift. Instead of: "*What* (wishes) are we defending against?"

He now asks: "*How* are we defending them?"

We know that we're defending against wishes because we're anxious. One has a wish; it sends a signal to the defensive part of the ego (the preconscious), the ego protects the person from the dangers associated with this wish.

This new reasoning is a total shift for Freud, and the symptom is outside of the self.

Next, Freud makes the observation that a symptom is a substitute for a wish's gratification (just like what occurs in a dream); the symptom is a substitute for a wish. The dream is a "prettied up" wish after it has been disguised by displacement and condensation. Freud now suggests that a symptom is also a substitute for a wish's gratification. It has been partially repressed and appears as a symptom.

Freud also asks: "Since repression comes from the ego, how does the ego perform this repressing?" Freud is beginning to ask new questions because he's shifting his whole understanding of how the mind works.

He says: "Here we have the id, here's the ego. Two parts to the ego: the perceptual system and the preconscious."

In effect, he's extending and expanding the model of the mind that he started when he first worked with dreams. Except that in dreams the person is asleep. In repression, the id is blocked by some part of the ego.

Freud follows up with more questions: "*How* does the ego do this? *Why* does the ego do this?" The major activity has shifted to the ego.

Freud answers these questions by reasoning:

"It's because of the ego's connection with perception, that is, the ego's connection with reality."

Freud reasons: "We know that in external danger, the ego takes flight." (You see a car coming at you; you get out of the way.) "But what happens if the danger is internal?"

Freud says it's the same process that occurs with an external danger; repression is just like flight. In external danger the whole ego (self) flees. In internal danger the ego "flees" by setting up a repression. That is, the wish is repressed. But because it's repressed, you have an internal battle going on. You have the energy of the id and you have the repressing mechanism of the ego burning a lot of energy in attempting to hold it back. I remind you of attempting to keep a basketball submerged in a bathtub filled with water. At first it may not be hard to do this, but over time it becomes very difficult. This is the same battle going on inside the ego. The instinct is repressed, but active. It continues to make demands on the ego. And the ego continues to defend against these demands.

Freud then asks: "Now what happens with this repression?"

He suggests that two things can happen:

(1.) The ego can make an attempt to adapt the symptom to the "self"/ego;
(2.) The ego can continue employing the defense of repression.

This is important, because if you adapt the symptom to the ego (personality), we're talking about people who have personality disorders. They're seemingly not in conflict.

STUDENT: Sorry. By "adapt the symptoms to the personality," do you mean, like, embed the symptom within the personality?
DR. M: Yes, it means that there will be no more fighting against the symptom by the ego.

With this situation, the person says of their symptom: "Oh, this is just the way I am." The person uses acting out, rationalization and externalization to convince themselves that the symptom belongs to the self. We know there are certain people who have a personality disorder. Some of these people can be unpleasant. One would suggest that perhaps in childhood, the person was traumatized, tried to be a good child but couldn't. So the person found a way to be angry all the time. There's no conflict. You might say to such a person, "You know you're a very angry person."

And they might answer:

"What do you mean? That is just who I am . . . and you aren't so nice either. It's a very bad world, so I am what I am."

There is seemingly no conflict and no insight, that is, this person is not in conflict with themselves. Instead, they are in conflict with the rest of the world. The person might state,
    "You just doesn't understand me." We'd say, if you take it to extreme, that the person is not neurotic but they are personality-disordered.

STUDENT: Are they accepting the impulse?
DR. M: No, they are adapting to it. Accepting it would mean a conscious accepting of it without acting on it, but instead finding ways to express the wishes, ideas and feelings. If you ask a "normal" person who's had therapy:

> "You seem angry. Are you?"

They might say:

> "Yes, and it can be a problem for me, but have you seen my stand-up comedy act? When I'm being sarcastic, I entertain, but sometimes I am not aware of myself. So thanks for letting me know; I've worked long and hard *not* to let my angry childhood father take control of my everyday life."

This is a person who accepts the defenses against anger and works with more mature defenses in an adaptive, conscious way instead of externalizing/alienating others. What about accepting one's sexuality? The kind of person that I've described would accept their defenses. What happens every time an impulse comes up? You consciously accept the defense, even though you may still be in some kind of an internal battle. Thus, for example, what about the kinds of natural, hormonal, glandular impulses that a priest would feel? I have a colleague. He's both a priest and a psychoanalyst. What does he do? There's a defense called sublimation. With sublimation, one finds ways of channeling impulses into something considered to be a higher calling.

STUDENT: You're making a differentiation between a symptom and a defense? I thought they were kind of similar?
DR. M: The impulse and the defense make a compromise that becomes a symptom, an inhibition or sublimation.
STUDENT: Right.
DR. M: This is why it's so complicated. Freud remained stuck with this energy system; he wasn't quite sure what to do with it. So in a certain way we can say that, particularly in this last theoretical work, Freud is doing a kind of mental gymnastics.

I suggest that Freud's quasi-positivist energy system provided both a good metaphor as well as a confusing connection to clinical reality, and this was (and still is) a constant struggle when it comes to his ideas. However, what also comes out of Freud's work is a series of absolutely brilliant observations about human beings, as well as ways of helping people (Bornstein, 2005). Perhaps we didn't need this energy stuff in its very specificity. In that way, perhaps it's better to view it as figurative/metaphorical.

Freud shifted the area of battle *from* dreams (the dream is a wish and a defense, you pretty up the dream images, and you get the manifest content. You unravel it via the patient's associations and you get the latent content) *to* "a symptom is a wish and a defense." There is an internal struggle and the mind produces a symptom.

On the other hand, if the person keeps adapting themselves to this symptom and rationalizes the symptom and externalizes the responsibility for their odd behavior, they might ultimately just say: "Well, I'm accepting that I'm a bad person and too bad for the rest of the world," and now you have a character problem. If the ego and id are no longer battling and this is part of the self, it's now a personality disorder. This is a lot harder to treat. The job of working with somebody with a personality disorder is to (figuratively speaking) help to make the person feel neurotic. That is, one has to help them make the impulse that has become part of the self become ego-alien.

For example, you remember that I saw someone who was an embezzler. I've worked with people with this kind of psychopathology, and a person is giving me a grand scheme and at some point he says "What do you think?" and I might say:

"I think if all wishes came true like they do in stories, you could wish yourself into being a millionaire."

I want them to be uncomfortable. The goal is to get the person to experience the signal anxiety in the ego that should be there but is missing. The goal is *not* to make the person comfortable. It's to make them uncomfortable with their style of living so they can figure out if they want to change this style, and have a better life as a result of the change.

STUDENT: In the case of borderlines, they would say that they're in pain. Right? Don't they say that?

DR. M: They'd say they're unhappy. However, the person would say that they're in pain because of how badly everyone is treating them. That's the personality disorder: "I'm in pain because you (and the world) treat me very badly."

STUDENT: So, the nature of the pain is not the same?

DR. M: The nature of the pain might be the same, but the locus of the pain is different. The reason this matters is that if a person with a personality disorder wants to feel better, they come to therapy to get you to change the other people in their world (like their life partner, their boss and the rest of their family).

STUDENT: You said that the ego is able to adapt the symptom to the personality?

DR. M: Uh-huh.

STUDENT: But I thought that the symptom is not part of the ego.

DR. M: The ego is trying to find a way to make it part of itself.

STUDENT: Trying to make the symptom a part of itself?

DR. M: Yes.

STUDENT: Wouldn't that be an inhibition?

DR. M: You are following the logic. Unfortunately, it is more complex: it could be an inhibition, or it could also be a personality disorder. However, in both cases the person is in effect saying: "I've been struggling to find a way to deal with this pathological demand on my ego." An example of adapting an impulse to the personality is the same as adapting a symptom, because the symptom is the compromise between the impulse and the defense fighting each other. So, adapting a defense is really not adapting a defense. The defense is working so well that the impulse is minimal. The difference here is that with an inhibition there is still an internal battle going on between the impulse and the symptom and energy is being expended; the whole ego then shrinks away (no pun intended) from the dangerous impulse. Why, then, would anyone want to go for help if their personality disorder works to keep them comfortable? Because the people close to them are complaining, or because they can't maintain relationships; they're feeling discomfort/abandonment; because they're having little or no interpersonal success. However, there are examples when adapting the impulse to the personality may not lead to a personality disorder or an inhibition. As an example of this, I have mentioned the priest who may have powerful demands on the ego, id demands on the ego, but has found a way to use certain defenses that make these demands less powerful or seemingly nonexistent. Now, we could say that that this priest is inhibited – or not. Another explanation is that the priest is sublimated. There are certain people who are very inhibited and others are sublimated. The point of your questions is that everybody is struggling with this because it's difficult. I think this is the problem Freud had with this energy system. Yet his observations about the defenses are wonderful, as are his observations about what the human being needs to do when their needs are too great. But his observations about "a system of energy" that can be measured? This is an ongoing problem within psychoanalysis.

Now, Freud looks at anxiety. He looks at several cases, including the case of the Wolfman, which we'll read. The Wolfman's symptom was terror that a wolf would bite him. As we will see with the Wolfman, this was his attempt to deal with castration anxiety. The patient has a childhood phobia. Repression is caused by castration anxiety, that is, a fear of castration. But the patient is not aware that he has a fear of castration. On first reading, these last paragraphs seems like a blow to Freud's entire system. Not only is the patient not aware of his impulses, the patient is also not even aware of fears that are a reaction to his impulse, fears that are causing the ego to employ the defense of repression. So in this example, anxiety doesn't seem to have originated from a wish: It comes instead from a fear. Can we see where Freud is going with this? The shift? I think this is brilliant even if Freud had to use these energy-system analogies to get there. So . . . anxiety doesn't come from the wish, but instead it comes from the repressing mechanism, that is, the fear. And fear is in the ego. This leads Freud to a change in his views: It's not repression that produces anxiety (the old toxic theory). It's the reverse: anxiety produces repression.

In other words, the anxiety doesn't come from a wish; it comes from a fear. But if the anxiety comes from a fear, Freud now thinks that this is much more complicated than he had originally thought, and he realizes that he is going to have to start revising things. Freud had originally felt that the repression of libido produces anxiety. He got this from observing the anxiety produced by certain sexual practices such as abstinence and coitus interruptus. In those cases he saw that somebody was anxious, and the patient had complained of sexual difficulties. Thus, he thought, it's the inhibition of these sexual feelings/wishes that caused the anxiety.

Next, Freud considers neuroses that occur without anxiety – the patient doesn't seem to experience anxiety. One of these is conversion hysteria. Those of you who have read an abnormal psychology textbook saw illustrations of Charcot hypnotizing a patient and afterwards the patient couldn't move their arm, and the patient showed no anxiety about it. This is called *la belle indifference*. Freud now says, in this case, little is seen of the ego's struggle against the symptom.

Next, Freud turns to the obsessional neurosis. But here there is a tremendous struggle against the symptom. As we'll see with the case of the Rat Man, a person in terrible suffering with many obsessions and compulsions (that is, torturous thoughts and rituals). Freud says that with the obsessional patient, the major defenses are regression, isolation and undoing – not repression. Freud is starting to distinguish between defense and repression. Remember, Freud previously used those terms interchangeably. Now he's saying there are a number of defenses and repression is only one of them. The major issue in the obsessive-compulsive (as we'll see in detail) is that the person has some kind of Oedipal feeling and they've regressed from the phallic stage to the anal-sadistic stage; there's a battle over hate and love. Defenses used are isolation of affect, reaction formation and undoing. Thus, the Rat Man, in order to stave off massive panic, performed magical acts and rituals. All of these rituals were employed for the magical *undoing* of hateful thoughts. The important point is that Freud is now saying that the terms *repression* and *defense* are no longer synonymous. He's distinguishing between different kinds of defenses; repression's only one of them.

Now Freud suggests: Anxiety is a signal. Anxiety is a signal indicating danger. One stops the danger by withdrawing from/avoiding the situation. Freud is saying out loud what I've been telling you he was going to say from our first lecture: With danger from the outside, we use our motoric system; that is, we flee an external danger. However, with danger from the inside, we also stop the danger by withdrawing from it.

Danger can be stimulated by the wishes of the id or it can be stimulated by the superego. The conscience part of the superego says that if you don't achieve something or in some other way you don't live up to your ego ideal, you'll be punished. So, if you have a strong superego, you are constantly feeling that you're not living up to your internalized standards. Here the superego is attacking the ego, castrating the ego. But Freud doesn't do what we're trying to do in these lectures. He doesn't systematize.

We have previously discussed: (1.) *On Narcissism;* (2.) *Mourning and Melancholia;* and (3.) *The Ego and the Id.* We are attempting to piece this all together – I hope we're doing that, piecing together how Freud formulated this new system. I hope the way he formulated is getting clearer even though he's stuck with his energy system.

If you're a neurotic, there are two ways to be neurotic:

(1.) You can have very powerful drives that cause inhibition/withdrawal via fixation and regression;
(2.) You can have very powerful defenses that don't let any of the drives get discharged without creating symptoms.

Thus, the ego flees internal danger with repression and creates symptoms. If you don't have repression, such as with obsessive compulsives, then you have regression, and isolation of affect, reaction formation and undoing. Whatever defenses you use, you need some kinds of protection in order to hide the wishes inside of you that are making you anxious. If you don't have repression and you have a "bare" impulse, drastic measures need to be carried out by the ego. That's when you have more severe psychopathology, and at that point, you're distorting reality.

Some of you have asked me, what's the difference between a primitive and a non-primitive defense? The answer lies in the amount of distortion of reality that occurs. You have to do a lot more reality distortion with a primitive defense.

For example, let's say you have two obsessive-compulsives – that is, two different people come to your office with the same obsessive-compulsive disorder. One is a highly functioning but neurotic person who is overly responsible. The second has severe body-image distortions and a severe eating disorder. Psychoanalysts would suggest that there is probably less repression, reaction formation, and undoing in the more severely disturbed person. That is, the ego needs more drastic measures to deal with living/survival. In this regard, I previously talked about a person who had to walk up 12 stairs to get to my office and she would walk up three, then walk down one, and then walk up four, etcetera. This was an example of primitive magical-obsessional rituals of doing and undoing. In this regard, Freud underestimated the psychopathology of the Rat Man (you'll be hearing about this soon), probably because Freud was somewhat identified with the Rat Man. Freud didn't see how this man suffered from borderline personality disorder, because we did not yet have a conceptualization of how a person can have aspects of both neuroses and psychoses at the same time, that one can have primitive-psychotic aspects in a seemingly "stable" personality.

In both phobia and the obsessive-compulsive, anxiety is a reaction to a situation of danger, which is stopped by the ego doing something to avoid the situation – withdrawing from it. Just like we withdraw from danger from the outside, the ego withdraws from danger from the inside. So symptoms are created to avoid a dangerous situation signaled by anxiety. Freud has moved from the idea that anxiety is created by a blocked libido, and that the libido somehow chemically turns/becomes poisoned into anxiety (toxic anxiety). Instead, the libido (that is, a wish) attempts to enter the ego. But the preconscious part of the ego says "Danger! Danger!" As a result, the ego has to run just like this ego would have to run if a bear was attacking. Now with all the twists and turns, you know this isn't so different from his dream theory.

STUDENT: Why does this matter in a clinical practice?
DR. M: We will be spending the rest of the lectures discussing this.
STUDENT: It's just like . . . what difference does it make for us? It's because it's supposed to be like, "Oh, you have anxiety, that's because you think your sexuality is, like, dangerous . . . and you have this, like, free-floating sexual energy."
DR. M: You are saying that the kind of interpretation you would use in the first theory of anxiety is different from what you might be saying in the second theory of anxiety. And here you might also add that the person "was traumatized, so of course they fear that sexual needs are frightening."
STUDENT: Yeah, that's actually what I was saying. Thanks, I get it.
DR. M: And in the second theory of anxiety, you would say: "It seems like you withdraw a lot from things. Why do you think that is?" The clinician's focus is now on the ego defenses, and on how and why it (the ego) withdraws from what it perceives to be danger. Thank you. Let's thank [student]! (*Class applauds.*) This example shows that the new theory puts the focus on ego functions. While in the first, the focus is essentially on wishes and impulses.

Now we come to another reason why *Inhibitions, Symptoms and Anxiety* is so important:

In the next part, Freud reminds us of what we know about anxiety. It is unpleasure. If you know what pleasure feels like, when you have anxiety it is very much the opposite.

Freud says that anxiety is a reproduction of some experience that contained the necessary conditions for a buildup of tension and then discharge (when you're hungry and you're a baby, you are desperate. You get more and more excitement/painful arousal. When you get a bottle or a nipple, the tension begins to drop).

Now he asks, What's the function of anxiety and on what occasions is it reproduced?

Anxiety arose originally as a reaction to a state of danger (the starving baby is in danger) and it is reproduced whenever a new danger situation occurs. The child is anxious when alone in the dark or with a stranger because the child is missing someone they love and long for.

For Freud, this is the key to anxiety: the loss of the love object (mother) is traumatic because the mother provides gratification. The danger is the accumulation of stimulation that needs to be discharged, and soon the danger shifts from the tension buildup itself to the consequences of the loss of the object.

The loss of the love object, the mother, is traumatic because the mother gratifies. Thus, through simple stimulus/response repetition, the infant is beginning to learn that when it's hungry, it needs to be looking for the object that is going to save it. Now the absence of the mother becomes the danger. So, as both an automatic reflex and a rescuing signal, anxiety is the product of the infant's helplessness. In other words, the loss of the object, the mother, becomes the traumatic danger because the mother provides gratification. The mother removes this tension buildup. The mother becomes essential.

As Modell (1988) suggests, Freud noted that the human child depends upon its caretakers to provide those signals of danger that are the instinctive endowment of other species. Now in a certain sense, this model sounds like a simple behaviorist model applied to human beings. But when we add the notion of unconscious identifications – for example, a mother who is depriving or anxious or incompetent – then we can reason that as this infant becomes a child and, later, an adult, if they are longing for someone to calm, contain and gratify them, what they've got in their head is "I'm not going to get calmed or gratified."

STUDENT: Was Freud the first to say what you just said? Was he first to come up with this? Does he ever get credit in the behavioral circles? I find it really interesting.

DR. M: Credit? Our faculty colleague, Bob Bornstein, speaks about this a bit later in our final lecture. While Freud gets a lot of things, I don't know if credit would be a major one of them. In this regard, Helen Block-Lewis (1988) wrote a paper where she wondered: *If Freud were alive now, what would he say differently? What ideas would he keep? What would he discard?* Some of the observations Freud made were said before we knew about the chromosomal differences between men and women, and these were accurate. And the REM research, about dreaming, shows that some of his observations about dream process were also accurate.

Freud continues that new anxiety situations are actually also separation anxiety, castration and loss of the superego. Earlier in this book, by the way, Freud had said these innovations were a total change in his views. Now he says they're not. One might say, as I said in the beginning of these lectures, that this is an example of Freud's unwillingness to break with the past. We might say that this is an example of Freud's separation anxiety.

Next Freud considers the relationship between the formation of symptoms and anxiety. This is a question some of you were asking about before. Freud says there are two views:

(1.) Anxiety itself is a symptom;
(2.) Symptoms are formed to avoid anxiety.

Both are true. Now he says that there's a danger situation interposed between the anxiety and the symptom. (Remember that a symptom is a way of fleeing an internal danger situation.) Therefore, symptom formation does in some way put an end to danger, at least temporarily. (You create the symptom so you don't have the danger). In this new model, symptom formation should be attributed to the defensive process, which is similar to the ego's motor defense of flight from reality danger.

STUDENT: Can you maybe give an example of, like, a case where anxiety is itself a symptom versus symptoms that are also formed to avoid anxiety? I mean, these could still be happening at the same time, but . . .?

DR. M: Sure, for example, Student XX was talking about a person who's nervous. So, there are a variety of ways to be nervous. When I talk in the next lecture about the nature of neurosis and the various ways that neurosis shows itself, I will say that there's hysteria versus obsessive-compulsive. In hysteria, you can have somebody who's nervous and who gets a conversion symptom. You can also get somebody else who has phobias, which means only very specific things make them nervous. You can have somebody else who has panic attacks, so it's not just a phobic situation that makes them nervous, but for some reason that's unclear, they're suddenly in a panic. You can have somebody who's always nervous. They have heightened anxiety. I think that, much of the time, if you ask a lot of questions of this person, you'll find it's not really that they're always nervous. They're nervous at certain times rather than at other times, perhaps for example only in social situations. Why are they more nervous sometimes and not at other times? There's probably a symptom there, but it is unclear what the symptom is, unless we dig deeper. But there are probably people who are chronically nervous. If you ask nonclinicians, "What's a neurotic?" They'd say, "A nervous person," because they don't understand that, with a hysteric, the person may have lots of anxiety, but you often don't see it. The average person sees a neurotic as chronically nervous.

STUDENT: Chronically nervous. And the discharge is happening. So it's not healthy for the person, but the discharge is happening. Isn't that what we're generalizing as anxiety too?

DR. M: Yes.

STUDENT: So, what would be . . . what would the approach be to create more defenses?

DR. M: Let's say that a person had a chronically anxious mother. We could say it's (to some extent) biologically inherited. We could also say that when that child felt danger (remember our new-mother model?), the mother couldn't sufficiently contain, gratify, help the child. This child took in (identified) the model of a mother who's nervous and can't contain them. This has now become part of this person's ego ideal. Some people can't be comforting. You also have other situations where somebody can't be comforting because . . .

let's say the mother who's trying to comfort you herself had a very critical mother or father. And this mother was always scared of her own internalized critical parent. Now she's communicating her scared self to you.

STUDENT: Why? Is she not going to make you feel safe?

DR. M: Yes, but I am also talking about someone who is already an adult. That is, whose mother was chronically anxious; she was not a person that stimulated protective/coping mechanisms. Instead, this person always falls back on their noncomforting mother inside of them. One new defense that psychoanalysis can do is to offer this person a new identification in the person of the clinician.

STUDENT: Is that like your explanation today about separation anxiety? It sounds like Freud is still pinning this object relations thing on, like, something more gratification-related.

DR. M: That's right. He's stuck in this model, and it will await others to move these brilliant observations along to more extensive explorations of object relations theory, but it starts with this.

In the last part of this paper, Freud says that there must be some factor that will explain why some people can control anxiety and some can't. He dismisses the work of other psychoanalysts and goes back to his earliest quantitative/energy model.

He says that whether or not a person can control anxiety depends on:

(1.) How much anxiety there is;
(2.) How strong the impulses (wishes) are;
(3.) How weak the ego is.

Then he says that there are three conditions that lay the groundwork for becoming neurotic, three reasons why human beings are more likely to become neurotic than other species. These are:

(1.) The biological fact about the human species' long state of helplessness. For example, those of you who have ever been on a farm and seen a horse being born, it's quickly up on its legs, walking around. With a human infant, it takes a long time to not be helpless. That means there's going to be a long and deep dependence on the mothering one;

(2.) The phylogenetic fact[4] is the existence of the latency period. Freud says all human beings, for reasons we don't understand, move developmentally into latency and then become good at reading, writing and arithmetic, that is, we learn sublimations. Our species developed mental skills, but while this gives us more survival advantages in the world, to do so we need to block our impulses for much of our childhood, and this makes us prone to neurosis;

(3.) The psychological fact is also evolutionary to the human species. That is, it's easier to flee from external danger than to flee from the danger of what is within us. Since we can think and be made aware of our inner experiences, we are forced to perceive internal danger; how does one flee from *that?* The only way that you can run from internal danger (if you have consciousness) is to develop defenses and symptoms, and thus we are prone to becoming neurotic.

Summary of lecture 8

In *Inhibitions, Symptoms and Anxiety* (1926), Freud returns to his model of the mind to question the role of anxiety in neurosis and personality development. Freud's first theory of anxiety (*Studies on Hysteria*) was that it was caused by blockages (fixations) of sexuality. Sexual tension couldn't be discharged in normal ways and was somehow converted into anxiety and symptoms. In *Inhibitions, Symptoms and Anxiety*, Freud suggests that anxiety doesn't come from this blocked sexuality (that is, anxiety does not reside in the id), but anxiety resides in the ego. Anxiety is now seen as a signal from the ego that danger threatens. Fear is a biological response to danger. In danger one can fight or flee. While fear is triggered by our perceptual system (for example, I step off the sidewalk, a car is barreling toward me, I flee from this danger by jumping back onto the sidewalk), anxiety is a response to another danger, which comes from inside me. Anxiety is a signal that a dangerous need/thought and/or feeling is attempting to come into my awareness. Yet, how can I flee from a danger that is internal? I can flee from this danger by a repression of the "dangerous" need, thought or feeling. In Freud's first model of anxiety, repression causes anxiety (and neurosis). Repression blocks sexual tension and it turns into anxiety. In Freud's second theory of anxiety, anxiety causes repression. Anxiety is a signal from the preconscious part of the ego that danger is approaching, and the ego flees the danger by turning away from the instinctual need via repression. Freud explores the nature of this danger. This leads him to look more deeply at the relationship between mother and child. When a young child "learns" that mother relieves tension buildup for them, the danger faced by the child shifts from the buildup of instinctual need to the consequences of the loss of the mother. Freud called the danger of the loss of the mother "separation anxiety" and believed that the signal given by the ego, which warns that danger is threatening from the id, is separation anxiety. Later, this danger is signaled by a thought or feeling, which has previously been associated with withdrawal of parental love. Freud continues to explore the ways in which the ego flees from anxiety. Originally, he'd used the words "defense" and "repression" interchangeably. Clinical experience has now shown him that there are many ways that the ego can defend itself against internal danger. Repression is only one of them. There is denial, reaction formation, projection, introjection, isolation of affect, undoing, devaluation, idealization and et cetera. Freud now views the concept of defense as overarching, including repression as one of many defenses.

Notes

1 I would like to thank Megan Parmenter for this delightful joke.
2 In his self-analysis, which Freud began while writing *The Interpretation of Dreams* (1900), he says that he was deeply affected by his grief following the death of his father in 1896. Regarding Freud's mother, the French/Scottish psychoanalyst Joyce McDougall (in Rothstein, 1986) hypothesized that for a very long time Freud neglected the traumatizing disturbances in the mother-infant dyad. In elaborating her view that even an apparently normal separation-individuation experience between the baby and mother can be traumatic, McDougall noted that Freud "gave lip service" to this phase of life. McDougall suggested that Freud's de-emphasis of this phase derived from an unanalyzed idealized relationship with his mother.
3 Otto Rank (1884–1939) (see Lieberman & Kramer, 2012) was an Austrian psychoanalyst, writer and teacher. Born in Vienna, he was one of Freud's closest colleagues for 20 years, a prolific writer on psychoanalytic themes, the editor of two psychoanalytic journals of the era, the managing director of Freud's publishing house and a creative theorist and therapist. In 1926, Rank left Vienna for Paris; for the remainder of his life he had a successful career as a lecturer, writer and therapist in France and the United States. In 1924 Rank published *Das Trauma der Geburt* (translated into English as *The Trauma of Birth* in 1929), exploring how art, myth, religion, philosophy and therapy were illuminated by separation anxiety before the development of the Oedipus complex. There had been no such phase in Freud's theories. The Oedipus complex, Freud had explained, was the nucleus of neurosis and the unconscious source of all art, myth, religion, philosophy and therapy – indeed of all human culture. This was the first time that anyone in Freud's inner circle had dared to suggest that the Oedipus complex might not be the supreme causal factor in psychoanalysis. Rank was the first to use the term *pre-Oedipal* in a public psychoanalytic forum in 1925 (Rank, 1996, p. 43). Ferenczi, with whom Rank had collaborated from 1920 through 1924 on new experiential, object relational and "here-and-now" approaches to therapy, vacillated on the significance of Rank's pre-Oedipal theory but not on Rank's objections to classical analytic technique.
4 The *phylogenetic* fact: Douglas (2010). In biology, phylogenetics addresses the inference of the evolutionary history and relationships among or within groups of organisms. These relationships are hypothesized by phylogenetic inference methods that evaluate observed heritable traits, such as DNA sequences or morphology, often under a specified model of evolution of these traits.

References

Block-Lewis, H. B. (1988). Freudian theory and new information in modern psychology. *Psychoanalytic Psychology, 5*(1), 7.

Bornstein, R. F. (2005). Reconnecting psychoanalysis to mainstream psychology: Challenges and opportunities. *Psychoanalytic Psychology, 22*(3), 323–340.

Breuer, J., & Freud, S. (1895). On the psychical mechanism of hysterical phenomena: Preliminary communication from studies on hysteria. In J. Strachey et al. (Trans.), *The standard edition of the complete psychological works of Sigmund Freud, Volume II (1893–1895): Studies on hysteria.* London: Hogarth, 1–17.

Douglas, H. (2010). *Phylogeny. Douglas Harper's online etymology dictionary.* www.etymonline.com.

Freud, S. (1900). The interpretation of dreams. In J. Strachey et al. (Trans.), *The standard edition of the complete psychological works of Sigmund Freud, Volume IV*. London: Hogarth, ix–627.

Freud, S. (1914). On narcissism. In J. Strachey et al. (Trans.), *The standard edition of the complete psychological works of Sigmund Freud, Volume XIV: On the history of the psycho analytic movement, papers on metapsychology and other works*. London: Hogarth, 67–102.

Freud, S. (1917). Mourning and melancholia. In J. Strachey et al. (Trans.), *The standard edition of the complete psychological works of Sigmund Freud, Volume XIV: On the history of the psycho analytic movement, papers on metapsychology and other works*. London: Hogarth, 237–258.

Freud, S. (1923). The ego and the id. In J. Strachey et al. (Trans.), *The standard edition of the complete psychological works of Sigmund Freud, Volume XIX*. London: Hogarth, 3–66.

Freud, S. (1926). Inhibitions, symptoms and anxiety. In J. Strachey et al. (Trans.), *The standard edition of the complete psychological works of Sigmund Freud, Volume XX*. London: Hogarth, 77–174.

Lieberman, E., & Kramer, R. (2012). *The letters of Sigmund Freud and Otto Rank*. Baltimore, MD: Johns Hopkins University.

Modell, A. H. (1988). The centrality of the psychoanalytic setting and the changing aims of treatment: a perspective from a theory of object relations. *Psychoanalytic Quarterly*, *57*, 577–596.

Rank, O. (1924). The trauma of birth in its importance for psychoanalytic therapy. *Psychoanalytic Review*, *11*(3), 241–245.

Rank, O. (1996). *A psychology of difference: The American lectures*. Princeton, NJ: Princeton University Press.

Rothstein, A. (1986). *The reconstruction of trauma*. Madison, CT: International Universities Press, Inc.

Chapter 9

Freud's case studies I

Hysteria

Source: *The Case of Dora*, 1905

The next two lectures will focus on Freud's case histories (most notably *Dora, Rat Man* and *Wolfman*). The main purpose in studying these cases is to directly observe how Freud employed what he learned from treatment to build a theory of neurosis, and then to broaden that into both a theory of technique and a theory of mind. As new clinicians you'll see how Freud used his understanding of each case to move from practice to technique as he developed talk psychotherapy.

"Dora"

Ida Bauer (1882–1945)

Today we'll be talking about the *Dora* case. Keep in mind, Freud's stated purpose for publishing this case was to show how to understand/work with a patient's dreams in psychoanalysis. While Freud's methods may not have been totally suitable for this young woman, no one before Freud had ever listened to her or taken her seriously. Of course, as we will see, it is true that Freud tried to symbolically shove his theories at her, and perhaps as a result, the case ended badly. That said, in this case as well as his other cases, Freud presented his theory of neurosis and its treatment.

Here is a summary of what Freud attempted to accomplish with his case histories:

First, Freud established that neurosis is worthy of study.

There were three theories about neurosis prior to Freud:

(1.) Neurotics are people who are faking illness for attention;
(2.) Neurosis is an acquired or hereditary physical disease

> The prognosis for hysteria was similar at that time to a number of other diseases that were prevalent when Freud first began his work (1880s–1900s). The belief was that little could be done to effectively treat some chronic

DOI: 10.4324/9781003171393-10

physical illnesses. Today, things are different and medical advances have meant that even illnesses that were, not so long ago, going to end in the quick death of the patient (such as AIDS, severe heart disease, many kinds of cancer) are now considered chronic diseases that can be managed with medical treatments to prolong one's life or even to cure the patient. For example, with the heart condition (aortic valve disease) that I was treated for with open-heart surgery several years ago before the pandemic, I was able to return to my gym and regular exercise routine. However, this same condition killed my grandpa at the age of 56. I am writing this to you now, more than 20 years older than he was on the day that a fatal heart attack took him. In any case, if neurosis was considered an incurable acquired or hereditary physical disease, it couldn't be treated. One could only help to make the patient comfortable.

(3.) Neurosis is some kind of moral degeneracy. One religious idea was that if one acted "oddly," they were controlled by Satan. Or, to the nonreligious, the patient was morally deficient.

By creating an approach for the treatment of the neuroses, Freud was openly rejecting all of these ideas.

The second contribution that Freud offered us was that he was able to categorize all of the symptoms of neurosis, dividing them into two major clinical types:

Obsessive-compulsive neurosis
Hysteria

Freud further subdivided hysteria into two types:

Conversion hysteria, where the patient converts their conflict into a physical symptom (Dora had some of these);
Anxiety hysteria, where the person converts the conflict into spells of anxiety. (Dora also manifested this type of hysteria. In our current diagnostic system, because she suffered from two types of hysteria, Dora would be diagnosed as mixed neurosis.)

Freud further divided anxiety hysteria into two types:

Phobia, where the patient has anxiety in specific situations, called phobic situations;
Free-floating anxiety, where the patient doesn't know what type of situation creates anxiety. Thus, free-floating anxiety is different from phobia because with phobia, the situation that brings anxiety is specific. If one avoids the situation one avoids the anxiety.

Finally, Freud further subdivided his last category (free-floating anxiety) into two subtypes:

Chronic anxiety state: what laypeople typically think of when they hear "neurotic." It refers to a person who always seems nervous;

Panic attack: People suffering from panic attack appear like someone with a phobia. They aren't chronically anxious; however, sometimes they have a spell of anxiety or panic. Unlike the phobic person, they are unable to pinpoint what precipitating event(s) have triggered the anxiety attack. (A clinician can often figure out what thoughts/feelings were the precipitating events for a panic attack. They're understood the way we understand a dream, by looking at the day residue that initiated the anxiety attack. The day residue is composed of some conflict between the conscious self and the unconscious wishes, and the compromise is a spell of anxiety.)

STUDENT: Can you say a little bit more about his idea of hysteria?

DR. M: We will be talking about this in an extended way as we go deeper into the *Dora* case, but for now, Freud suggested that an internal conflict is converted into a physical symptom, for example, migraine headaches. Physicians who are not psychologically sophisticated (some are) might tell a migraine sufferer that along with the physical factors, another irritant that causes a migraine is stress. We will soon see that Dora had headaches and a chronic cough and other more vague physical symptoms. As I suggested, by understanding this as a treatable condition, Freud was also attempting to remove the social stigma from neurosis. This understanding allows the clinician to be more empathic to the patient, and makes it easier to understand the dynamics of the problem.

Freud's next contribution from the case histories was that he showed us that neurosis is treatable by psychoanalysis. Freud suggested that the psychoanalyzability of the neurotic results because the neurotic forms transferences. These transferences can then be worked through in psychoanalysis. What do these terms mean? Here is an example:

A couple begin to recognize that, as a result of their histories, and in particular, the kind of marriages each saw with their parents, that whenever they are intimate, they later start a fight. It is, by the way, very easy to start a fight with one's partner. Feelings are contagious, and if you have ever been part of a couple or have ever known a couple, one certainly finds oneself fighting with one's partner and wondering, How did this happen?

With this couple's therapy, the three of us have been working on this dynamic. After having had several powerful couple-therapy meetings about it, they arrive at the office for their session and he's very proud. He'd originally been rejecting of this idea, that is, that they might be enacting their own parental histories via their current marital relationship. However, today he starts the session proudly stating that they'd had a very passionate weekend, both sexually and emotionally, but then started arguing. He said to her: "See, look, that's what Bob told us." They talked about this, and now feel closer. They're working this dynamic through. Thus, as clinicians we can ask ourselves, What's one goal of psychological treatment? The goal for this couple is to no longer need me ("That's what

Bob told us"). They will have taken what they needed from me (identified with this new understanding of themselves) and they can work with it themselves. You might not be surprised to learn that this goal of learning how to be self-reliant is particularly important for this man. Thus, in a certain way, this couple is being "trained" to become their own psychoanalysts, with their marriage as their "patient."

As you know from previous lectures, as Freud explored aspects of the transference neurosis, he was able to suggest that, with some cases, the transference cannot be worked through in psychoanalysis. He was dividing psychopathology into two types, based on a treatment's severity and treatability:

> Transference neurosis, where the person has transferences that are worked through in a psychoanalytic treatment;
> Narcissistic neurosis, where the person cannot form a therapeutic transference to the psychoanalyst because they are too narcissistic; that is, too self-centered (See lecture 6).

In this regard, if you walk through the locked ward of a psychiatric inpatient unit, you'll see people staring off into space. They're not able to form transferences to a clinician because they're not in contact with others. They don't have the emotional/cognitive capacity to be interested in another human being.

However, what is unfortunate about Freud's way of categorizing these types is that it makes it seem as if the narcissistic person is self-loving. That's not the case. What we now understand from Freud's *On Narcissism* is that a psychotic person is in a desperate fight to try to survive as an independent entity but that there is not enough "ego strength" in the person to become connected/stay connected to others. What Freud called the "narcissistic neuroses" is what we might now refer to as severe character disorders, affective disorders in the psychotic range, severe borderlines and schizophrenics. We have now understood that there *are* ways that one can contact a narcissistic neurotic (psychotic) person. In actuality it's not that such a person is unable to form transferences, it's that the \transferences that they form are different from those seen in verbal, somewhat self-differentiated neurotics. Ego psychology (and its offshoots in object relations, self-psychology and relational psychoanalysis) helps the clinician understand the functioning of the ego, so we now know that it is hard, but not impossible, to work with somebody whose ego is barely holding on.

When we read the *Wolfman* case (next lecture), you'll see that it is remarkable that Freud successfully treated Wolfman. Wolfman was very disturbed, by any standard. In fact, at his first session with Freud, Wolfman suggested that he and Freud have anal intercourse, and that Wolfman would then defecate on Freud's head. In the interests of science, Freud had declined. The important point I want to emphasize at this stage of Freud's work is that by describing neurosis as two types – narcissistic or transference – Freud is describing each type of psychopathology based on a therapeutic understanding. In this way, Freud moved from a descriptive definition of mental illness to a therapeutic definition. The best psychiatry had been able to do up to that point was to simply classify psychopathology by making lists of signs and symptoms for every disorder. In science, the first thing one does is label and categorize; this is called taxonomy. Freud added something very different and helpful, also describing disorders based on how the clinician can treat them.

Freud's next contribution was that he employed his libido theory to explain neurosis. He said that in every developmental process there are certain weak spots. He suggested that these weak spots form the basis for later emotional problems. The weak spots may differ from person to person, but we all have such weak spots. Freud called them "fixations." Freud suggested that in times of stress, a neurotic regresses (falls backward) to one of these points of fixation. In this regard, we all know that before doing something that one is nervous about, a person might bite their fingernails, or suddenly have to go to the bathroom or tidy up their desk. These are examples of temporary regressions to points of fixation. If the regression is a typical pattern that continually interferes with one's functioning, then this is a psychopathology. If not, it is what we have been calling symptomatic acts. Freud said all of these fixations are in the developmental period of infantile sexuality. Freud saw the Oedipal fixation as the most important fixation, and therefore the most common form of neurotic problem. Until what we saw in the last few lectures, Freud had been less interested in looking at very early childhood phenomena. When he (finally) looked at pre-Oedipal fixations and earlier stages of development, Freud recognized the powerful influence that the mothering one has on the development of the child.

Freud felt that each type of neurosis could be related to a specific fixation point, and he assigned Karl Abraham to look at the relationship between fixation point and psychopathology.[1] Freud respected Abraham; Freud had trained him. They had a very deep connection. The general schema that Abraham and Freud developed is that hysteria is a fixation at the phallic stage, the obsessive-compulsive neurosis is a fixation at the anal-sadistic stage and the deeper pathology (what was then called paranoia and dementia praecox, and is what we now call the severe character disorders, the borderline conditions, and schizophrenia) are all fixations of the oral stage. Now while this model isn't precise, the general idea of it still holds true: The earlier the trouble (the fixation), the more severe the psychopathology. Thus, the essence of Freud's model of the etiology of neurosis is that it is a fixation on and then a regression to infantile sexuality. While it is often difficult to see this directly with neurotic people, we can see derivatives of it. It is easier to see this in the more disturbed patient. In the neurotic patient, these processes are hidden. In the psychotic they are transparent. This is the origin of the expression:

"Neurotics build castles in the air, psychotics live in them."

I'm hoping that by the end of today's lecture, we'll understand what Freud was correct about and what Freud missed in the treatment of hysteria. With the *Dora* case, we have an advantage: a second psychoanalyst, Dr. Felix Deutsch, treated her 22 years after her first contacts with Freud. We'll see that some of what Freud said was confirmed, but also that (at this early point in psychoanalytic work, Freud was not diagnostically sophisticated) he labeled (really, mislabeled) everything as hysteria. He would sometimes use the term as a catch-all phrase meaning neurosis before he talked about defenses. This is particularly important because now, as you've seen with the development of ego psychology, psychoanalysts are less interested in *what* it is that one is defending against and more interested in *how* the person is defending. The implications of this will become clearer, for now: One can manifest a hysterical style and hysterical symptoms and be neurotic, character-disordered or psychotic, depending on the person's ego strength.

Ego psychology uncovered an error in Freud's first work. Originally, Freud suggested that the two components of psychodynamic treatment are abreaction and insight and that there's improvement in both of these processes if the clinician works to remove or weaken a patient's defenses. What ego psychology showed us is that one doesn't want to remove every defense, particularly in patients who operate with primitive defenses and poor ego strength. To some degree every person needs at least some of their defenses. There are several implications for psychoanalytic therapy once we understand this. First, whether one is working with more-disturbed people or neurotic people, there are only a limited number of affects and conflicts that human beings display: love, success/power, aggression, closeness, emotional survival, autonomy. The figure/ground then shifts from what the conflicts are to how these conflicts are dealt with by the person's ego. This shift has revolutionized how psychoanalysis works.

STUDENT: Can I ask: Do Freud's ideas about psychoanalytic therapy apply to people of color?

DR. M: Yes, this is a complex question that deserves a detailed answer: Freud was a Jew who spent most of his life in an anti-Semitic country (Austria). Freud credited his Jewish background and life as an outsider with helping him to develop and maintain a different perspective about the human condition, and to embrace his ideas despite considerable opposition. Freud also made several attempts to apply his psychoanalytic method and theory to cultures other than those of Victorian western Europe, but the results were unsatisfactory (Freud, 1913). While psychoanalysis had been practiced successfully in the developed Western world, there was doubt expressed about the universality of Freudian ideas and therapy to other cultures, and even to marginalized populations in Western culture. Altman (1993) notes that there are few attempts to apply psychoanalysis to people of lower socioeconomic backgrounds. In the United States, psychoanalytic treatment typically takes place in private practice where the poor patient cannot afford the fee. Yet economic factors don't fully explain the traditional exclusion of these patients. Even in low-fee training clinics attached to institutions, lower-class patients have sometimes been "selected out" if they applied for treatment. Criteria of "psychoanalyzability" were often cited. As early as the 1950s, sociologists were recognizing that psychoanalysis had become a treatment for white, educated, middle- to-upper-class patients (Hollingshead & Redlich, 1958). In recent decades there's been some reversal of this tendency to exclude lower-socioeconomic patients, as well as patients of color. As fewer people seek out psychoanalysis, patients from lower-class and minority backgrounds have more often been accepted in training clinics, often out of necessity. Moreover, clinicians with psychoanalytic training often spend part of their professional time in public clinics where such patients are increasingly the vast majority, no matter where the clinic is located. As a dramatic example, recent research (Strauss et al., 2015) has shown that psychodynamic psychotherapy is not only helpful to African-American males diagnosed with depression, but also that it may be more helpful than other traditional treatments (such as psychotropic medication). As psychoanalysts have embarked on work with people in public clinics, and with people of diverse backgrounds and ethnicity, they often wondered about the extent to which the psychoanalytic treatment model is applicable or adaptable in these contexts. Altman suggests that the psychoanalytic model is essential to work with such patients. I applaud his work and direct you to it. I also want to direct you to several recent powerful (and inspirational) documentaries and programs, such as one on YouTube: *Black Psychoanalysts Speak* (Winograd, 2020) and another, *Psychoanalysis in the Barrio* (Winograd, 2017).[2] As I've said repeatedly throughout these lectures, it is important to understand Freud and his work in the context of his time. I hope this adds some clarity to your question.

I want to now return to the focus on hysteria. As we've seen, there are two major categories (and several subcategories).Conversion hysteria is where the person develops a somatic symptom. In this regard, in some studies (Escobar et al., 1998) visits to internal medicine and family practitioners were often for an unspecified, stress-related malady (translated for our purposes into neurotic/hysterical symptomatology). People get migraines; a person's immune resistance gets low and they get the flu; some people have chronic migraines; others have an illness that seems to come "out of nowhere." But if one looks closely at the person's emotional issues, their immune system has often been weakened because they are fending off crippling anxiety and/or depression. This is not a conscious process, so we are not blaming someone for being sick. Another way to put this is that there are people who get anxious because they are afraid that they will get sick. However, there are others who get sick because they're anxious and a third group who get sick because they can't let themselves experience anxiety.

To proceed, there are two types of hysteria: the aforementioned conversion hysteria, where the person develops a somatic symptom, and anxiety hysteria, where the person reacts with chronic anxiety or with free-floating anxiety, or the person is chronically anxious or has phobias or panic attacks. Aside from the difference in the formation of the symptoms, Freud saw these different anxiety disorders from a psychoanalytic point of view. That is, Freud understood them as memories of past traumatic experiences; they are a substitute for the return of these experiences. This is an extension of the processes that we see in the formation dreams.

Dreams: "I'm sleeping, but I've got a problem. I don't know how to solve it, so I'm going to go back into the attic of my mind, which contains a storehouse of old images – wishes, thoughts, as well as the problem-solving methods available to me in my childhood. Then I'm going to take an image that solves my current problem but doesn't arouse me, so I don't have to wake up."

Neurotic Symptom: "I'm awake. I've got a problem. I have these conflicting emotions and feelings, but instead of confronting them head-on I'll have a convulsive-like attack. That'll be my solution." In this second circumstance, the solution will be a substitute for the return of the repressed childhood experiences. It will return as a symptom, like a dream, or it will return as a slip, or a symptomatic act, but in whatever form it returns, it will be a partial fulfillment of an unconscious wish by the realization of an unconscious fantasy. Like a dream, it will be my attempt to solve a problem by going back to a childish wish-fulfillment method of solution.

Hysterical attacks and chronic symptoms are the same. The unconscious fantasy is being acted out just as in a dream. Thus, the formula is: infantile sexuality, failure of the repression and, finally, what Freud called "the return of the repressed" in the form of a symptom. In this regard, Erdelyi (2006) states that repression is an empirical fact.[3] In Freud's time, before the popularity of psychoanalysis in the culture, it was often easier to see this, but here is an example of what might happen in a clinician's office today:

A man has a lovely dinner with his best friend and best friend's wife. But when he goes home, he has a massive anxiety attack. He doesn't understand why. The next day he goes to his psychoanalyst, Dr. XX, and talks about his panic attack:

DOCTOR: "You had an anxiety attack. What preceded it? Did anything happen at work?"

PATIENTR: "No, nothing."

DOCTOR: "Well, what did you do yesterday?" (the day residue)

PATIENTR: "Oh, I went to dinner with my buddy and my girlfriend . . . I mean with my buddy and his wife."

DOCTOR: "Well, is she your girlfriend or is she his girlfriend . . . or his wife?"

PATIENTR: "Why are you asking me that, you know I don't have a girlfriend."

DOCTOR: "Well, you had a slip of the tongue."

PATIENTR: "You're always picking on my every word."

DOCTOR: "Well, do you think the anxiety attack was related to the dinner?"

PATIENTR: "No, absolutely not. Wait . . . oh, I haven't thought about this for a very long time. When my buddy and his future wife first met – and I'm embarrassed to say this – my buddy and I were at a party when they met, and I was moving toward talking to her, and he talked to her first."

DOCTOR: "Have you ever told him that?"

PATIENTR: "No."

DOCTOR: "So, like you've done in other situations, you punish yourself by going to these dinners without at least working this out, either in your own mind or with your friend. And, then, by never having told him, you have created another Oedipal-type triangle."

The encounter between our imaginary psychoanalyst/patient pair might or might not go this way, but you get the idea. In this instance, the psychoanalyst is employing questions, free association, detailed inquiry, a technique called the paradigmatic technique[4] (a kind of exaggerated emphasis on the patient's comments) and interpretation. The clinician's techniques are designed to help the patient to look at his history of triangulation, and in this case he is reminding the patient that he's done this before, that there was a triangulation between the patient's parents and the patient, so that he's created another off-limits woman that he pines over. The woman of this fantasy may have some wonderful attributes, but is she the only attractive woman on Earth? As of now, she is for him. She is the only woman on Earth, and she is unavailable, just like his mother was unavailable. And a further diagnostic question might be: Is she the only woman on Earth because she has the right combination of attributes, or is it because she's unavailable so he can create castles in the air in order to perpetuate his childhood conflicts?

STUDENT: But, what's the purpose of the panic attack in that situation?

DR. M: Going to dinner reignited a longing for his friend's wife. He was stimulated and guilty about it. He didn't want to become conscious of this, so he had a spell of anxiety when his preconscious started to become aware of his thoughts and feelings. In other words, the danger shifted from his longing and triangulation history to the dinner with the couple. The dinner became the trigger and the dinner was mentioned in the discussion of the residue of the previous day.

STUDENT: Can we talk about the difference between an unconscious fantasy and a wish?

DR. M: There is no difference. The wish is being played out: as a dream or as a symptom. In this case, the anxiety has replaced a picture/fantasy of his friend's wife and the patient running off "in love," living in bliss together. This would be similar to this man's childhood fantasies. Or, in a dream, he went to sleep thirsty and he was crawling in the desert when he found an oasis that serves Miller Extra Dry beer (please note the play on words). The wish becomes a fantasy using displacement and condensation, and when one unravels the images we see that the dream images are a substitute for the latent content/wish that's now in danger of becoming manifest. If these fantasies had been conscious, he wouldn't need to have an anxiety attack – he could rationalize (that is, employ secondary defenses) to resolve this. He might ultimately be able to say: "Damn, I like her, I should have gotten there first, but, you know what? They're doing so great, and I'm not really her type and she's not mine. She's actually a bit too tall/short, skinny/not skinny, intellectual/not intellectual enough for me. What am I doing spending my time thinking about *her*? Why don't I get a girlfriend of my own?" That is, he'd be using higher-level defenses like reasoning and rationalization and intellectualization to soothe and encourage himself, and these defenses, as we can see here are useful, if not overused, to self-soothe and help one deal with blockages, symptoms and inhibitions. If we use higher-level defenses and something bad happens to us, we can pick ourselves up, brush ourselves off, and go on. The problem for all humans is that we don't have access to these kinds of defenses until we are adults, and so when we regress to an earlier fixation point, we also regress to older and less mature ways of solving conflictual problems.

STUDENT: What accounts for the fact that we don't see the other kinds of hysteria?

DR. M: I think that there are a lot of reasons, but one of the reasons is that the culture has changed. The physicians that we once called general practitioners – now we call them internal medicine physicians – just don't have the time or the patience (no pun intended) for people with vague, clearly medically untenable physical complaints. Psychologists' biggest source of referrals is internal medicine and gastroenterologist doctors. They refer people that they just don't have the time or the professional interest to listen to. Doctors don't like to feel helpless or unable to treat someone. After these physicians have done the workup and there's nothing physical, and/or stress is exacerbating the physical symptoms, these doctors (essentially) say: I want you to go to somebody who has the patience to listen to this. In this regard, one of the things that's happened in medicine is that there is more screening out of hysteria, so people who have hysterical symptoms with little or no medical intervention needed get sent for psychotropic meds and/or talk therapy. We'll later also see that there are other ailments that Freud might have called "hysteria" during his time, that we now know have other emotional components, such as chronic fatigue syndrome and, with some, migraines. Further, with some people the disorders are both organic and psychological. Also, more people are sophisticated about basic medicine, and with a click or two they "graduate" from Google Medical School. You're all graduates of Google Medical School, right? With more knowledge, there is more of an understanding that some of a person's symptoms, while they may appear to be so, are probably not organic.

STUDENT: I worked in a lab doing trauma research, and we had a participant who was shouting out words, some trauma-primed and some neutral, and she came out of the MRI, and she said, "There's something wrong with the machine, the screen kept going black." She couldn't see every time the trauma words came up.

DR. M: Was she a known trauma survivor?

STUDENT: She said that she was a trauma survivor, and during the trauma words she just saw black.

DR. M: From what we now know about trauma, that method of coping may have saved her life. Her ability to black out might be how she coped. Remember the example of the girl who saw the dark and gloomy basement wall with its tiny flashing light? That was a dramatic example of how that young woman used mechanisms to hold onto her sanity. As we know, certain trauma survivors might act in very strange ways, but they are not clinically mentally ill in the developmental sense. What these people have done to survive was develop certain coping mechanisms to keep themselves sane and protected in an insane life; this underscores what children will do to survive. Early on, this woman had learned a coping strategy to screen out dangerous/painful reality.

The case of Dora

This is the first case that Freud published after *Studies on Hysteria*. At the end of my presentation of what Freud did in this case, I will tell you my own 21st-century understanding of it, based on Freud's concept of identification. Freud had not fully developed this concept when he wrote this case.

Freud's intention was to show the role of dreams in the analysis of hysteria. While critics of Freud present this as a finished product, it's not a complete case and was never presented as complete, yet this work often gets criticized as being incomplete. As he noted, the purpose was to introduce psychoanalysis, and to show how dreams are used in a psychoanalytic therapy.

STUDENT: Some feminist writers find Freud's therapy with Dora to be problematic.
DR. M: Yes. Early second-wave feminists (Simone de Beauvoir, 1989) discredited Freud. They argued that Freudian theory worked to perpetuate sexual difference and reinforce the belief that inferiority was an inherent quality of the female. Freud's reputation was particularly diminished when his ideas were employed by conservative neo-Freudian (primarily American) psychoanalysts to persuade unhappy women that their social fate was biologically determined. However, feminist psychoanalysts (Benjamin, 1988a, 1998b) have attempted to reconcile Freud's patriarchal and somewhat naive understanding of gender and sexuality with his brilliant and valuable insights into our humanity. As I have said regarding Freud's misogyny, one thing that walking in Freud's shoes can help us to do is see him in the context of his time.

Dora's history

Dora was the younger of two children. Her brother was a year and a half older. Her father was in his 40s and had suffered from a number of illnesses throughout his life. Father had been Freud's patient. He treated the father for symptoms related to syphilis; Freud had cleared up the symptoms. This was before the major antibiotics, so Freud had used other methods with Father. After he successfully treated the father (Dora was 16) Father brought Dora to Freud. However, Dora refused to begin treatment. Two years after that, Dora did start treatment with Freud, and she stayed with him for three months. This was three months at six sessions per week. That was the way psychoanalysis was practiced. While it's not over a great period of time, there were many meetings. Dora was now 18 years old, and had suffered from many hysterical symptoms since she was eight. She had breathing problems, a nervous cough, loss of voice for up to five weeks (apropos of your questions about conversion hysteria, a person could have symptoms like this then: If you couldn't speak for five weeks, the doctor might say: "Oh, it must be 'can't-talk-er-itis'"). Dora also had migraines, depression, suicidal ideas and what Freud noted as "a general dissatisfaction with life."

Dora's mother suffered from what doctors called "housewife's disease," an obsessive concern with household chores. In Dora's mind, Mother was cold and psychologically unavailable to the family. Dora's parents had become friendly with another family, the "Ks." To Dora, evidence pointed to her father having an affair with Mrs. K. This emerged in Dora's treatment. What Freud suggests is that everybody in Dora's family was telling Dora she was crazy. While all of this drama was occurring, Mr. K. had made sexual advances to Dora, and had implied marriage. Freud believed that Dora's symptoms were connected to her love for her father and the proposals of Mr. K., as well as a homosexual longing Freud believed Dora had for Mrs. K., representative of her longing for her unavailable mother. Although Freud didn't relate these problems to Dora's Oedipal conflicts, he worked on what he thought were adolescent issues centering around struggles to become an adult woman without a decent maternal identification figure. In footnotes written in a later edition of the case, Freud discusses his errors in not talking about Oedipal issues or the transference.

Dora worked with Freud for three months. She abruptly terminated the therapy. Fifteen months later she returned to treatment, and there had been a lessening of the symptoms. In 1922, *22 years* after her first contact with Freud, Dora was seen by Dr. Felix Deutsch (1957), an Austrian psychoanalyst whose other claim to fame (besides his having treated Dora) was that he was married to Dr. Helene Deutsch (1942) Helene Deutsch was also trained at the Vienna Psychoanalytic Institute. (She and her husband later fled to America. In the early 1940s, by the way, Helene Deutsch wrote a paper called the "As-If Personality." This paper is cited as the first true description of patients presenting with what is now called borderline personality disorder.)

Felix Deutsch later wrote a paper in which he compared what actually happened to Dora in her adulthood to what one might predict based on Freud's writing. What Deutsch observed was Dora's frigidity and negative attitudes toward marriage. The improvement that Freud saw in Dora did not hold up long. A kind of rapid improvement and relapse occurred again with Deutsch's treatment. At the end of the paper, Freud talks about his mistake in not dealing with Dora's transference. But Freud's error (dare I say this) was that he also didn't understand his countertransference to Dora.

Let me explain what I mean: Despite it all, in Dora's history she had a loving relationship with her father and a not-so-loving relationship with her mother. That is, until Dora entered puberty, at which point Dora became sexual.

Let me say this a bit differently: what happens in some families is, as long as a little girl stays a little girl, it doesn't make her father crazy. When she becomes a woman, any (unconscious) attraction the father has to his daughter becomes horrifying because of what it implies. Now, if Father had been able to sublimate this he would've been able to say: "My Dora, she's so adorable, look how pretty she is, I'm sure that she's going to have a wonderful mate." However, if one is repressed (everyone was repressed in the time that Freud worked), one is going to have many confusing feelings, but won't know how to deal with them. I'm suggesting that for Dora's father, everything was fine with him and Dora until she began to make him nervous, at which point he emotionally cut her off/rejected her. I have a bit of evidence for this: In the transference with a patient, what happens is a reenactment of the kind of traumatic experiences that happened between the child and a parent. We also have a bit of data about Freud that is very interesting: After he completed the treatment with Dora, Freud could never quite remember the exact year that he had treated her. This is an example of a parapraxis. Why would Freud have had a parapraxis about this patient?

Let me propose the following:

Prior to the writeup of the Dora case, Freud hadn't written any psychoanalytic cases as a solo author, just the related work he had done with Josef Breuer (*Studies on Hysteria*). Now he was working with a new case and he got an idea:

> "She's an interesting girl, I'm going to write up her dreams. I'm going to show the world my new procedures and present the patient's innermost life, her dreams. I'm excited, I'm going to write up her dreams!"

Then, Dora appears at what *she* knows to be her final session and says: "Today is our last session."

I suggest that Dora did to Freud what her father had done to her. I propose the following: Father symbolically dumped Dora when he got too excited by her budding sexuality. Dora dumped Freud when he got "excited" by her case.

Here was what I believe to be Dora's unconscious transference revenge:

> (1.) Freud got excited by Dora; (2.) She dumped Freud suddenly and for seemingly no reason; (3.) Based on evidence of Freud's parapraxis, Freud never quite got over it.

How do I know this? I don't know it. It's my (perhaps ridiculous) theory.

A similar clinical example

Many years ago, a woman began to work with me; she was a college professor and I saw her twice a week. She was a very interesting person. I was a young man beginning my clinical practice, and I really liked her. She was in her 50s, and in our first meeting she told me the following story.

She had thought that she had a good marriage. One night nearing their 25th anniversary, she and her husband made passionate love, but the following morning her husband served her with a subpoena: He was filing for divorce. She was devastated.

We began the therapy and (I thought) we were working on her need to mourn the loss of her marriage (you will see that – in a way – we were). Therapy was going along swimmingly as far as I could see. Then, in what seemed to me to come out of nowhere, she came to a session and said:

"I've made a decision, I'm going to see *the other one.*"
    I said: "What other one?"
    She said, "I'm also seeing another therapist, at the same time that I have been seeing *you.*"
    "Oh!" I said. "Well (*attempting to regain what little composure I could*), can I ask you a few questions? Is the other therapist female?"

PATIENTR: "Yes."
ME: "And, she knows that you are working with me, but I didn't know about her?"
PATIENTR: "Yes."
ME: "Had she suggested that you tell me?"
PATIENTR: "Well . . . no."
ME: "I guess I was just served the subpoena."
PATIENTR: (*laughs at my comment*) "I really am appreciative of your understanding, and despite this, you've helped me a lot."

She left, never to return.
    Please notice that I never asked the patient anything about her own feelings, her thoughts or about her decision, as I thought that any patient has the right to leave any therapist whenever they want to. My concern with this person, and with others where something like this has happened, is not *when* the person leaves, but *how* they leave. By the way, my comment at the end of the session, ('I was just served a subpoena') is called a paradigmatic technique.[5]
    Also, I thought that the other therapist's behavior was unconscionable, but I felt that any attempt to tell the patient this would not be helpful to her.
    How does this example relate to Freud's case of Dora? I believe that, just like Dora, this woman had to do to someone what had been done to her, to surprise, reject and hurt a man like she had been rejected by her husband.
    In the Dora case, when she said, "Today is our last session," Freud said some version of "Okay, well, let's talk about the feelings about the dream that you had a fortnight ago, the fortnight dream." That is, Freud kept working in the remaining time to make meaning out of a bewildering and upsetting experience for him. This is what is now called an inducement and an enactment, and I believe that, with the snippet of the case that I just presented to you, I was in good company: It happened to Freud and it also happened to me.

Summary of lecture 9

Freud used the single-case-study method to present a theory of neurosis. He reasoned that normality and neurosis are only different in degree, removing the social stigma from neurosis. Freud demonstrated that neurosis is amenable to psychoanalytic treatment. He suggested that the psychoanalyzability of the neurotic rests on the fact that the neurotic forms transferences that can be worked through (analyzed and resolved) in psychoanalysis. Freud differentiated between a transference neurosis, where the patient forms transference, and a narcissistic neurosis, where the patient cannot form transferences because they are too self-centered. Patients suffering from what Freud referred to as the "transference neurosis" would now be considered to be neurotic, while patients who suffered from narcissistic neurosis would now be understood to be suffering from severe character disorders (such as borderline personality disorder) or psychotic disorders (such as schizophrenia). In categorizing emotional illness in this way, Freud rejected a descriptive definition of psychopathology in favor of a therapeutic definition, and demonstrated the connection between theory and treatment. Freud took the symptoms of neurosis and classified them into two major clinical types: obsessional neurosis and hysteria. He further subdivided hysteria into two subtypes: conversion hysteria and anxiety hysteria. Aside from the differences in the formation of the symptoms, Freud saw all hysteria as a result of a fixation of infantile sexuality, repression of sexuality, a failure of the repression and the breaking through of the repressed sexuality in the form of a neurotic symptom. In the case of Dora (1905), which is a fragment of the full case, Freud's stated purpose was to show how to understand and work with a patient's dreams in psychoanalysis, as well as to present a first look at the psychoanalytic method. In this case, as with his other case histories, Freud outlined and gave examples of his theory of neurosis and its treatment.

Notes

1 Karl Abraham (1877–1925) was an influential German psychoanalyst and a collaborator of Sigmund Freud, who called him his "best pupil." "Frequently Asked Questions." London: Freud Museum. Archived from *the original* on June 26, 2007.
2 *Black Psychoanalysis Speak* is directed by Basia Winograd and features Drs. C. Jama Adams, Janice Bennett, Anton Hart, Annie Lee Jones, Delores Morris, Michael Moskowitz, Craig Polite, Richard Reichbart, Cheryl Thompson, Kirkland Vaughans, Cleonie White and Kathleen White. A number of these people happen to have been or are affiliated with our doctoral program, and Dr. Kirkland Vaughns is a member of our faculty and a graduate of our doctoral and postgraduate programs. The video *Psychoanalysis in the Barrio*, also directed by Basia Winograd, challenges the unfounded notion that Latinx people who are poor are so consumed by the pressures of everyday survival that they cannot make use of psychoanalysis and can benefit only from time-limited, symptom-focused interventions. The video features Ricardo Ainslie, Daniel Gaztambide, Patricia Gherovici, Rafael Javier, Ernesto Mujica (a former member of the Derner faculty), Lourdes Mattei, Carlos Padrón and David Ramirez.
3 Erdelyi (2006) states that repression is an "empirical fact." He cautions that fragmented clinical and laboratory traditions and disputed terminology have resulted in misunderstandings and false distinctions. For Erdelyi, repression designates the nondefensive inhibition of ideas by other ideas in the struggle for consciousness. Freud adapted repression to the defensive inhibition of intolerable mental contents. Substantial experimental literatures exist on "attentional" biases, thought avoidance, interference and intentional forgetting. As psychoanalytic clinicians have long suggested, inaccessible ideas are often available and emerge indirectly (e.g., implicitly).

4 Helene Deutsch (1884–1982) was a Polish-American psychoanalyst and colleague of Sigmund Freud. She founded the Vienna Psychoanalytic Institute. In 1935 she came to Cambridge, Massachusetts, where she maintained a practice. Deutsch was one of the first psychoanalysts to specialize in working with women.

5 Paradigmatic techniques are a technical innovation first suggested by Coleman-Nelson (Coleman-Nelson, 1981; Sherman, 1981; Spotnitz, 1976, 2004), who introduced the psychoanalytic model known as paradigmatic psychotherapy. In paradigmatic treatment the psychoanalyst is understood to enact different roles that are induced by various ego states of the clinician. These techniques are seen as helpful with distrustful patients; the clinician joins the patient's system (that is, their distrustful ideas) but also continues to support the patient's manifest negative feelings. When this is done empathically, the patient experiences that the clinician understands them. From this, a more positive transference can evolve; one result is the patient begins to question their distrustful ideas/beliefs.

References

Altman, N. (1993). Psychoanalysis and the urban poor. *Psychoanalytic Dialogues*, *3*, 29–49.

Benjamin, J. (1988a). *The bonds of love*. New York: Pantheon Books.

Benjamin, J. (1998b). *Like subjects, love objects*. New Haven: Yale University Press.

Coleman-Nelson, M. (1981). The paradigmatic approach: A parallel development. *Modern Psychoanalysis*, *6*(1), 9–26.

de Beauvoir, S. (1989). *The second sex* (H. M. Parshley, Trans.). New York: Vintage Books (1953).

Deutsch, F. (1957). A footnote to Freud's "Fragment of an analysis of a case of hysteria." *The Psychoanalytic Quarterly*, *26*(2), 159–167.

Deutsch, H. (1942). Some forms of emotional disturbance and their relationship to schizophrenia. *The Psychoanalytic Quarterly*, *11*(3), 301–321.

Erdelyi, M. (2006). The unified theory of repression. *Behavioral and Brain Sciences*, *29*, 499–551.

Escobar, J. I., Gara, M., Waitzkin, H., Silver, R. C., Holman, A., & Compton, W. (1998). DSM IV hypochondriasis in primary care. *General Hospital Psychiatry*, *20*(3), 155–159.

Freud, S. (1905). Fragments of an analysis of a case of hysteria. In J. Strachey et al. (Trans.), *The standard edition of the complete psychological works of Sigmund Freud, Volume VII: ("Dora")*. London: Hogarth, 1–122.

Freud, S. (1913). Totem and taboo: Some points of agreement between the mental lives of savages and neurotics. In J. Strachey et al. (Trans.), *The standard edition of the complete psychological works of Sigmund Freud, Volume XIII*. London: Hogarth, VII–162.

Hollingshead, A. B., & Redlich, F. C. (1958). *Social class and mental illness: A community study*. New York: Wiley.

Sherman, M. H. (1981). Siding with the resistance in paradigmatic psychotherapy. *Modern Psychoanalysis*, *6*(1), 47–64.

Spotnitz, H. (1976). *Psychotherapy of preoedipal conditions*. New York: Jason Aronson.

Spotnitz, H. (2004). *Modern psychoanalysis of the schizophrenic patient: Theory of the technique*. New York: YBK Publishers, Inc.

Strauss, B., Barber, J. P., & Castonguay, L. G. (Eds.). (2015). *Visions in psychotherapy research and practice: Reflections from the presidents of the society for psychotherapy research*. New York: Routledge Press.

Winograd, B. (2017, June 28). *Psychoanalysis in el barrio* [Video]. YouTube. www.youtube.com/watch?v=Po3G7_xYBjM

Winograd, B. (2020, July 2). *Black psychoanalysts speak* [Video]. YouTube. www.youtube.com/watch?v=N8-VIi7tb44

Chapter 10

Freud's case studies II

Obsessional neurosis, phobia and reconstruction

Sources: *The Rat Man*, 1909, and *The Wolfman*, 1918

As we talk about Freud's case material, I want to mention my belief that each of you should have experience with hospital work. Although this kind of setting can be emotionally challenging, if your ultimate goal is clinic work and/or office practice, and you're not planning to work with seriously disturbed patients, then it's particularly important to have hospital experience and be able to have first-hand knowledge about very disturbed patients who aren't currently functioning. Having experience working with disturbed people is a good way to know how to access those people that need more management and monitoring than office practice allows, versus those who can do well with psychodynamic talk therapy and/ or talk therapy and medication.

I once worked with a young man, a practicing attorney. In the middle of the first interview, during my questioning, this man began to act very oddly. I knew from hospital experiences that he was not psychotic, in the formal sense of blunted affect and thought disorder, but he was certainly acting crazy. I also knew I could work with him, but if I hadn't had hospital experience, I don't know that I would have known this. He certainly did odd things. Yet because of what I had previously learned in terms of affect blunting and/or loss of control over affect, as well relatedness versus psychotic withdrawal, I had a high degree of confidence that we could work with what he was presenting.

The episode of what I have called "oddness" (an enactment) occurred when he was describing his childhood. He'd said that his parents were always yelling and critical, but when I inquired about this, he said, "Like this," and started yelling at the top of his voice and making barely recognizable howling sounds like a ferocious creature.

I want to be clear: What he did was very odd. I'm not suggesting otherwise. It was odd enough for me to go back into my mental files about hospitalized patients, to say to myself: *no blunted affect, makes eye contact, tolerated it when I moved my chair just a bit closer to him, had a coherent description of his history, had until this point in the intake interview manifested the ability to test reality.* He had, by the way, graduated from an excellent college and law school, but that

DOI: 10.4324/9781003171393-11

data might lead one to draw conclusions only about his *prior* level of functioning: I had to make a decision about how he was acting at present. After a few seconds of this yelling, he sat back in his chair and reassured me that, while he had been making weird sounds, "I don't usually act like this."

Thus, I observed that he had critical ego functions in that he was able to describe what he had done. (In regard to this yelling, I suggested to him that this behavior made him seem unattractive and a bit frightening. I also suggested that perhaps his acting unpredictable and irrational had been a tactic that he developed in childhood to protect himself from being killed by his toxic family. While he neither confirmed nor denied my remark, he then went on to describe how none of his three siblings had fared as well in their own lives. That felt like a preconscious confirmation of what I'd just said, and later work with this man was also confirmatory of these preliminary thoughts about him.

STUDENT: Your comments sounded poetically beautiful, but how do you know whether they had anything to do with this patient?

DR. M: I didn't have great confidence that my comments were accurate, near accurate or off the mark. This is one of the important things that we will be talking about today, that in Freud's case histories he introduces the technique of reconstruction, that is, taking the person's current symptoms, character traits and defenses and reconstructing what kind of history the person might have had based on their current adjustment and symptomatology and behavior in the session.

I thank you for your question because it provides us with a kind of prelude to how Freud's case histories tell us about how each of you can apply what we've learned so far in your training to become psychodynamic clinicians. Here is more of my answer to your question: Some of you will want to do direct services (clinical work), some of you will want to do research, some of you may also want to teach, either in a formal academic job or teaching and supervising part-time in hospitals/clinics. It seems from your writings that a few of you strongly disliked the Dora case. This got me thinking about a paper I wrote with a colleague a number of years ago. The paper is called "The Interviewer's Presenting Problems in the Initial Interview." (Billow & Mendelsohn, 1990).

The paper suggests that it's not only the patient who has presenting problems at a first interview; the interviewer also has presenting problems! Here's one presenting problem: I'm bringing this up to make a point about the Freud cases that we already have heard (Freud, 1905), cases of his that come next and cases you have heard about from me during these lectures.

A young man, the interviewer, is starting a practice, has a doctorate, a couple of years of postdoctoral experience, and has just opened an office. He's feeling excited to start private clinical work. In this example, he gets a call from a respected senior male colleague who had been his clinical supervisor several years before. This senior colleague says the following:

"I'm supervising a guy who reminds me of you, at your early training when I worked with you. He's delightful, eager to learn, he's smart like you . . . he's terrific. I want to send him for therapy, he needs a lower fee and I thought that since you are just starting your practice, you might consider this. Are you willing?"

Not only are you willing, you are both delighted and thrilled. Here's your presenting problem:

This new patient – highly praised by your former supervisor – arrives for a first meeting. The first thing he does is growl about the terrible directions that you gave him to the office. (The navigation apps now make it harder to give directions to the office. In the past, one way to assess how well a new patient might take directions in the therapy was to give extremely clear and accurate directions and wait to see if and how your new patient had taken the directions. This seemingly innocuous direction giving was employed to gather information about the new patient, and in this case it was.)

Next, the new patient sits down and starts questioning you about your credentials. He seems nasty and defensive.

Here's this clinician's presenting problem: *Who* is the new patient? Is it the guy that his respected senior supervisor/now colleague called him about, or is it the person that is seated across from him?

That's the clinician's presenting problem. This man certainly doesn't sound the way he was described by the supervisor. One solution to this presenting problem would be to become convinced that your former supervisor is senile, that he is in fact now out of his mind. Yet that doesn't really sound right, because the former supervisor was very thoughtful on the phone, and also you saw him at a professional meeting recently and he was making a lot of sense. Well, then, here's another "solution": Perhaps you're not yet polished and skilled enough and this new patient (a person beginning in the field and thus probably a clinically sensitive person) saw right through you. What you experienced and thought you understood about him was in fact inaccurate. Yet that doesn't sound right, either. So, what is going on here? What is going on is that we've stumbled onto an important clinical truth: There are *two patients* in this situation, and actually there might soon be *three*. What I am saying is that there is one patient who has different aspects to their presentation. The first patient is the person that your former supervisor described, and this person acted the way he did with this older, respected male teacher (the dynamics might have been a bit different had the former supervisor been female, but maybe not). The second patient is the person that you now see: aggressive, competitive, contemptuous and devaluing.

Here are some common errors that a clinician might make: If one stays focused on what the supervisor told you and ignore what's occurred in front of you, I might label this an obsessive-compulsive style, bogged down in/blocked by old details. If, on the other hand, one drops everything they were told and is concerned only with what occurred at the moment (living exclusively in this current moment), that would be a hysterical or manic style.

The interviewer's presenting problem is that they're going to need to find a way to incorporate both what they were told *and* what they see, into a new patient. That new ("third") patient will combine some aspects of the other two patients.

Why am I bringing this up in relation to today's cases/Dora? Because either of these styles, obsessive-compulsive or hysterical/manic, will have at least one negative result: It will inhibit the clinician's curiosity. Once one loses curiosity (the same curiosity that I was encouraging in this young man about his unusual behavior in the session), we limit what we can discover about our patient. I believe that is the issue with Freud and his case of Dora. It is clear that Freud made a number of mistakes in the treatment. That said, I urge you to stay curious. Perhaps, then, you can figure out what Freud actually said, what he meant and what the Dora case was actually about. If one loses one's intellectual/emotional curiosity, it's hard to make psychological meaning out of each clinical situation, and it is harder to help one's patient. In this regard, one of the more controversial things I have to say to you is that one danger with "victimology" is the mistaken belief that patients who were traumatized were *only* traumatized, that they don't also have a psychology of their own, that they can't also then traumatize others. This mistake leads to a related error: that the only way one can understand a victim of trauma is by assuming that their trauma is the only thing we need to know about them.

All humans have a psychology that is largely based upon their psychological development, such questions as: At what age was this person exposed to trauma? What were they like *pre-morbid* (before the trauma)? How much, if at all, did the person collude in the trauma? (This is a very delicate question that can make it seem like we are blaming the victim, when in fact, no matter how much a person may have colluded with their traumatizer, it is always the fault of the traumatizer rather than the person who was traumatized.) What sources of support were available to the traumatized person, and were they able to use these resources? If not, why not? Just as we have seen with the issue of the presenting problem, everything that we hypothesize in every clinical session with a patient is absolutely true, and also may not be quite true at the same time. In this regard I would suggest that Dora was both a victim and a colluder, although Dora's parents and the Ks were the *only* perpetrators of the moral transgressions that occurred. If you think of Dora only as a victim, then you miss the colluder, and you can't fully help her. If you see only the colluder and not the victim, you can't fully help her. Dora's interesting and dramatic history can encourage one to lose curiosity and become either an unthinking devoted follower of Freud or, on the other hand, a skeptic of Freud and an ardent defender of those misunderstood by him. In other words, can we be objective about Freud and recognize both his insights and his errors?

One more thing before we look at the remainder of Freud's cases: A few of you asked about Freud's dividing psychopathology into two clinical types: the narcissistic neuroses versus the transference neuroses. This is what I wrote to a number of you:

"Freud worked at a time when the patients we now describe as having borderline personality disorder didn't get diagnosed with this, because our
understanding of this character problem wasn't yet known. Simply put, these
patients inhabit a kind of border area between the neuroses and the psychoses. They are capable, under certain conditions, of being able to function
well, while under other circumstances they can present as quite disturbed
with problems in emotional regulation and disordered thinking. In Freud's
time, these people where commonly misunderstood and diagnosed as hysterics. Some of these people had all sorts of dissociative symptoms. In this context, Freud thought that the patients he called narcissistic neurotics, whom
he believed couldn't form a transference, were more like the kind of overtly
psychotic patients that one sees in a hospital setting before they are stabilized with medication and the safe space of the institution. Or they are the
chronically hospitalized, withdrawn patients. That is, Freud thought psychotics were not treatable (narcissistic neurosis). Yet Freud also had only limited
success with borderline patients like Dora, because he thought they were neurotic (transference neurosis). Ironically, Freud underdiagnosed the pathology
of those he thought he could treat, and labeled as untreatable patients we now
see as treatable and capable of change with the right kinds of medicine and
modifications in the way one does talk therapy."

With this as a context, we're going to talk later about Freud's case of the Wolfman
(S. Pankejeff), and most clinicians today would see Wolfman as treatable but quite
disturbed. However, first we will discuss the Rat Man.

The Obsessional Neurosis: Rat Man,
Ernst Lanzer[1] (1878–1914)

A description of the structure of the obsessional neurosis is first found in Freud's
case history *The Rat Man*. The title of this work is: Notes Upon a Case of Obsessional Neurosis. I want to say, with some irony, that this is the only complete
and successful psychoanalytic case that Freud wrote about. There is certainly
evidence that Freud had obsessive-compulsive aspects to *his* personality. Freud
seems to have very much valued this man. If we glance at the bottom of the last
page of this book, we see Freud's footnote. In the footnote, Freud talks about Rat
Man, and one can almost feel the sadness in Freud's comments about Lanzer's
untimely death in World War I.

During our last lecture we talked about the structure of hysteria as exemplified
by the case of Dora. With today's material we complete Freud's understanding of
the neuroses by talking about the obsessive-compulsive patient, and the patient
suffering from a phobia.

Freud begins the case by saying that in the year 1896 he reasoned that obsessive
ideas are self-reproaches that emerged from repression (and that they are probably) connected to infantile sexuality–childhood masturbation. Freud suggests

that the adult has thoughts that take the form of a repetition of the kind of phrases that one hears as a child:

"No, no!" or "Bad boy!" or "Bad girl!"

In other words, Freud's original understanding of the obsessive-compulsive process is that the child had taken in the prohibitions of the parents and is now using these prohibitions against the self. (One sees, even in 1896, Freud's beginning understanding of what he'll later call identification=superego.)

In *The Rat Man*, written later (in 1909), Freud deepens this understanding. He says that the obsessional neurotic not only represses upsetting thoughts/feelings but also isolates the feelings that belong to these thoughts, that is, the obsessional keeps the thoughts and feelings separated from each other. If one's feelings are kept separate from one's thoughts, then the person will be shielded from the emotional impact of the thoughts. This can be both a good thing and a bad thing. In this case, Freud believes that the obsessive-compulsive separates (isolates) their love feelings for a parent from their hate feelings for the parent.

STUDENT: OK, so the idea is that there is both love and hate for the mother?

DR. M: Yes. Frustration leads to anger, aggression and hate. No mothering one – forgetting what gender – is perfect. No mothering one is devoid of ambivalence, makes no mistakes, is always able to totally detoxify their own ambivalence or their child's ambivalent feelings. A mother who deeply loves her child, who hasn't had sleep for weeks with her newborn and is forced awake by the infant's cries, has hate and ambivalence, but is typically able to contain and detoxify these feelings because they also deeply love this child. In the best of circumstances, the mother makes all sorts of accommodations. However, there is still a problem, because even with the best-fit mother the child is faced with a dilemma: "I'm frustrated, I'm furious." If the conditions are such that the mother is as close to perfect as a mother can be, and the child's temperament is perfect for this particular type of mother, and no very disruptive circumstances occur (like a COVID-19 pandemic), there's not going to be unmanageable frustration. If it's not a perfect fit, then the child's own anger and hate at the mother is going to seep through as a threat to this child's security. In other words, if we extend Freud's ideas, built into all relationships is ambivalence. If you're very frustrated and therefore you've got a large amount of hate, then this hate tips the balance against the love. That's dangerous. What does the child do? The child could have a total reaction formation (as an adult they become a person in a higher calling, and never have one bit of conscious anger). Where does the anger go? (As an aside, I'm always a little skeptical of people who show no anger in them.)

STUDENT: So, can I ask: It's basically that within every child, like, there's some ratio of actual love and actual hate?

DR. M: Yes. We hope that this hate can get channeled into the kind of outlets that happen in latency-age kids like sports, particularly competitive sports. That is one way to channel one's rage and frustration, aggression and hate, but there are other channels, like turning the aggression into academic competitiveness, wanting to be the best student in class, to be smart, to be successful. There are channels for aggression in an optimal life. If you're loved enough, you're frustrated but within bounds, your temperament is such that you're able to tolerate frustration without using all sorts of overly harsh defenses, you can use these channels to discharge your feelings.

Freud sees obsessive-compulsive neurotics as fixated at the anal-sadistic stage; as the child develops, the same conflicts that bothered them about anality now recur as they enter the phallic stage, where there is stress not only about messy bowels but also now about having messy longings to touch the genitals. The conflict moves from not wanting to touch messy bowel movements to not wanting to touch one's genitals, to not wanting to be touched emotionally by feelings. As one might imagine, this system can now become an elaborate system designed so that the person does not feel any upsetting feelings. If one listens to the subtext: hysterics feel too much, that is, they are showy, unclear in their thinking, overly emotional and overly anxious; obsessive-compulsives feel too little. Obsessional thinking uses secondary defenses against the primary obsessional thought(s).

When we get to the Rat Man case history, the primary obsessional thought for Rat Man is what he calls the "rat torture." Rat Man had to perform many mental maneuvers in order to *not* have the rat-torture thoughts. Rat Man traveled hither and yon on various trains, paid money to an attendant, all in order to not owe money to another soldier. In order to deal with his obsessional thoughts (the primary obsessional thoughts of the rat torture), Rat Man performed many mental gymnastics (obsessions) and rituals (compulsive acts) in an attempt to control his frustration and hate. While Freud doesn't talk about this directly in *The Rat Man*, he implies something that we now know from clinical work. That is, with certain obsessional processes the person has all sorts of vague worries, not just a single, primary obsessional idea like the rat torture. Thus, for example, the person may also worry about dying from many diseases. The obsessive-compulsive's life is often a great struggle. One can feel like saying to an OCD patient, "It must be so hard to be you." In this current COVID-19 pandemic, one can only guess what's happening to people who are already struggling with OCD and germ worries!

Along with the primary obsessional idea and the defense of isolation of affect – these are employed to make the primary obsessional idea devoid of upsetting feeling – there are also secondary defenses of reaction formation and undoing. With these mechanisms, the patient first turns the hatred into its opposite, into caring and love (reaction formation), and then treats their thoughts like they have a magical power (via the mechanism of undoing).

There is a game that children play on the sidewalk: "Step on a crack, break your mother's back." The child is magically protecting their mother from their own hatred. There is also the example that I presented in an early lecture: a mother who counted all the knives in the kitchen, worrying that if she miscounted a knife, one of her children might cut themselves. Now we can more fully understand that by focusing on the external dangers of a misplaced knife, this mother could blunt her ambivalence toward her children, a love mixed with ambivalence that would have been unacceptable to her conscious mind. Freud describes these two new mechanisms of reaction formation and undoing as processes that develop in the child to promote something called the "omnipotence of thought." That is, the child begins to treat thoughts as if they are real, instead of treating them as simply ideas in the head. Freud also suggests that this magical thinking and "omnipotence" (or what is commonly called superstition) is evidence of a similarity between obsessive-compulsives and certain rituals observed in religious observance. Further, he suggests that there is a similarity between the rituals of the obsessive-compulsive patient and the religious and/or tribal rituals of what were then called primitive cultures. In these cultures, Freud suggests, the primary obsessional thought is incest (infantile sexuality). In order to avoid the temptation and acting out of incest, a tribe will create complicated lineages for marriage and reproduction.

One might ask: Why do all cultures seem to have an incest taboo? Remember, Freud was influenced by Darwin's evolution theory. He would answer anyone who asked the purpose of the incest taboo by saying that incest is bad for the species. As a psychobiologist Freud said that rules about mating and reproduction are created for the preservation and advancement of our species.

STUDENT: But people start having OC behaviors where you can't always draw a direct connection to something that happened when you were a child.

DR. M: While we can't easily draw a direct connection to child-rearing – and to the anal stage – if somebody has OC behaviors, we do know that some person (some object) early on in this person's development was controlling and critical of them – just as the person's superego is controlling and critical of them now. How do we know this? Because when the person later comes to therapy and becomes involved emotionally with the psychoanalyst, they are soon in a struggle with the therapist over control and they are soon seeing the therapist as critical. The patient is in an internal struggle and an external struggle. One hundred and twenty years of clinical observation and psychological test data show that this kind of patient is hypersensitive to controlling and being controlled, and handles their sensitivity in ways similar to how Rat Man functioned. Hysterical patients are hypersensitive to sexuality and triangulation; these dynamics are enacted in the hysteric's treatment. Borderline patients are extremely reactive to affect dysregulation and terror of abandonment, and employ defenses of projective identification, enactment, denial and splitting. Manic patients are hypersensitive to anything that suggests loss, and they become reckless and flee feelings of loss and sadness. We know all of this because of the advances made since the work Freud did in his (albeit rudimentary) understanding of psychodynamics.

To return to our current topic, the obsessive-compulsive disorder: If a psycho-analyst hasn't done anything to control this patient that merits their temporarily "hating" the clinician, but the patient is reacting to the doctor as if the clinician did do this, one might draw the conclusion that the patient had at least one critical and controlling parent who attempted to totally control the patient's life and limit their sense of autonomy. And that at some point the patient battled with the parent, but they ultimately gave in. The patient needed to stifle any feelings of hatred toward this frustrating parent. The patient loved and needed the parent, even if they didn't always like the parent. That is a conclusion that one can draw. And, most likely, the person has come to the therapist talking about interpersonal problems and frustrations where they feel that others (a mate, friends, coworkers, the boss, et cetera) are trying to control them, interfering with their autonomy. The therapist might not see this in the early stages of the therapy, but will see the specifics of the origin of conflicts over rage and control, and will also get some sense of a personality style: A style will suggest the presence of a particular complex of defenses. Thus, in my work, a person with this kind of style will quickly sniffle at me, or look askance, or be impatient and annoyed about something. I will begin to realize that anything that I do is potentially heard as a kind of malevolent control over them. That means they most likely had a history of malevolent control, or the belief that there was malevolent control. Thus, while I have yet to know their history, I can assume that we will get there. Therefore, what Freud introduces from his case histories is the concept of reconstruction. (Freud, 1937). In reconstruction the psychoanalyst assesses the current symptoms and forms hypotheses about what the person's childhood family must have been like to influence what they are like now. If somebody sees me as controlling them malevolently, and, as a reference point, no one else I am currently working with sees me this way, then this new patient probably has some history of being malevolently controlled.

As the model for this, we turn to Freud's case of the Rat Man. *The Rat Man* is the only full, complete and successful case that Freud published (it's clear that Freud had a deep fondness for this man, as seen in Freud's footnote). Dora can't be considered a complete analysis, since she stopped the treatment prematurely, and it wasn't totally successful. Other cases that Freud published were only fragments.

The title of this paper is *Notes Upon a Case of Obsessional Neurosis* (Freud, 1909). Freud's purpose in writing the paper was to demonstrate the obsessional neurosis. The analysis began on October 1, 1907, and lasted 11 months (remember that this is 11 months, six times a week – over 200 sessions). The treatment ended successfully, the symptoms cleared up, the patient returned to work, his love life improved. Unfortunately, he was killed in World War I. The nickname the "Rat Man" comes from the patient's obsessive fears, which brought him to Freud. The patient was a lawyer of 30 who had been drafted into the army. During maneuvers he had a number of obsessional ideas, but they had always passed. However, after one long march, he met some officers and at the same time he lost his pince-nez. At that stop, he talked with two officers; one was a sadistic person. This cruel soldier described a torture used in Asia in which a criminal is tied up and a pot of rats is turned upside down on the patient's buttocks, allowing the rats to bore their way into the criminal's anus. Clearly this is a horrific way to die. As Rat Man heard the officer tell of this torture, the idea went through his mind that the torture was happening to the woman he loved and was planning to marry. This was clearly an irrational worry. Even more irrational was a second thought that Rat Man had, that the rat torture might happen to Rat Man's father. Both of these thoughts were nonsensical, but the thought about his father was particularly bizarre: Rat Man's father had died several months before. Further, based on what we're talking about today, both of these relationships – with the father and the girlfriend – were somewhat frustrating, conflictual and ambivalent. That is, both of these relationships stimulated not only love but also frustration and hatred; in fact, Rat Man could only now become engaged to his girlfriend because he'd accumulated a certain amount of money upon the death of his father. He was both emotionally and sexually frustrated by this (therefore by her). Concerning his father, Rat Man's history suggests that his father was critical and controlling, some-times nasty and mean. These are the kinds of dynamics that can be a breeding ground for ambivalence/hatred and obsessive-compulsive symptomatology.

After this incident with the sadistic officer, whenever the patient thought that the rat torture could be happening to either his fiancée or his father, he felt forced to think of a sanction. To Rat Man a sanction was a defensive measure that he had to think of and perform to magically prevent this fantasy from being fulfilled. This is what Freud calls "undoing." This is totally ridiculous, just as avoiding cracks in the sidewalk doesn't do much for Mother's spinal column. However, these prohibitions and sanctions are part of the ritualization seen in obsessional symptomatology as well as in religious rituals. We can also see that they're the same mechanisms that someone with an obsessive-compulsive disorder might be performing. Again, by the way, I am talking about the similarities between certain religious rituals and certain OCD rituals: yet, because they are similar does not mean that the religious ones are pathological, but we can certainly say that the OCD ones are. Rat Man was not an observant religious person but had to perform lots of sanctions in order to prevent the fantasy of the rat torture from happening to these two important people in his life.

It is worth asking: Was Rat Man psychotic? I don't think so, but Freud did not have the advantage we now have of understanding that some patients can have *both* neurotic *and* psychotic features in their personality. How would a psychotic process manifest? I would contend that (unlike Wolfman, whom I believe *did* have psychotic features) if in a clinical interview we asked Rat Man,

"If you didn't perform these sanctions, would the rat torture actually occur?"

Rat Man would probably answer in the following way:

"I don't know . . . maybe not, but I can't stand how painful it is to think about this. I can't stop thinking about it so I don't know if it could *really* happen, but that doesn't matter because I just want these torturous thoughts to stop."

By this, Rat Man would be showing us that while he *did* have critical ego functions (the ability of the ego to perform reality testing) and that he most likely could distinguish reality from fantasy, he was dysregulated by upsetting affect; therefore, he had borderline features to his personality (whereby under the press of powerful thoughts and affect, he would temporarily lose the ability to use secondary, that is, reality-based, defenses). In effect, Rat Man would be saying that it is better to think of – even perform – these sanctions so he didn't have to go through the excruciating pain of anxiety/self-torture that he would experience if he had to keep thinking about the rat torture. In this regard, thinking about the rat torture might lead this patient to the intolerable experience of what the rat torture implied about his ambivalent feelings for both his fiancée and his father (including perhaps about the infantile sexual longings and fears about the anal cavities of each of these important people in his life).[2]

This case reveals many of the features that are seen in the obsessional patient. For example, in the first few minutes at the beginning of Rat Man's first session with Freud, the patient detailed the things that happened to him concerning his sexual experiences from childhood. He pictured a scene of sex play with a governess when he was four or five years old (a hysteric might also believe *or* feel that this experience is somewhere in their history, but they would not remember the details due to the use of repression and dissociation. However, Rat Man remembered the scene clearly. Yet because of the defense of isolation of affect, the experience was devoid of feeling (and therefore devoid of any emotional implications).

STUDENT: I feel like in every story there's a governess involved.

DR. M: As with many of life's issues, it's complicated. In every era, unfortunately, some of the people who have access to the care of young children are not good people. The people employed as caretakers for children are often low-paid and undereducated, and sometimes they were traumatized as children; they may be envious of their richer employers. That said, we don't know what is true versus what the person fantasized about in their childhood. We don't know what actually happened. In either case, we want to understand the patient's experience (whether or not it was all a wish-fulfilled longing that colored their experience, or a clear memory of what occurred or, most likely, a partly clear/partly distorted memory of what happened). In this regard, I want to remind you about the story that I told you about the young woman I briefly treated who kept having flashback images of a dark and dingy wall with a flashing light. We don't actually know what occurred in her history. We do know that my concern as her therapist was that I would not be able to help her have the opportunity to mourn the loss of her own view of her parents as protectors. Because of this, I saw her at risk for depression, and I kept in contact with her over several years, worrying about her.

STUDENT: So the hysteric – not remembering – that's because they're repressing the thoughts?

DR. M: Yes. A hysteric is repressing powerfully upsetting thoughts and feelings. This is opposed to obsessive-compulsives, who use isolation of affect as their major defense.

Now, back to Rat Man and his remembering childhood sexual experiences without the affect that ought to have accompanied these memories. At age six he had the idea that his parents could read his thoughts. This was most likely a projection of his guilty thoughts about being both angry and sexual, magical thinking that Freud calls the "omnipotence of thoughts."

The theoretical explanations that Freud gave about the obsessional process are still mostly accepted. We can now add to Freud's ideas that a child who was raised by someone who entered into battles over control and therefore did not soothe the child but instead stayed in the battle over toilet training, probably wasn't great at helping the child navigate through the battle over the prior (oral) stage, or the later stage of discovering the differences between the genitals. And the child themselves probably brought into this mother/child mix some sensitivity and proneness as more easily frustrated and harder to soothe than many children. All of this probably led to larger amounts of frustration, which led to greater amounts of hate, and more hate led to more drastic measures the child needed to employ. We understand that it's always much more complex than the patient's narrative suggests. That doesn't mean that their narrative isn't valuable, but it suggests that the narrative is probably not the whole story. In other words, I can't emphasize enough that a skilled clinician needs to remain curious. Being curious means not taking the patient's story as the end of, but rather as the beginning of, what the patient will tell us, while also comparing the patient's story with what we currently feel about them and their narrative.[3]

We have finished *The Rat Man*.

With regard to *The Wolfman*, the key psychoanalytic notion is the process of identification. By understanding and applying identification we'll be able to see how Freud helped initiate a process of positive change in his patients' lives.

Before we continue with today's material, I want to do a follow-up from the weekly emails, because I find them helpful in terms of having a clear sense of what you understand. Someone asked me about whether or not there's significance in Rat Man's fixation on rats, i.e., is his fixation on rats arbitrary or do rats signify something unique to Rat Man? Rats have to do with oral aggression. When Freud focuses on the zones of the body, the first zone is about orality. What can one do with one's mouth? Swallow, spit out, tear and bite. Hearing someone talk about the rat torture would be uncomfortable for anyone. It was particularly horrible to hear for Rat Man because he had a difficult time with powerful feelings that might at times cause him to have a tenuous hold on reality, what Freud called "the omnipotence of thoughts." With omnipotence of thoughts, thoughts are experienced as real instead of abstractions in the mind. Rat Man also had trouble dealing with frustration and angry feelings; he was desperately trying to control them. When he thought of someone who frustrated him, instead of flying into a rage (the kind of person that flies into rages would be an impulse disorder) or flying into panics (one who flies into panics is an anxiety disorder or an hysteric) Rat Man "flew into worries and rituals." This is called an obsessive-compulsive disorder. Throughout Rat Man's development, when he was faced with a conflict over an erogenous zone that made him upset and anxious, he became unglued. As with those people who suffer from severe OCD, he had a particular problem with rage. Thinking of the rat torture stimulated rageful wishes toward the important people in his life who frustrated him, and this sent Rat Man flying into OCD.

STUDENT: It's a sublimation of the wish?

DR. M: Here's why it's not a sublimation: because Rat Man was trying to hold back the expression of the wish. By doing so, the wish caused a conflict that interfered with Rat Man's routine functioning. If instead Rat Man had heard about the rat torture and, being a lawyer, had written a powerful legal brief proposing to outlaw this primitive punishment, that would be a sublimation. But it wouldn't quite matter whether or not Rat Man's legal brief was a fruitful experience for the world; one mistake made about the defense of sublimation is that it is often mistakenly defined by its outcome, i.e., it's a sublimation because it's good for society. It can be this, but is also more than this. Rituals of train travel from here to there, that's not functioning in life. If Rat Man had been able to discharge the pent-up anxiety and blocked up feelings of frustration and rage by legal work – or some other reality activity – that would be sublimation.

STUDENT: My dad doesn't want to retire because he's scared that he will – he doesn't call it becoming depressed – but he's afraid that's what will happen.

DR. M: In some way, he might be right. That's why some successful people don't retire, or they find an avocation, because their activity burns off powerful emotional needs; needs to express competitiveness, creativity and aggression; needs to function, achieve and produce. They need to find new sublimations.

The Wolfman

Sergei Konstantinovitch Pankejeff (December 24, 1886 – May 7, 1979)

The Wolfman was the last of Freud's case histories. Freud's goal was to show the development in childhood of an adult neurosis. In attempting to piece together the relationship between a person's current problems and their childhood development, the patient and psychoanalyst engage in the process of reconstruction. In reconstruction the psychoanalyst *and* the patient look at a symptom/personality style in adulthood and then reconstruct (like putting together pieces in a puzzle) what they think should have or might have occurred in childhood. They reconstruct the history in a similar way to how a detective might reconstruct the way that a crime took place. However, what Freud calls a "neurosis" here is from my point of view far from the kind of psychopathology as mild (in relative terms) as a neurosis. Further, Freud treats this patient as if he had a transference neurosis while there are a number of narcissistic neurosis features in this man.

The full title is *A Case History of an Infantile Neurosis*, and the nickname of the patient, "the Wolfman," comes from the patient's childhood phobia of wolves. Wolfman only knew about wolves from books/stories. He was a wealthy, titled Russian nobleman (in czarist Russia) who was completely handicapped by his "neurosis." At the time he came to Freud, Wolfman was 23 years old, and for years he'd traveled Europe with a valet and a doctor, as he needed constant care. In fact, Wolfman was so bizarre that in the first hour of treatment with Freud he offered to have anal intercourse with Freud and then to defecate on Freud's head. In the interests of science, Freud declined. Wolfman was in treatment with Freud for five years (from 1909 to 1914, six times per week) and fully recovered from his original phobic symptoms, but the story does not end with the termination of this treatment. The Russian Revolution of 1917 left the family penniless, and Wolfman lost his czarist Russian nobleman title. In 1919 the patient was able to escape from Russia to Vienna. This time, Freud psychoanalyzed Wolfman for four months (from November 1919 to February of 1920) for symptoms of constipation. At the end of these sessions, this symptom disappeared. One of the clinical issues that happened in this second therapy is that Freud did something he'd never done before. He set a time limit for the treatment and he promised that he could cure the patient of his constipation symptoms. Freud undertook what we now call the first short-term psychoanalysis. Freud not only treated the patient free of charge during this period (because Wolfman's only "skill" was being a titled nobleman and he had no paid employment). For the next five years Freud collected money for the patient from friends and colleagues, so Freud supported Wolfman both emotionally and financially. For several years after Freud's first treatment, Wolfman was free of mental illness, but then Wolfman developed a paranoid psychotic episode, a delusion that someone was drilling a hole into his nose and through his skull. This coincides with Wolfman learning that Freud was suffering from cancer of the jaw. I would suggest that if you're going to work with someone who is capable of regressing into psychotic-like magical thinking, and promise a cure (imply you are godlike/omnipotent), then don't get cancer of the jaw. The patient's psychotic delusion mimics the kind of surgical treatment required for Freud's cancer. With the development of a psychosis, this time the patient saw Dr. Ruth Mack Brunswick,[4] a psychoanalyst trained in Vienna who treated Wolfman for five months (from October 1926 to February 1927). Two years later he returned to Mack Brunswick, and she treated him on and off for several more years.

Wolfman's later life and his "profession"

Because Wolfman had been Freud's patient, and for several other reasons I will tell you about, his case was followed for over 50 years. From his first meetings with Freud to his death in 1979, many psychoanalysts interviewed Wolfman.

Freud never published the entire history of this case, as he had done with the Rat Man, only the reconstruction of the case material. However, while Freud's focus was narrow, the patient himself wrote a book titled *Wolfman: My Analysis with Freud* (Pankejeff, 1971). Wolfman traveled the world lecturing about this treatment.

As I mentioned, the issue of identification is quite important here. While Wolfman lost his title of Russian nobleman, by virtue of his long relationship/psychoanalysis with Freud, the patient achieved another "title," that of "Freud's patient." Using this new title, Wolfman traveled the world, lecturing and getting royalties from speaking and from his book: the money supported him. In effect, we can say that this patient got cured via identification as patient-of-Freud.

As for Wolfman's symptoms, he had a severe phobia of animals, particularly wolves. In order to understand the patient's symptoms and to correlate them with infantile sexuality, Freud took the patient's memories of childhood and reconstructed what the patient's history of trauma must have been. Freud traced the patient's wolf phobia to a childhood dream the patient had when Wolfman was four years old. Freud understood this dream as stemming from the patient's fear of his father. The form taken in the dream to present the fear of the father is Wolfman's fear of being eaten by a wolf. Freud reasoned that this fear, like the fearful content that one sees in dreams, is a representation of the turning around of a wish. Freud reconstructed the following: the wish is to have intercourse with the father, that is, to submit to the father, get strength from him and to blunt any competition with Father. This wish was then turned into a fear: the patient regresses from the phallic stage to oral stage (intercourse to eating). Finally, this wish was projected outward as a phobia.

STUDENT: I want to understand what this means. Is it really a sexual wish or longing for a strong father?

DR. M: You are asking another version of what should come out of reconstruction. Let's understand the role of fantasy in a person's life. Freud began to reason that a patient might present one fantasy as a substitute for another fantasy. As an example, a man has pathological jealousy about his wife. He's positive she's having sex with his best friend, his neighbor, an old boyfriend. In therapy he begins to understand that these fantasies center on feelings of inadequacy; the fear of inadequacy is represented by a fear of not being able to sexually satisfy his wife, not being "man enough" for her. The fantasy/belief that another man will take her off his hands might then be both reassuring and torturing. He must then surrender his masculinity to another man. However, what if, in reconstructing his history, we also find that his father was absent much of the time and that his mother was frustrated and that he sometimes felt that she wanted him to make up for the love that she wasn't getting from her husband (his father). While Mother probably didn't think about this in a sexual way, a young child might be concretely relating to his mother's longings by saying to himself:

"I'm just a little boy with a little penis. I can't replace Daddy."

In the same way that this man had wished that his father had been more of a force with his mother, who was controlling, overbearing, filled with longing for him and powerful, he may now feel this about his wife. This is a quasi-homosexual wish, meaning he may or may not be homosexual, but he longs for the protection and power of a daddy and this takes the form of a longing for Daddy's penis. The patient's longing, whether it involves his wanting to have sexual intercourse with his father and/or whether he wants his father's power and protection as symbolized by the longing for sexual intercourse, can be understood as being related to Wolfman's belief that he didn't have a father who was available and strong and that, until Freud, Wolfman had no helpful identification figure that he could take in to help with his inadequacy feelings. All he had when he came to Freud was a soon-to-be-useless title as a Russian nobleman who didn't feel very noble and also didn't feel like a man.

What Freud didn't know about the patient's childhood – and these facts would only emerge later in the Wolfman's story – was that Wolfman had probably been sexually abused/or at least taunted and viciously teased in childhood by his sadistic and disturbed older sister. She committed suicide in her young adulthood and so did Wolfman's father, some years after the sister killed herself. Later, a brother committed suicide. Because of Freud and the psychoanalysis, Wolfman's adjustment seems to have not been as awful as it could have been, given this seriously disturbed family. Although this slightly alters the patient's history, it doesn't actually change the patient's dynamics, as it suggests that Wolfman needed a father to protect him – not necessarily from the father, but from Wolfman's sister. In sum, I would suggest that Freud's reconstruction, based as it was on the patient's dreams and associations to the dreams, might have been incorrect in some of the precise historical details, but not in the psychological meaning of the patient's dynamics and psychopathology.

Keep in mind that Freud's stated purpose was to make the patient's adult problems understandable based on the infantile material. Freud likened these memories to pictures/memories the patient had of sexual intercourse between his parents. Wolfman believed that he had been in his parents' bedroom at some period of time and claimed that he saw his parents having sex. Given the examples of poor boundaries and disturbance in the family, this is possible. Freud felt that this experience left a powerful and traumatic effect on the patient; that as a result, the patient was fixated on these sexual longings. However, we don't even have to talk about them as sexual. They are sexual in the way that a young child might imagine sex.

In this regard, I want to also tell you of a patient of mine whose jealousy fantasy was more of a metaphor than an actual wish. It was more along the order of: "Somebody help me with my [mother/wife who I can't deal with]. Why don't you take her? Take her off my hands because I'm not man enough for her." This is a case of pathological jealousy (which appears in my couples book, Mendelsohn, 2017). This kind of jealousy is sometimes considered by those who work with couples hard to treat. The person who is pathologically jealous is viewed as quite troubled. However, I have found that this isn't necessarily true. First, everyone has some jealousy, but pathological jealousy is often overdetermined. Some couples collude, with the mate who is encouraging jealousy worrying that they're not interesting/desirable enough for their partner. If they can get the mate jealous, this helps them feel more secure . . . unless the problem becomes overwhelming (keep in mind the notion "be careful what you wish for"). In any event, the nonjealous mate finds ways to keep the jealous partner interested. This mate doesn't think to themselves:

> "First, I'll make them pathologically jealous, and then they will make my life miserable."

What they want is for the other to be only a little jealous. That said, the important take-away from this case and others is the following: Freud's emphasis was on tracing the connections between the patient's symptom(s) and his or her infantile history.

STUDENT: In these reconstructions, it sounds like what's more important is creating meaning for the patient, rather than an actual pinpointing of episodes in time.

DR. M: Yes, that is the point. However, this a very complex issue, because one needs to understand what the patient's meaning is. Freud *did* make meaning out of Wolfman's phobia and make meaning out of Wolfman's history. There are certain things that can happen that are key moments in the person's life; they are often used as key metaphors in the therapy. These are like screen memories – you probably don't need a whole lot of these memories to focus on in the therapy. The patient keeps going back to the same memories over again. It doesn't mean that each memory is totally accurate, it means that each memory is totally meaningful. Sometimes the traumatized child in the memory identifies with the abuser, becomes like them.

As an example, in a previous lecture I mentioned that I once did an intake interview with a disbarred attorney who was now planning a scheme to embezzle money in stock transactions. I will now expand on this case, saying more of what I had reconstructed, more of what I said to him than I previously shared with the class.

This man had a very difficult childhood. His mother had been very nasty to him; his father was never around and, while he never said so directly, he made it clear that in his mind he believed he had the right to swindle money. As I mentioned before, I listened for the entire session without commenting (this is unusual for me), then I said there would be no charge for the session, because I didn't think I had much of value to add to what he already believed.

He said: "You don't have any advice for me?"

I will now add things I hadn't told you when I previously presented this case:

> I told him that I didn't feel that I could work with him because it seemed that he was very much identified with a mother who was a nasty bitch as a mother, and it seemed as if his father had been no protection for him, and that during our session he had acted just like his mother: that he had been a nasty bitch to me. But, worse than that, it seemed as if he was on his way to becoming a nasty bitch to himself. That if one's wishes always came true, he could become rich with his plan, but I doubted it. And I thought that one way he was a nasty bitch to himself was that he was going to wind up in prison.

He listened intently and then, as if he hadn't taken in a word I said, he repeated: "But you still haven't given me any advice."

I SAID: "Well, I don't want to be harsh to you so I have been holding myself back to not be a nasty bitch to you, but if you want advice, then here it is: You should take martial arts lessons."

HE SAID: "What's so good about martial arts?"

I SAID: "Because I think that you're going to wind up in prison. You can use martial arts to defend yourself."

I've given you this example in a past lecture, but today I gave you more details because I want to emphasize again the following: the clinician's job is to use all data, including reconstruction, to make meaning in the therapy. Equally important to what the person has told you about their history is how they are treating you, the therapist. This man was treating me as if he was embezzling me. I let this happen (no charge for the session) because underneath this, he was filled (in a kind of identification with his mother) with a compensatory grandiosity, omnipotence and disdain for others. By telling him that he was unworkable with talk therapy I was attempting to create meaning with a person who was intent on making the session meaningless (because for him, any meaning that occurred would have made him feel awful about his life). There was a part of me that hoped against hope that he could be shocked into being interested in what I had to say; that he would want to actually receive some of the wisdom I believed I could offer him. In fact, in this regard, I actually did do a bit of therapy with him, even during the very brief time that we met, and, even though I'd told him I wasn't going to. That is, I made a few trial interpretations ("nasty bitch to yourself") that could have brought meaning into the session, but he refused it.

Let's return to Wolfman.

As I said, Wolfman later wrote a book called *The Wolfman: My Analysis with Freud*. I saw a film of Wolfman lecturing; it was just before Wolfman died in the late 1970s. He had a thick German-Russian accent but was quite clear and cogent in his description of his psychoanalysis with Freud. Following his last meetings with Freud (as well as his later therapy with Dr. Ruth Mack Brunswick), for the rest of Wolfman's (long) life he traveled the world describing his analysis with Freud. Wolfman lost one title in czarist Russia and gained a new title because of his deep and intimate connection with Freud. He assumed the title of "Freud's patient." In other words, Wolfman identified with Freud as a child identifies with a father. And Freud took care of Wolfman: not only figuratively, but literally when Wolfman was too disturbed to work, and later, Freud "took care" of Wolfman by providing the patient with the treatment Wolfman subsequently used to write, lecture and live off the title of "Freud's patient."

Many of you found Freud's speculations in *The Wolfman* difficult to under-stand, much less to believe. Yet, as I've said throughout these lectures, I hope you'll be able to maintain curiosity and openness to Freud's ideas, even dif-ficult ideas such as these. The method of psychoanalytic reconstruction has yielded important clinical results. What Freud gave us in his case histories was a deep and unending curiosity about the details of his patients' lives and, in particular, an interest and curiosity about each patient's childhood. Except in very rare circumstances (such as autobiographies of people who later became famous) no one before Freud had ever taken such an interest in the histories of ordinary people. Also, Freud gave us another valuable tool: the concept of the transference.

A summary statement about Freud's case histories

Each of Freud's case histories we studied was written with a specific focus:

(1.) The *Dora* case (Freud, 1905) was written to show how dreams are used in psychoanalysis;
(2.) *The Rat Man* was written to demonstrate the structure of obsessional neurosis;
(3.) *The Wolfman* was written as a political commentary. Freud wrote it as his counterargument to Jung's theories. Freud was trying to show exactly how the reconstruction of the patient's infantile sexuality confirms Freud's hypothesis of psychosexual development.

Some of you have indicated that in your view Freud was filled with biases; that he was motivated to find the things that he found. While this might be so, there is now 120 years of amassed clinical and research data to suggest that many of Freud's clinical observations are at least partly true.

However, Freud also introduced a very important clinical technique: talk ther-apy. This psychoanalytic technique comprises the following:

(1.) Free association;(2.) Detailed inquiry;(3.) Reconstruction;(4.) Interpretation (correlating reconstructions to symptoms).

That said, with all the brilliance that Freud displayed in these case histories, Fine suggests (1987) that there are several problems with them:

(1.) Many of the patients in *Studies on Hysteria* we would now diagnose as suffering from what Freud called the narcissistic neurosis. Dora, Wolfman, and Rat Man would probably now be diagnosed as borderline or mixed neurotic with borderline features;(2.) A major omission in Freud's case histories is there is no discussion/analysis of the patient's defenses, the overall character structure. What does this mean? When I talked about the reconstruction of the embezzler patient and I said: "Nasty bitch to yourself," I was saying he had met the enemy: "It is yourself." This describes an understanding of a patient's particular defenses, how they work to protect this person from pain and suffering while ironically causing the person even more pain and suffering. This defensive structure is character as it developed in childhood via identification with early objects. At this particular point in Freud's work, he was only interested in working with the patient's symptoms, not with the total personality.

As we know, when talking about a series of defenses the person uses, we're talking about their character/personality.

To summarize, what Freud did in his case histories was:

(1.) He classified the clinical material;(2.) He correlated the symptoms with infantile sexuality;(3.) He called this process "reconstruction";(4.) He created the therapeutic technique of psychoanalysis as a talk therapy.

Summary of lecture 10

Freud believed that the processes described in *Hysteria* were the same as what occurs in the obsessional neurosis and phobia. However, in the obsessional neurotic – as seen in *The Rat Man* (1909) – there is a regression to the anal-sadistic stage of infantile sexuality, and the person struggles with both sexual impulses and sadistic hatred. Following this regression, there is the same failure of repression, breakthrough of repressed impulses and formation of symptoms. In *The Wolfman* (1918) Freud attempts to show how the process of reconstruction of infantile sexuality confirms Freud's hypothesis of psychosexual development. Freud presented neurosis as an extension of a normal psychical process. Yet if neurosis is the result of a universal process (that is, if all human beings employ a certain amount of repression), is everyone neurotic? To understand Freud's answer to this question, we note Freud was ambivalent about psychology. While Freud made many brilliant psychological observations in his career, he hoped that science would discover a biological underpinning to neurosis. One consequence of this is that whenever Freud couldn't explain a psychological phenomenon psychologically, he'd fall back on a biological explanation. Thus, to the question, Why does one person become neurotic while another doesn't? Freud answers that neurotics are inherently (biologically) more easily frustrated/more easily gratified at the bodily zones. Because of this inherited predisposition, neurotics are more likely to have strong fixations, more likely to have more frequent and pervasive failures of repression, and therefore more frequent neurosis.

Notes

1 Dr. Ernst Lanzer is more widely known by the pseudonym the "Rat Man," given him by Freud (1909). He is the subject of Freud's case history. (During military maneuvers from August through September 1907, Lanzer first suffered from an obsession with rats.
2 The point is that conflicts that occurred during toilet training had stimulated frustration and hate that needed drastic defensive measures.
3 "Narrative as we listen to their story" is a process found in the work of reconstruction.
4 Dr. Ruth Mack Brunswick (1897–1946) born Ruth Mack, was an American psychiatrist. Mack was initially a student and later a close confidante and collaborator of Freud. After Wolfman's second treatment with Freud ended, Dr. Mack Brunswick treated Wolfman.

References

Billow, R. M., & Mendelsohn, R. (1990). The interviewer's "presenting problems" in the initial interview. *Bulletin of the Menninger Clinic, 54*(3), 391–414.

Fine, R. (1987). *The development of Freud's thought: From the beginnings (1886–1900) through id psychology (1900–1914) to ego psychology (1914–1939)*. Lanham, MD: Rowman & Littlefield.

Freud, S. (1905). Fragments of an analysis of a case of hysteria. In J. Strachey et al. (Trans.), *The standard edition of the complete psychological works of Sigmund Freud, Volume VII: ("Dora")*. London: Hogarth, 1–122.

Freud, S. (1909). Notes upon a case of obsessional neurosis. In J. Strachey et al. (Trans.), *The standard edition of the complete psychological works of Sigmund Freud, Volume X: Two Case Histories ("Little Hans" and the "Rat Man")*. London: Hogarth, 151–318.

Freud, S. (1918). From the history of an infantile neurosis. In J. Strachey et al. (Trans.), *The standard edition of the complete psychological works of Sigmund Freud, Volume XVII ("Wolf Man")*. London: Hogarth, 7–122.

Freud, S. (1937). Construction in analysis. In J. Strachey et al. (Trans.), *The standard edition of the complete psychological works of Sigmund Freud, Volume XXIII*. London: Hogarth, 255–270.

Mendelsohn, R. (2017). *A three-factor model of couples therapy*. Lantham, MD: Lexington Books/Rowman & Littlefield.

Pankejeff, S. (1971). *The wolf-man: Pankejeff's memoirs, along with essays by Freud and Ruth Mack Brunswick*. New York: Basic Books.

Chapter 11

Conclusion

Freud's psychoanalysis: a "talk therapy" for the 21st century

At the dawn of the 21st century, Reisner (1999)[1] noted: Freud's psychoanalysis has been criticized for reflecting a zeitgeist of scientism that's being challenged as we enter the 21st century.

However, in opposite fashion, Bornstein (2005) noted that it is ironic that one key tenet of psychoanalysis – the primacy of subjective narrative truth – has been used by other scientific researchers to co-opt psychoanalytic ideas at the same time as they criticize them.

Throughout our lectures, I've posed questions highlighted by these two psychoanalytic scholars:

> *Why have Freud's ideas not been readily accessible to the current student/clinician?*
> *Why have so many of Freud's psychoanalytic ideas been either co-opted or discarded?*

Is it for the reasons that each is describing?

In part, yes. I suggest two other reasons as well:

(1.) Because of Freud's arcane language;
(2.) Because reflected in Freud's work are the outdated cultural mores of the late 19th and early 20th centuries.

Throughout this book I've asked that the reader walk in Freud's shoes. This is an example of what is called "the theory of mind." I've presented Freud's ideas with more modern language. Only you can judge if I've accomplished this. Regarding Freud's ignorance about gender, misogyny and his cultural milieu, I've said that walking in Freud's shoes helps us to see him in the context of his time. This does not make his wrong-headed ideas disappear, but allows for a space between ways of thinking we now consider socially wrong, with ways of thinking that were socially acceptable then.

A lot has changed since Freud worked. Yet, as Brickman (2010) and Woods (2020) suggest, psychoanalysis has always thought of itself as an instrument

DOI: 10.4324/9781003171393-12

of freedom; yet it can become obstructive without self-consciousness. It can be unconsciously white and Eurocentric, patriarchal and heteronormative. In short, it can fail when the psychoanalyst is not doing his or her own work within themselves.

To return to our previous comments prior to the criticisms described by Brickman and Woods, in the current understanding of Freud's work, two criticisms one often hears are:

(1.) His work is an example of scientism (too much emphasis on science as an explanation for complex human phenomena);
(2.) His work is not scientific enough (other "more objective" models and methods are more reliable and more valid).

We could present these criticisms so that each one cancels out the other argument. However, there is substance and truth to both. That's why we need a clearer understanding of what Freud actually said and why he said it. The reality is, Freud's ideas haven't been accessible to the current reader, the current practicing clinician and the current student. This has contributed to his ideas being co-opted and marginalized. Because of this I have worked to make Freud's concepts more accessible, and to show the path Freud traveled from his early clinical/theoretical work to the ideas seen in his last papers.

Another purpose of this book has been to demonstrate Freud's theoretical ideas and their technical implications. I believe Freud did his best theoretical work when he stayed connected to the basic clinical data; this data includes the clinical data of the unconscious and the preconscious processes. As a corollary I believe the further Freud strayed from this clinical data, the less accessible are his ideas and the less defensible are his observations.

To continue, I have seen my role to present a more accessible Freud, and to leave it to others to more closely describe the social, political, cultural and other forces that have also contributed to the marginalization of Freud's work.

The current state of psychoanalysis

From its inception, psychoanalysis has been the object of criticism and controversy. However, current psychoanalysts suggest that our treatment is the most effective approach to working with problems of intimacy and attachment. More recent advances in psychoanalytic theory, following from both the post-Freudian ego psychologists and the object relations theorists (two approaches that you have heard about during these lectures) include both self-psychology[2] (Kohut, 1971) and relational psychoanalysis[3] (Aron, 1996).

Next is a clinical example and a review of many of the theoretical and technical advances that followed from Freud's final work; an example of how the theoretical advances in psychoanalysis had, as a corollary, several major advances in psychoanalytic theory and technique:

Clinical example

Two women present themselves for psychotherapy. The first is a young hetero-sexual woman (age 18) in her freshman year of college and living in a college dormitory 1,000 miles from home. She presents at her university's psychological clinic because she is abusing laxatives. She is horrified by her behavior, views herself and this new habit as disgusting but can't seem to stop because of recent struggles with weight gain. She tells the middle-aged male intake worker in the initial consultation that she's even having difficulty describing these behaviors to him because she is humiliated and embarrassed, yet feels too weak to stop.

This same male therapist ends his workday at the university to go to his own office in order to see private patients. The first person that he meets there has come for an initial interview. She is a 35-year-old heterosexual woman, happy in her professional career, and wanting to find a suitable (male) life partner. She tells this same male therapist about her frustrations in romance, and while discussing this she casually mentions that she occasionally uses laxatives as a method of weight control. When he inquires about this, she flies into a rage, saying that he has no idea of the pressures placed on women to be thin and attractive, while men like him experience no such pressure.

When one poses a question to clinicians – even to student clinicians – asking them which of these people might present the greater challenge for treatment, it's clear to most that the second person presents significantly greater challenges. The first patient's problems are what is now called "ego alien" (seen as a symptom of a neurotic disorder) while the second patient's problems are seen as "ego syntonic" (viewed as a symptom of a characterological problem; the symptom is not seen as a "symptom" but as a part of the self). This presents an additional technical problem with the second patient: the therapy also requires a modification to the patient's defensive (character) processes.

STUDENT: How do you help the person to make it "not part of the self"?

DR. M: This is an important question and the answer will seem counterintuitive. All of our lectures about Freud have been about how to help a person feel that their inner experiences are not intolerable so they can be free of emotional pain. With a personality problem, this is the ultimate goal. At first one needs to help the patient feel that their thoughts, feelings and behavior are not pain-ful enough to the self because the locus of the pain is external; it is in "the other" (that is, with the second patient, the locus of the pain was in the male therapist who asked the question about laxatives). This person is angered by the male clinician's worries about her laxatives, not worried about it herself. She first needs to stop projecting and externalizing her conflicts into the other, thereby avoiding her inner pain. After she feels the intolerable experience, she can be helped to understand how she came to associate weight gain with a lack of being lovable. Perhaps a parent projected a hatred of their own appetites 'piggishness' into her, and this style of projecting and externalizing made her desperate to avoid "overeating" at all costs – even at a detriment to her health and well-being.

Further advances in theory and technique

In elaborating Freud's ideas, ego psychologists began to reevaluate Freud's model of psychological development, suggesting that children are born with an innate potential that unfolds naturally in a receptive environment. This opened up an important question pursued by developmental ego psychologists such as Bowlby (1953) and Mahler (1973). These theorists began to ask: What are the elements in an average expectable environment required for the person's psychic apparatus to develop normally? This led to an exploration of the influence of healthy and unhealthy attachment.

Mahler (1975) initiated an exploration of severe disturbances in childhood, emphasizing the importance of the environment on the child. She was especially interested in mother-infant duality, carefully documenting the impact of early separations of children from their mothers. This documentation of separation-individuation was Mahler's most important contribution to the development of psychoanalysis. Separation-individuation is now viewed as the psychological birth of a child, occurring over a period of time after the child's physical birth. The child begins to emotionally separate from the mother, and will also individuate (become psychologically aware of their separation). Mahler shed light on the normal and abnormal features of separation as part of developmental ego psychology.

Along with an increased focus on the environmental (particularly maternal) influences of child-rearing, other psychoanalytic theorists began asking another question:

What are the social and cultural factors that influence parental practices? Erikson (1963), an analysand and later student of Anna Freud, is most credited with this. Although Erikson accepted the essential aspects of Freud's theory, he didn't focus solely on the parent-child relationship. He gave equal importance to the role of the ego and the person's progression of selfhood. Erikson suggested that the environment in which a child lives is crucial to providing growth, adjustment, a source of self-awareness and identity. He questioned whether there are factors in a child's early relationship with their environment that facilitate the process of drive neutralization, toning down instinctual conflicts and making energy sources available to fuel the ego's nonconflictual activities. Earlier, Hartmann (1939) had suggested that adaptation, which had previously been studied from the point of view of mental conflict, should also be understood from the viewpoint of normality. He suggested that there is a sphere without conflict.

The subsequent development of ego psychology within psychoanalysis brought a shift from instinct theory to this new focus on the adaptive functions of the ego. This allowed psychoanalysis and psychology to move closer to each other. For the next half-century, ego psychology became the dominant psychoanalytic theory in America, before object relations theory gained more influence. Ego psychology also formed the basis for the self-psychology of Heinz Kohut, which opposed but was rooted in Hartmann's theory of libido. Self-psychology was conceived in the 1970s as a contemporary form of psychoanalytic treatment. In self-psychology the effort is made to understand an individual from within their subjective experience via vicarious introspection, basing interpretations on the understanding of the self as the central agency of the human psyche. This was seen as a major break from traditional psychoanalysis and is considered the beginnings of the relational approach to psychoanalysis. Kohut maintained that a parent's failure to empathize with their child, and the response of the child to this failure, lies at the root of psychopathology. He suggested that those suffering from unempathic parents search for a "selfobject" where they feel validated, adored and cared about. He also believed that it is a selfobject transference that is the curative factor in psychoanalysis, as it repairs the patient's damaged sense of self.

All of these contributions led psychoanalysts to a further revision in their thinking: a change in emphasis from the intrapsychic fantasy life of the patient to an exploration of actual events originating in childhood and displayed in the current relationship with the psychoanalyst. In this regard, Alexander and French (1946) suggested that Freud's insights had from the beginning actually been leading psychoanalysis in the direction of such changes. He reasoned that Freud recognized a principle known in immunology. The organism, receiving small quantities of injected toxins, develops defenses against them. These antibodies enable the organism to protect itself against the invasion of the original toxins when reexposed to infection. Analogously, in the transference, the patient learns to deal with small quantities of the same emotional tensions they couldn't master in the past and had defended against by repression (excluding intolerable emotions from consciousness). After Freud recognized that the emotional patterns in effect *are* the patient's personality, and that they come into expression during the treatment as the defenses against them are overcome, the transference was seen as the dynamic reenactment of this pathogenic past. Alexander understood this as the basis of modern psychoanalytic therapy. Transference analysis transformed therapy into a kind of retraining of the ego, gradually enabling patients to deal with conflictful psychological situations they had previously avoided. Both principles – the old etiological reconstruction of the past and the newer analysis of its transference manifestations – continue side by side in theory and practice. The technique of psychoanalysis changed from an exclusive focus on the patient's fantasy life to a focus on the patient's real relating as it unfolds in the here-and-now relationship with the psychoanalyst.

STUDENT: How is this done?

DR. M: Remember the embezzler? In the session I suggested that he was being a nasty bitch to himself when he was sneering at me?

STUDENT: Oh, right!

DR. M: However, coincident with such changes, others continued to explore fantasy. Klein (1963), a child psychoanalyst, suggested that a preverbal anxiety occurs in infancy resulting in the formation of an unconscious splitting of the world into good and bad idealizations. How the child resolves this splitting depends on both the constitution of the child and the nurturing the child experiences; the quality of resolution can inform the kinds of distress that the child experiences later in life. By observing and analyzing the play and interactions of children, Klein built onto the work of Freud's unconscious mind. Bion (1962) further expanded these ideas with the concept of a maternal "reverie" as the capacity to sense and make sense of what goes on inside the patient. This is an important element in post-Kleinian thought. Bion suggested that reverie is an act of faith in unconscious process. In therapy, the psychoanalyst's use of reverie is an important tool in the response to the patient's material. It's this capacity for "playing with" the patient's images that Bion encouraged. Another of Klein's students, Winnicott (1960), a pediatrician and psychoanalyst, worked with children and their mothers. This led to the development of an influential concept that he called "the holding environment." Winnicott viewed the work of the psychoanalyst as offering a substitute holding environment based on the mother-infant bond.

STUDENT: What does this mean?

DR. M: The psychoanalyst will sometimes be silently listening or simply saying a phrase like: "Well, un . . ."

The patient will feel held, understood and protected the way they felt as a child with their mother.

In current psychoanalysis, the emphasis has shifted even further toward an object relations/relational therapy, where the real relating that occurs between patient and psychoanalyst is seen as the best way to understand the psychopathology that developed in childhood. As one step along the way, Bowlby (1953), observing infants, came to believe that the tendency for primate infants to develop attachments to familiar caregivers was the result of evolutionary pressures, since attachment behavior facilitates the infant's survival in the face of dangers such as predation or exposure to the elements. Bowlby's work influenced Mahler and led to the development of attachment theory, a psychological model describing the dynamics of long-term and short-term interpersonal relationships between humans. In infants, attachment as a motivational and behavioral system directs the child to seek proximity with a familiar caregiver when they are alarmed, with expectation that they will receive protection and emotional support (in this regard, remember Freud's comments about separation anxiety in inhibitions, symptoms and anxiety). The most important tenet of attachment theory is that an infant needs to develop a relationship with at least one primary caregiver for their successful social and emotional development, particularly for learning how to regulate their feelings. Any caregiver is likely to become the principal attachment figure if they provide most of the childcare and related social interaction. In the presence of a sensitive and responsive caregiver, the infant will use this caregiver as a "safe base" from which to explore. Attachment theory was built by Bowlby as an attempt to link psychoanalysis with the wider world of evolutionary theory. Initially this was rejected by the psychoanalytic establishment, but there was a gradual rapprochement (Holmes, 2015).

Otto Kernberg's (1998) integrative writings also became central to the development of modern object relations theory, the theory that is perhaps most widely accepted among modern psychoanalysts. Kernberg designed an intensive form of psychoanalytic psychotherapy known as transference-focused psychotherapy (TFP), meant to be most suitable for patients diagnosed with borderline personality organization (BPO). Borderline personality disordered patients are described as experiencing so-called splits in their affect and thinking (Klein, 1963). The intended aim of Kernberg's treatment is the integration of split-off parts of the patient's self and object representations. To do this, the patient's affectively charged internal representations of previous relationships are consistently interpreted as the therapist becomes aware of them in the therapeutic relationship, e.g., in the transference.

In a further advance, Greenberg and Mitchell's (1983) important book *Object Relations in Psychoanalytic Theory* distinguished between psychoanalytic theories emphasizing biological drives (sexuality/aggression) and theories emphasizing human relationships. The former are referred to as "drive/conflict theories," and the latter are termed "relational/conflict theories." Greenberg and Mitchell (1983) argued that drive theories and relational theories are conceptually incompatible, that psychoanalysis must choose between them. After their book, the ideas of Mitchell and Greenberg diverged. Mitchell became acknowledged as the founder of the school of psychoanalysis known as relational psychoanalysis. Relational psychoanalysis sought to bridge the traditions of interpersonal relations, as developed within interpersonal psychoanalysis, *and* object relations, as developed within British object relations theory. Various tributaries – interpersonal psychoanalysis, object relations theory, self-psychology, empirical infancy research, and elements of contemporary Freudian and Kleinian/Bionian thought – flowed into this tradition, which now understands relational configurations between self and others, both real and fantasized, as the primary subject of psychoanalytic investigation.

Finally, in a very thoughtful paper, Lettieri (2005) restates what I've suggested to you: that the psychic agencies of id, ego and superego are now seen as metaphors of psychological functions rather than as structures and that they are utilized to organize clinical observation and understand conflict. Yet the ego remains a valuable metaphor for the psychoanalyst. What are the treatment implications of this? Lettieri cautions that – from the viewpoint of the ego as an organizing principle – if the psychoanalyst engages exclusively in natural and spontaneous relational exchanges (that is, the more modern relational approach of psychoanalysis), this may lessen interpersonal/intrapsychic tensions. However, it may also inhibit the patient's "ego" from fully using the analytic process (and prevent the discovery of aspects of the patient's inner experience that would not otherwise appear and be known). The *neutrality* of the psychoanalyst still provides space that not only protects the patient's individuality but also provides an opportunity for new aspects of the person to be discovered. Lettieri suggests that the art of psychoanalysis is in the balance that each psychoanalytic dyad achieves between what may be called optimal neutrality coupled with psychoanalytic authenticity.

Research in psychoanalysis

In the field of psychoanalytic research, exploration into infant and child development has led to many new insights (Beebe, 2018). There is a recent meta-analysis on the efficacy of psychoanalysis-demonstrated evidence that psychoanalytic treatment yields significant pre/post and pre/follow-up change in patients presenting with complex mental disorders (Castonguay & Muran, 2016) and Shedler (2010). While the original approach of psychoanalysis as a multiple-sessions-per-week process is no longer the way treatment is typically practiced, psychoanalytic theory and technique continue to inform numerous time-limited psychodynamic psychotherapies (Lipner et al., 2016). Further, multiple meta-analyses (Strauss et al., 2015) have demonstrated that psychoanalytic therapy is efficacious in treating depressive, anxiety and personality disorders. Psychoanalytic theory has also led to empirical research that is now integrated into a comprehensive psychoanalytic understanding of human psychology and a vibrant technique that can be used to help eliminate human suffering (Bornstein, 2005; Weinberger & Stoycheva, In Press).

Summary of lecture 11

I have posed the following questions: Why have Freud's ideas not been readily accessible to the current student/clinician? Why have so many of Freud's ideas been either co-opted or discarded? I suggest that Freud's arcane language and his outdated cultural mores make it difficult to embrace his wonderful insights. I also suggest that the reader attempt to walk in Freud's shoes. Walking in Freud's shoes can help us to see him in the context of his time with regard to his ignorance about gender, misogyny and his cultural milieu. In an elaboration of Freud's ideas, ego psychologists reevaluated Freud's model of psychological development, suggesting the child is born with an innate potential that unfolds naturally in a receptive environment. Developmental ego psychologists (Bowlby, 1953; Mahler, 1973) began asking: What are the elements in an average expectable environment required for the person's psychic apparatus to develop normally? These ideas led to an exploration of the influence of healthy and unhealthy attachment and an increased focus on the environmental (particularly maternal) influences of child-rearing. Other psychoanalytic theorists began asking another question: What are the social and cultural factors that influence parental practices? Erikson (1963) questioned whether there are factors in a child's early relationship with their environment that facilitate the process of drive neutralization. The subsequent development of ego psychology within psychoanalysis, with its shift from instinct theory to a focus on the adaptive functions of the ego, allowed psychoanalysis and psychology to move closer to one another. Ego psychology also formed the starting point for the self-psychology of Heinz Kohut. In self-psychology the effort is made to understand an individual from within their subjective experience via vicarious introspection, while basing interpretations on the understanding of the self. This was the beginning of the relational approaches to psychoanalysis. This contribution led psychoanalysts to a further revision in their thinking: a change in emphasis from the intrapsychic, or fantasy, life of the patient to an exploration of actual events originating in childhood and displayed in the current relationship with the psychoanalyst. The technique of psychoanalysis began to change from an exclusive focus on the patient's fantasy life to a focus on the patient's real relating as it unfolds in the here-and-now relationship with the psychoanalyst. However, Klein (1963), in observing and analyzing the play and interactions of children, built onto the work of Freud's unconscious mind (Freud, 1900). Her explorations into the unconscious mind of the infant yielded a suggestion of the possible developmental roots of the superego. Further, one of Klein's students, Winnicott (1960), working with children and their mothers, proposed an influential concept that he called the holding environment. Winnicott viewed the work of the psychoanalyst as offering a substitute holding environment based on the mother/infant bond. In current psychoanalysis, the emphasis has shifted even further toward an object relations/relational therapy, where the real relating that occurs between patient and psychoanalyst is seen as the best way to understand the psychopathology that originally developed in the patient's childhood. In a further advance, Greenberg & Mitchell's (1983) important book Object Relations in Psychoanalytic Theory distinguished between psychoanalytic theories that emphasize biological drives such as sexuality and aggression versus theories that emphasize human relationships. The former were referred to as "drive/conflict theories" and the latter were termed "relational/conflict theories." This led to the growth of the school of psychoanalysis known as relational psychoanalysis. Additionally, psychoanalytic research into infant and child development has led to many new insights (Beebe, 2018), and a recent meta-analysis on the efficacy of psychoanalysis demonstrated evidence that psychoanalytic treatment yields significant pre/post- and pre/follow-up changes in patients presenting with complex mental disorders (Castonguay & Muran, 2016). Research has also demonstrated that psychoanalytic therapy is effective in the treatment of depressive, anxiety and personality disorders (Shedler, 2010). As we have seen, psychoanalytic theory has led to empirical research integrated into a vibrant and comprehensive psychoanalytic understanding of human psychology, and a vibrant technique helpful to eliminate human suffering (Bornstein, 2005; Weinberger & Stoycheva, In Press).

Notes

1   Scientism (*Merriam-Webster Dictionary*) is the promotion of science as the best or only objective means by which society should determine normative and epistemological values. The term *scientism* is generally used critically, implying a cosmetic application of science in unwarranted situations considered not amenable to application of the scientific method or similar scientific standards.

2 Self-psychology is a psychoanalytic theory that was conceived by Heinz Kohut (1971) in the 1970s. It was an effort to understand individuals from within their subjective experience via vicarious introspection, basing interpretations on the understanding of the self as the central agency of the human psyche. Though self-psychology recognizes certain drives, conflicts and complexes present in Freudian psychodynamic theory, these are understood within a different framework. Self-psychology was seen as a major break from traditional psychoanalysis and is considered the beginnings of the relational approach to psychoanalysis.
3 Relational psychoanalysis (Mitchell, 1988; Aron, 1996) is a school of psychoanalysis that emphasizes the role of real and imagined relationships with others in both psychopathology and psychotherapy. Relational psychoanalysis began in the 1980s as an attempt to focus on the detailed exploration of interpersonal interactions (interpersonal psychoanalysis) with ideas about the psychological importance of internalized relationships with other people (object relations theory).

References

Alexander, F., & French, T. (1946). *Psychoanalytic therapy*. New York: Ronald Press.

Aron, L. (1996). *A meeting of minds: Mutuality in psychoanalysis*. New York: Routledge.

Beebe, B. (2018). Comment on microanalysis of multimodal communication in therapy: A case of relational trauma in parent-infant psychoanalytic psychotherapy. *Journal of Infant, Child and Adolescent Psychotherapy, 17*(1), 14.

Bion, W. R. (1962). *Learning from experience*. London: William Heinemann.

Bornstein, R. F. (2005). Reconnecting psychoanalysis to mainstream psychology: Challenges and opportunities. *Psychoanalytic Psychology, 22*(3), 323–340.

Bowlby, J. (1953). *Child care and the growth of love*. London: Penguin Books.

Brickman, C. (2010). Psychoanalysis and Judaism in context. In L. Aron & L. Henik (Eds.), *Answering a question with a question: Contemporary psychoanalysis and Jewish thought*. Brighton, MA: Academic Studies Press, 25–54.

Castonguay, L. G., & Muran, J. C. (Eds.). (2016). *Practice-oriented research in psychotherapy: Building partnerships between clinicians and researchers (Special issue reprint from Psychotherapy Research)*. Oxford: Routledge.

Erikson, E. H. (1963). *Childhood and society* (2nd ed.). New York: W. W. Norton & Company.

Freud, Sigmund. (1900). "The interpretation of dreams." *The standard edition of the complete psychological works of Sigmund Freud, Volume IV*. London: Hogarth Press, ix–627.

Greenberg, J. R., & Mitchell, S. A. (1983). *Object relations in psychoanalytic theory*. Cambridge, MA: Harvard University Press.

Hartmann, H. (1939). *Ego psychology and the problem of adaptation*. New York: International Universities Press.

Holmes, J. (2015). Attachment theory in clinical practice: A personal account. *British Journal of Psychotherapy, 31*(2), 208–228.

Kernberg, O. F. (1998). *Love relations: Normality and pathology*. New Haven, CT: Yale University Press.

Klein, M. (1963). *Envy and gratitude, and other works, 1946–1963*. London: Hogarth Press.

Kohut, H. (1971). *The analysis of the self: A systematic approach to the psychoanalytic treatment of narcissistic personality disorders*. New York: International Universities Press.

Lettieri, R. (2005). The ego revisited. *Psychoanalytic Psychology*, *22*(3), 370–381.

Lipner, L. M., Mendelsohn, R., & Muran, J. C. (2016). Psychoanalysis. In A. E.Wenzel (Ed.), *Sage encyclopedia of abnormal and clinical psychology*. New York: Sage Publications.

Mahler, M. S. (1975). On the current status of the infantile neurosis. *Journal of the American Psychoanalytic Association*, *23*(2), 327–333.

Mahler, M. S., Pine, F., & Bergman, A. (1973). *The psychological birth of the human infant: Symbiosis and individuation*. New York: Basic Books.

Reisner, S. (1999). Freud and psychoanalysis: Into the 21st century. *Journal of the American Psychoanalytic Association*, *47*, 1037–1060.

Shedler, J. (2010). The efficacy of psychodynamic psychotherapy. *American Psychologist*, *65*(2), 98–109.

Strauss, B., Barber, J. P., & Castonguay, L. G. (Eds.). (2015). *Visions in psychotherapy research and practice: Reflections from the presidents of the society for psychotherapy research*. New York, NY: Routledge Press.

Weinberger, J., & Stoycheva, V. (In Press). *The unconscious: Theory, research, and clinical implications*. New York: Guilford Press.

Winnicott, D. (1960). *The maturational processes and the facilitating environment*. New York: International Universities Press.

Woods, A. (2020). The work before us: Whiteness and the psychoanalytic institute. *Psychoanalysis, Culture & Society*, *25*, 230–249.

Index

Page numbers in *italic* indicate a figure on the corresponding page.

For Product Safety Concerns and Information please contact our EU
representative GPSR@taylorandfrancis.com
Taylor & Francis Verlag GmbH, Kaufingerstraße 24, 80331 München, Germany